INCURSION

ALEX PAKNADEL | ANDY DIGGLE | DOUG BRAITHWAITE | DIEGO RODRIGUEZ

CONTENTS

5 INCURSION #1

Story: Andy Diggle and Alex Paknadel
Script: Alex Paknadel
Pencils: Doug Braithwaite
Colors: José Vilarrubia and Diego Rodriguez
Letters: Marshall Dillon
Cover Artists: Doug Braithwaite
with Diego Rodriguez

27 INCURSION #2

Story: Andy Diggle and Alex Paknadel
Script: Alex Paknadel
Pencils: Doug Braithwaite
Colors: Diego Rodriguez
Letters: Marshall Dillon
Cover Artists: Doug Braithwaite
with Diego Rodriguez

49 INCURSION #3

Story: Andy Diggle and Alex Paknadel
Script: Alex Paknadel
Pencils: Doug Braithwaite
Colors: Diego Rodriguez
Letters: Marshall Dillon
Cover Artists: Doug Braithwaite
with Leonardo Paciarotti

71 INCURSION #4

Story: Andy Diggle and Alex Paknadel
Script: Alex Paknadel
Pencils: Doug Braithwaite
Colors: Diego Rodriguez
with Leonardo Paciarotti
Letters: Marshall Dillon
Cover Artists: Doug Braithwaite
with Diego Rodriguez

Collection Cover Art: Doug Braithwaite
with Diego Rodriguez

93 BEHIND THE SCENES

CHARACTER DESIGNS
INCURSION #1-3 PRE-ORDER EDITIONS

INVASION PLAN
INCURSION #1 PRE-ORDER EDITION

DEADSIDE QUESTS
INCURSION #2 PRE-ORDER EDITION

ANATOMY OF A SCENE
INCURSION #4 PRE-ORDER EDITION

Writers: Andy Diggle and Alex Paknadel
Commentary: Drew Baumgartner
Artists: Doug Braithwaite with Diego Rodriguez

101 GALLERY

Ryan Bodenheim
Doug Braithwaite
Andrew Dalhouse
Roberto de la Torre
Renato Guedes
Tonci Zonjic

Assistant Editor: Drew Baumgartner
Editors: David Menchel (#1-4) with
Joseph Illidge (#1) and Robert Meyers (#2-4)

Dan Mintz
Chairman

Fred Pierce
Publisher

Walter Black
VP Operations

Matthew Klein
VP Sales & Marketing

Robert Meyers
Senior Editorial Director

Mel Caylo
Director of Marketing

Travis Escarfullery
Director of Design & Production

Peter Stern
Director of International Publishing & Merchandising

Karl Bollers
Senior Editor

Lysa Hawkins
Heather Antos
Editors

David Menchel
Associate Editor

Drew Baumgartner
Assistant Editor

Jeff Walker
Production & Design Manager

Julia Walchuk
Sales & Live Events Manager

Emily Hecht
Sales & Social Media Manager

Connor Hill
Sales Operations Coordinator

Danielle Ward
Sales Manager

Gregg Katzman
Marketing Coordinator

Ivan Cohen
Collection Editor

Steve Blackwell
Collection Designer

Russ Brown
President, Consumer Products,
Promotions & Ad Sales

Oliver Taylor
International Licensing Coordinator

Zane Warman
Domestic Licensing Coordinator

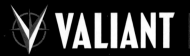

VALIANT

ANDY DIGGLE | ALEX PAKNADEL
DOUG BRAITHWAITE

#1

INCURSION™

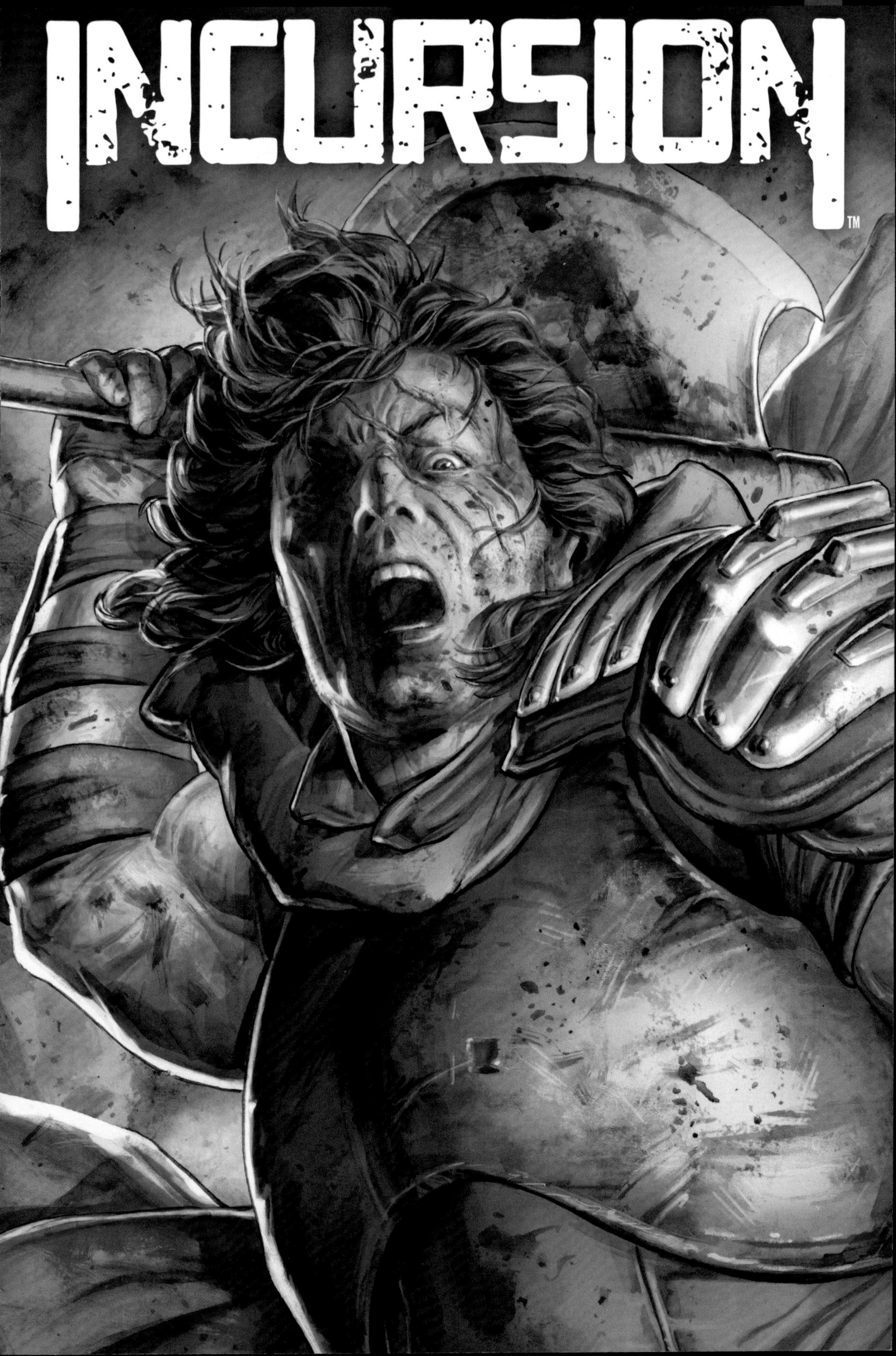

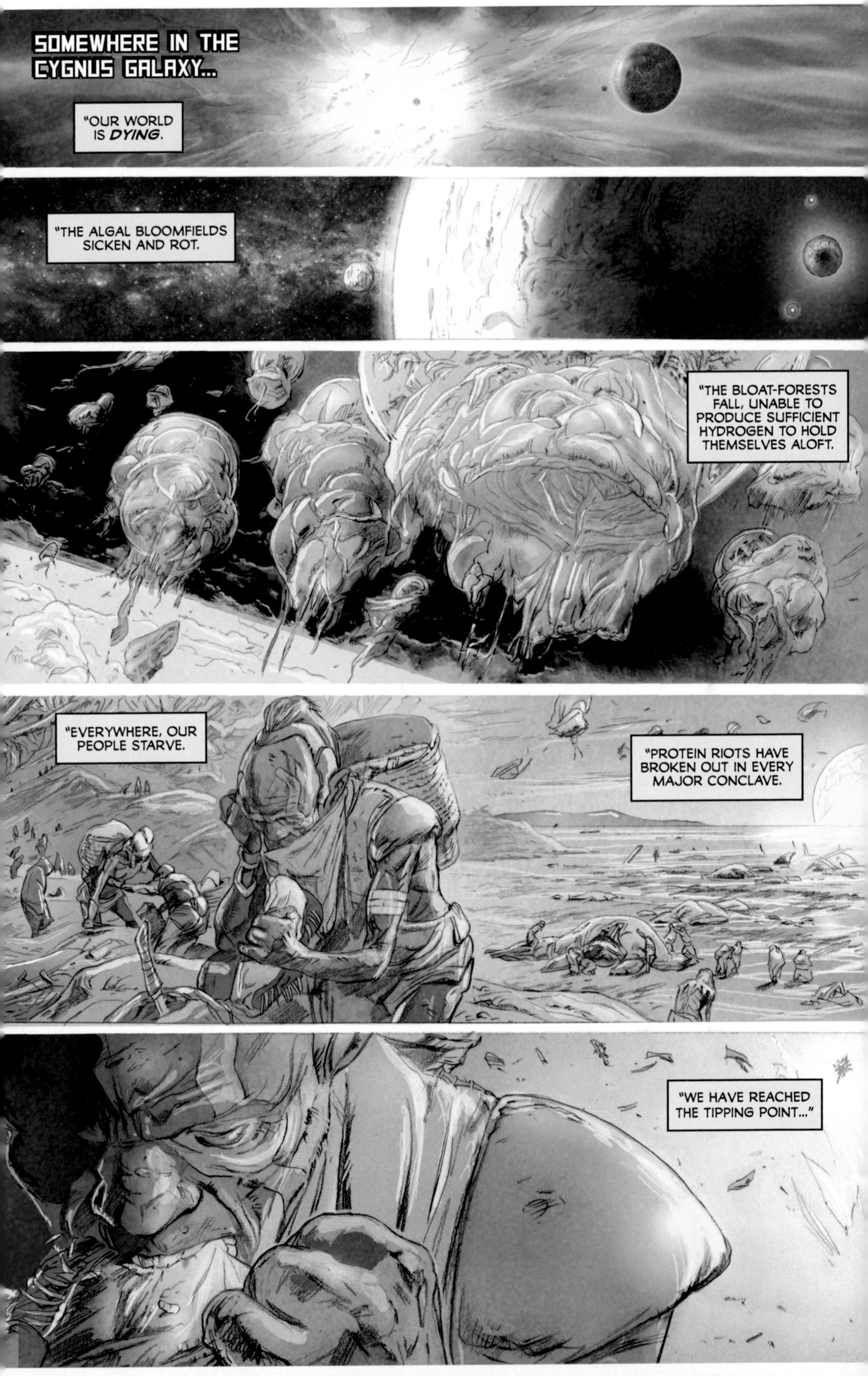
SOMEWHERE IN THE CYGNUS GALAXY...
"OUR WORLD IS *DYING*.
"THE ALGAL BLOOMFIELDS SICKEN AND ROT.
"THE BLOAT-FORESTS FALL, UNABLE TO PRODUCE SUFFICIENT HYDROGEN TO HOLD THEMSELVES ALOFT.
"EVERYWHERE, OUR PEOPLE STARVE.
"PROTEIN RIOTS HAVE BROKEN OUT IN EVERY MAJOR CONCLAVE.
"WE HAVE REACHED THE TIPPING POINT..."

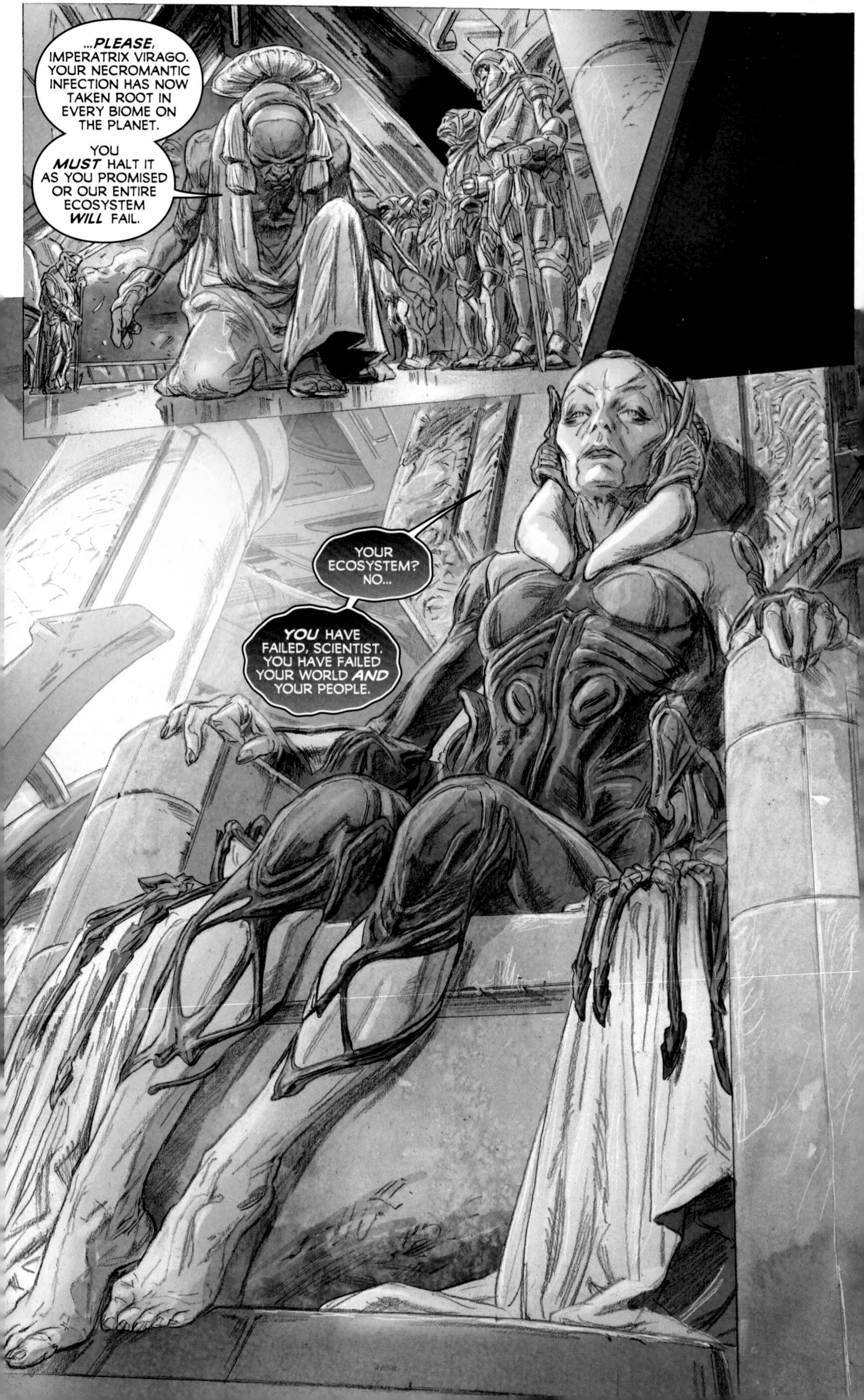
...PLEASE, IMPERATRIX VIRAGO. YOUR NECROMANTIC INFECTION HAS NOW TAKEN ROOT IN EVERY BIOME ON THE PLANET.
YOU MUST HALT IT AS YOU PROMISED OR OUR ENTIRE ECOSYSTEM WILL FAIL.
YOUR ECOSYSTEM? NO...
YOU HAVE FAILED, SCIENTIST. YOU HAVE FAILED YOUR WORLD AND YOUR PEOPLE.

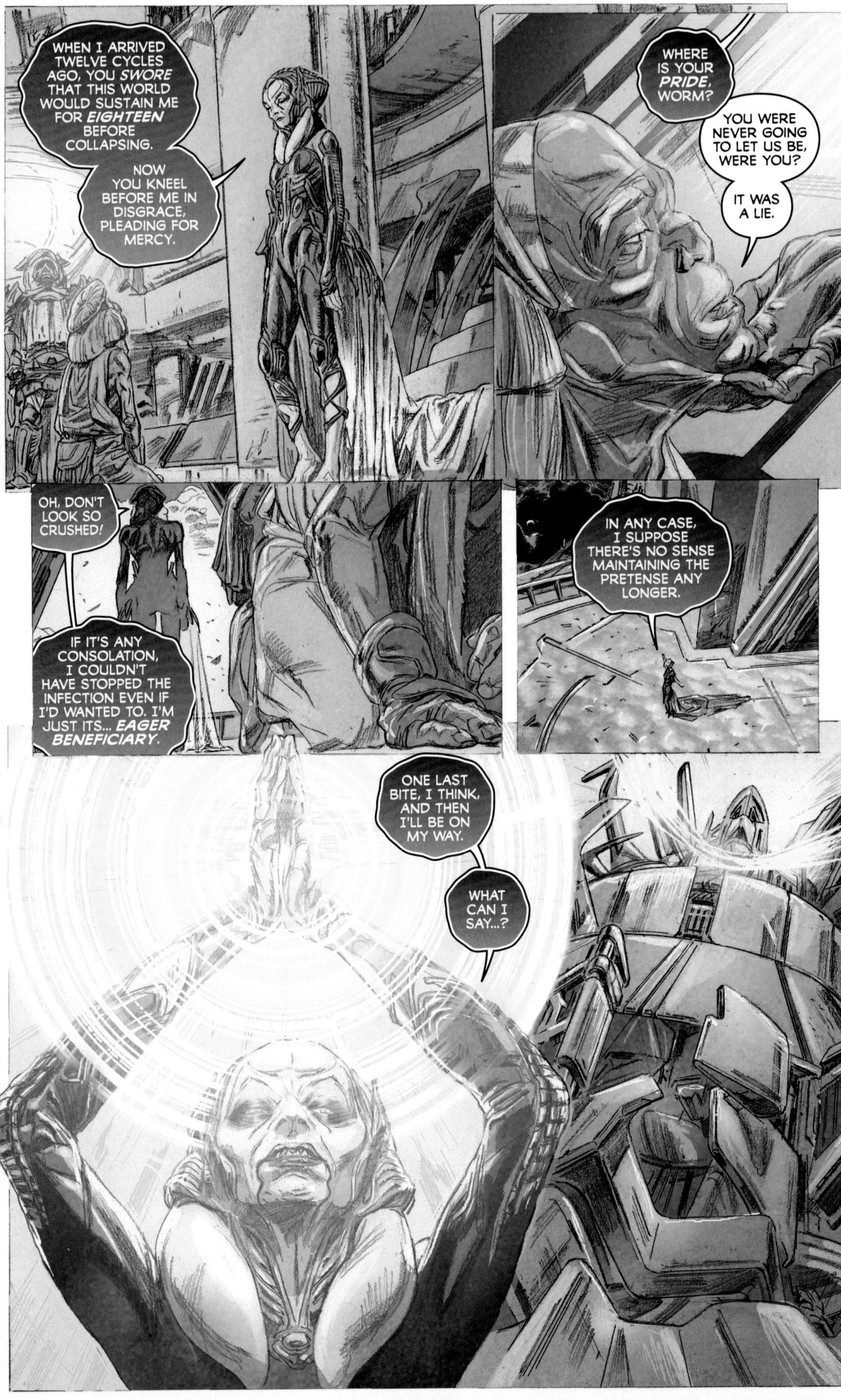
WHEN I ARRIVED TWELVE CYCLES AGO, YOU SWORE THAT THIS WORLD WOULD SUSTAIN ME FOR EIGHTEEN BEFORE COLLAPSING.
NOW YOU KNEEL BEFORE ME IN DISGRACE, PLEADING FOR MERCY.
WHERE IS YOUR PRIDE, WORM?
YOU WERE NEVER GOING TO LET US BE, WERE YOU?
IT WAS A LIE.
OH, DON'T LOOK SO CRUSHED!
IF IT'S ANY CONSOLATION, I COULDN'T HAVE STOPPED THE INFECTION EVEN IF I'D WANTED TO. I'M JUST ITS... EAGER BENEFICIARY.
IN ANY CASE, I SUPPOSE THERE'S NO SENSE MAINTAINING THE PRETENSE ANY LONGER.
ONE LAST BITE, I THINK, AND THEN I'LL BE ON MY WAY.
WHAT CAN I SAY...?

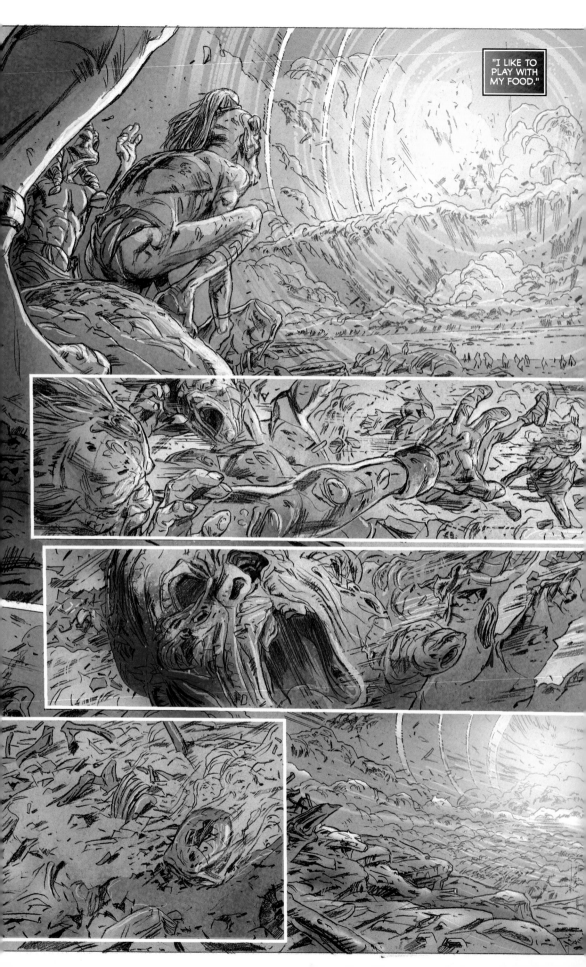

"I LIKE TO PLAY WITH MY FOOD."

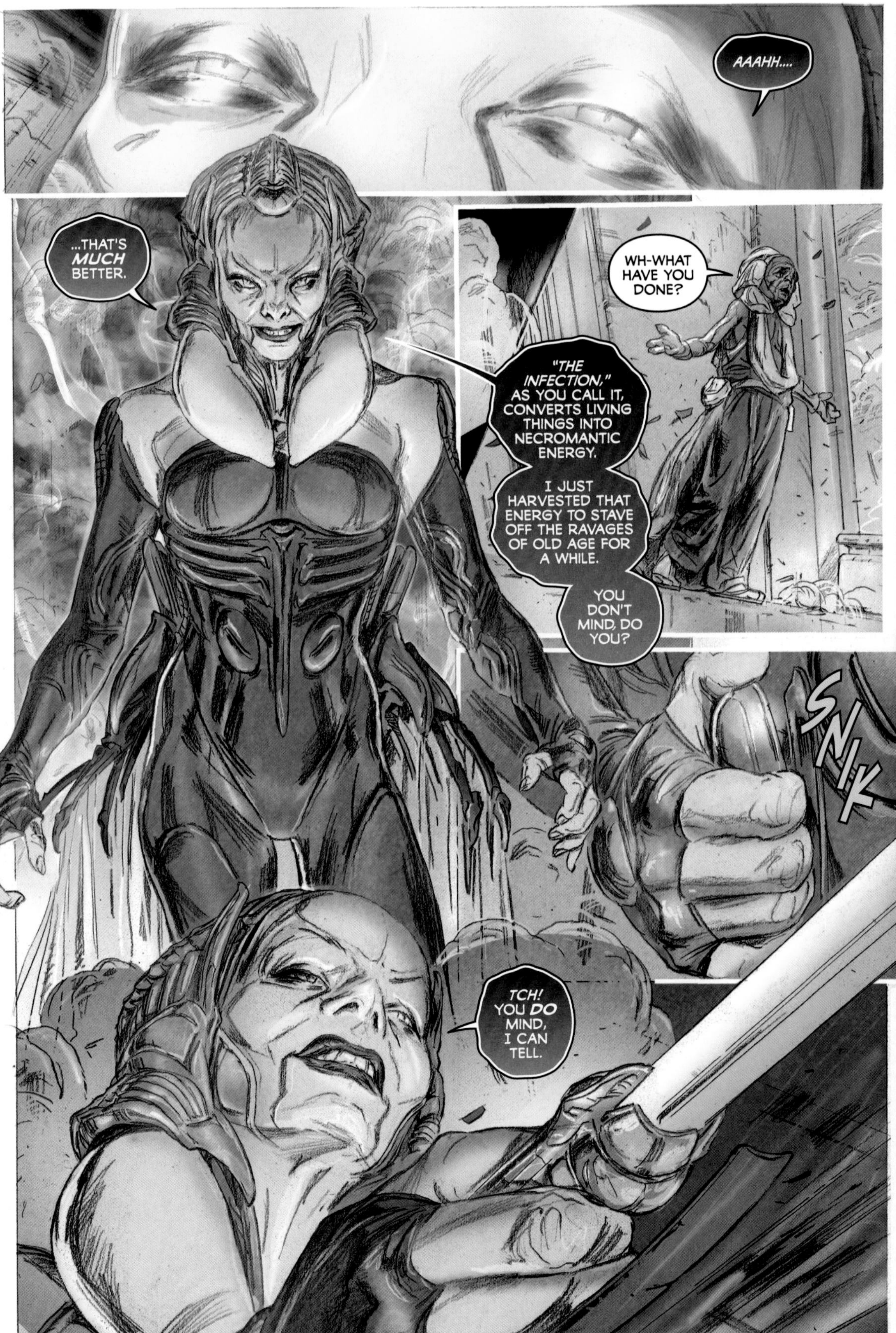
AAAHH....
...THAT'S MUCH BETTER.
WH-WHAT HAVE YOU DONE?
"THE INFECTION," AS YOU CALL IT, CONVERTS LIVING THINGS INTO NECROMANTIC ENERGY.
I JUST HARVESTED THAT ENERGY TO STAVE OFF THE RAVAGES OF OLD AGE FOR A WHILE.
YOU DON'T MIND, DO YOU?
SNIK
TCH! YOU DO MIND, I CAN TELL.

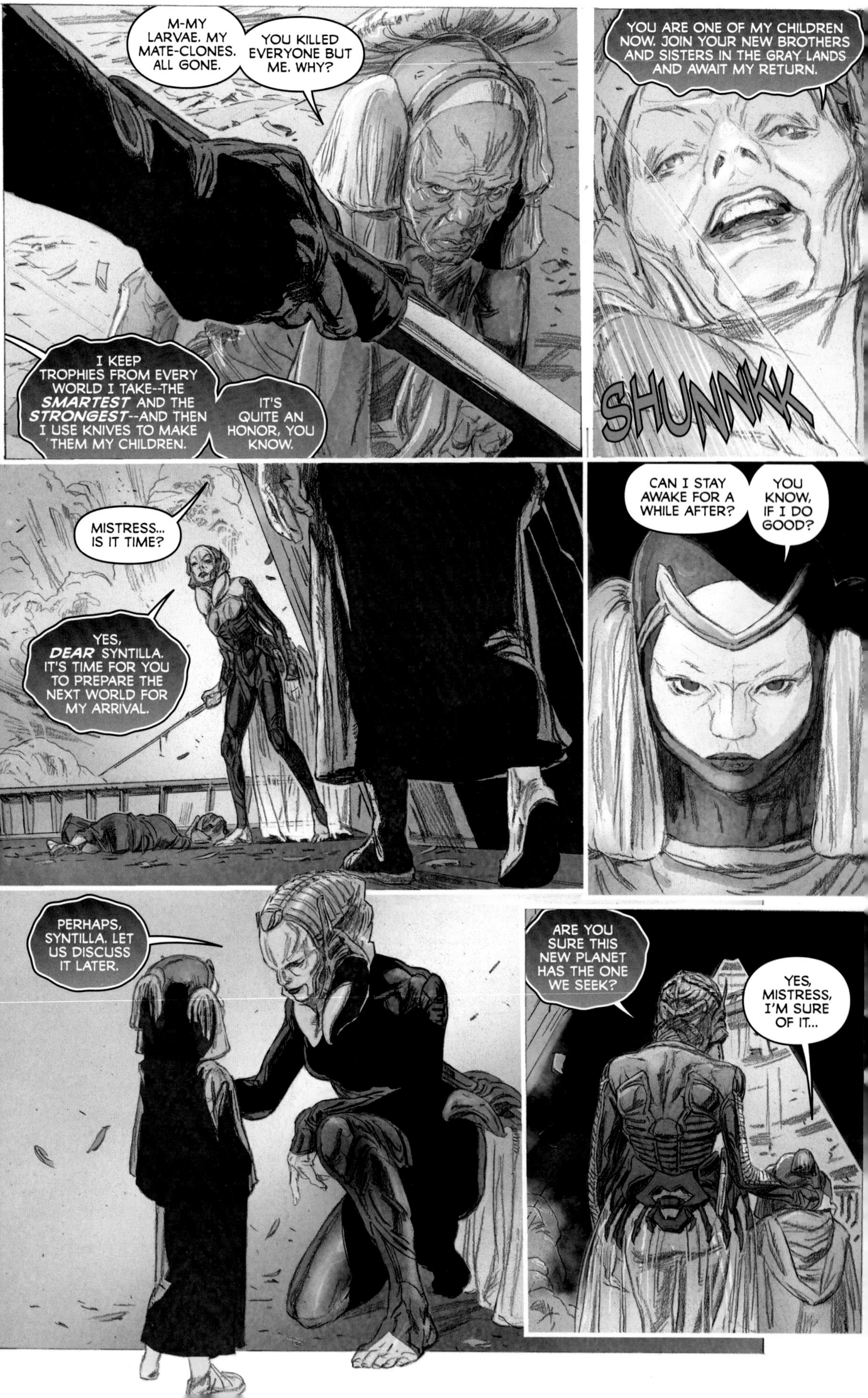
M-MY LARVAE. MY MATE-CLONES. ALL GONE.
YOU KILLED EVERYONE BUT ME. WHY?
I KEEP TROPHIES FROM EVERY WORLD I TAKE--THE SMARTEST AND THE STRONGEST--AND THEN I USE KNIVES TO MAKE THEM MY CHILDREN.
IT'S QUITE AN HONOR, YOU KNOW.
YOU ARE ONE OF MY CHILDREN NOW. JOIN YOUR NEW BROTHERS AND SISTERS IN THE GRAY LANDS AND AWAIT MY RETURN.
SHUNNKK
MISTRESS... IS IT TIME?
YES, DEAR SYNTILLA. IT'S TIME FOR YOU TO PREPARE THE NEXT WORLD FOR MY ARRIVAL.
CAN I STAY AWAKE FOR A WHILE AFTER?
YOU KNOW, IF I DO GOOD?
PERHAPS, SYNTILLA. LET US DISCUSS IT LATER.
ARE YOU SURE THIS NEW PLANET HAS THE ONE WE SEEK?
YES, MISTRESS, I'M SURE OF IT...

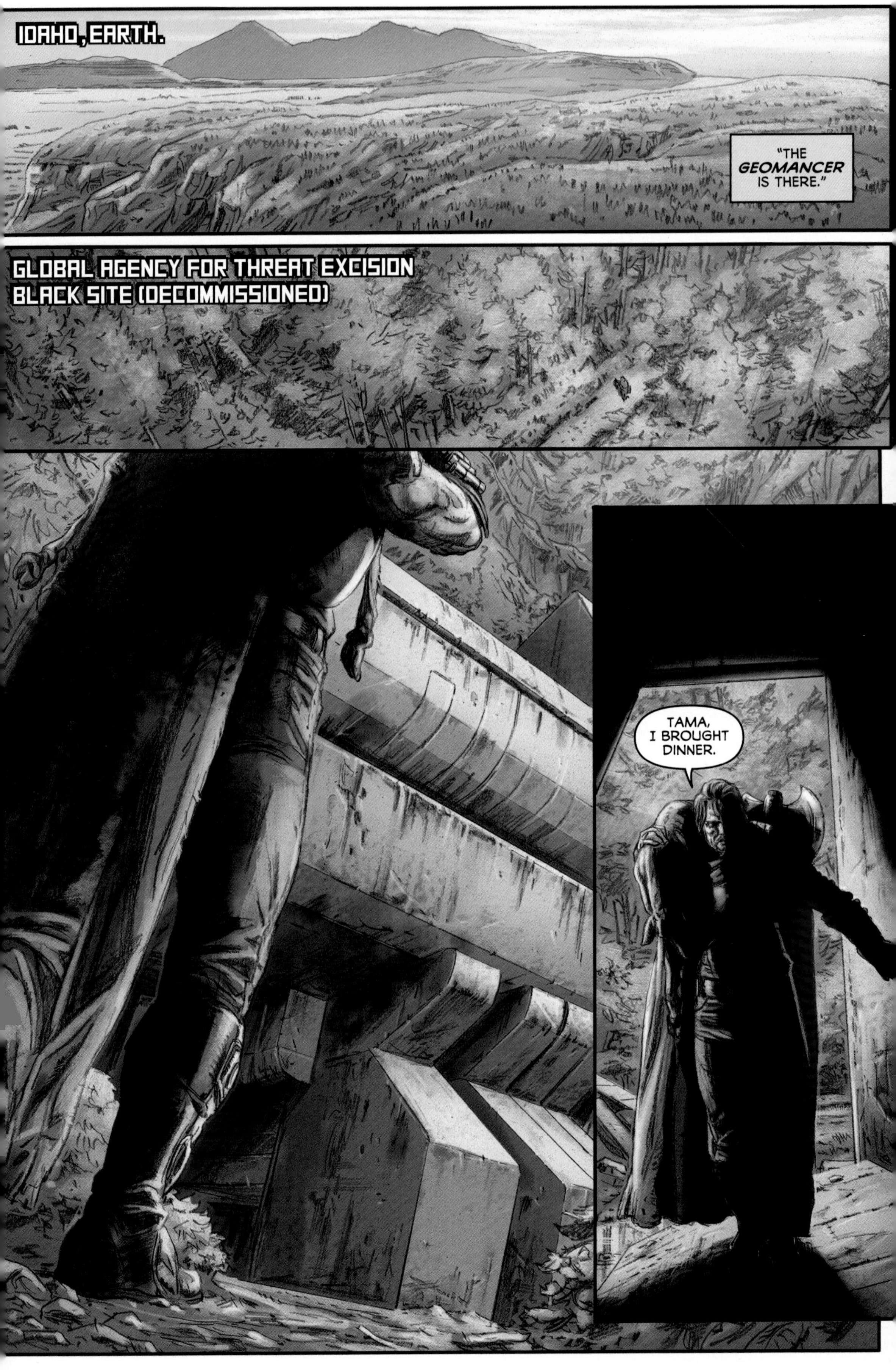
IDAHO, EARTH.
"THE GEOMANCER IS THERE."
GLOBAL AGENCY FOR THREAT EXCISION BLACK SITE (DECOMMISSIONED)
TAMA, I BROUGHT DINNER.

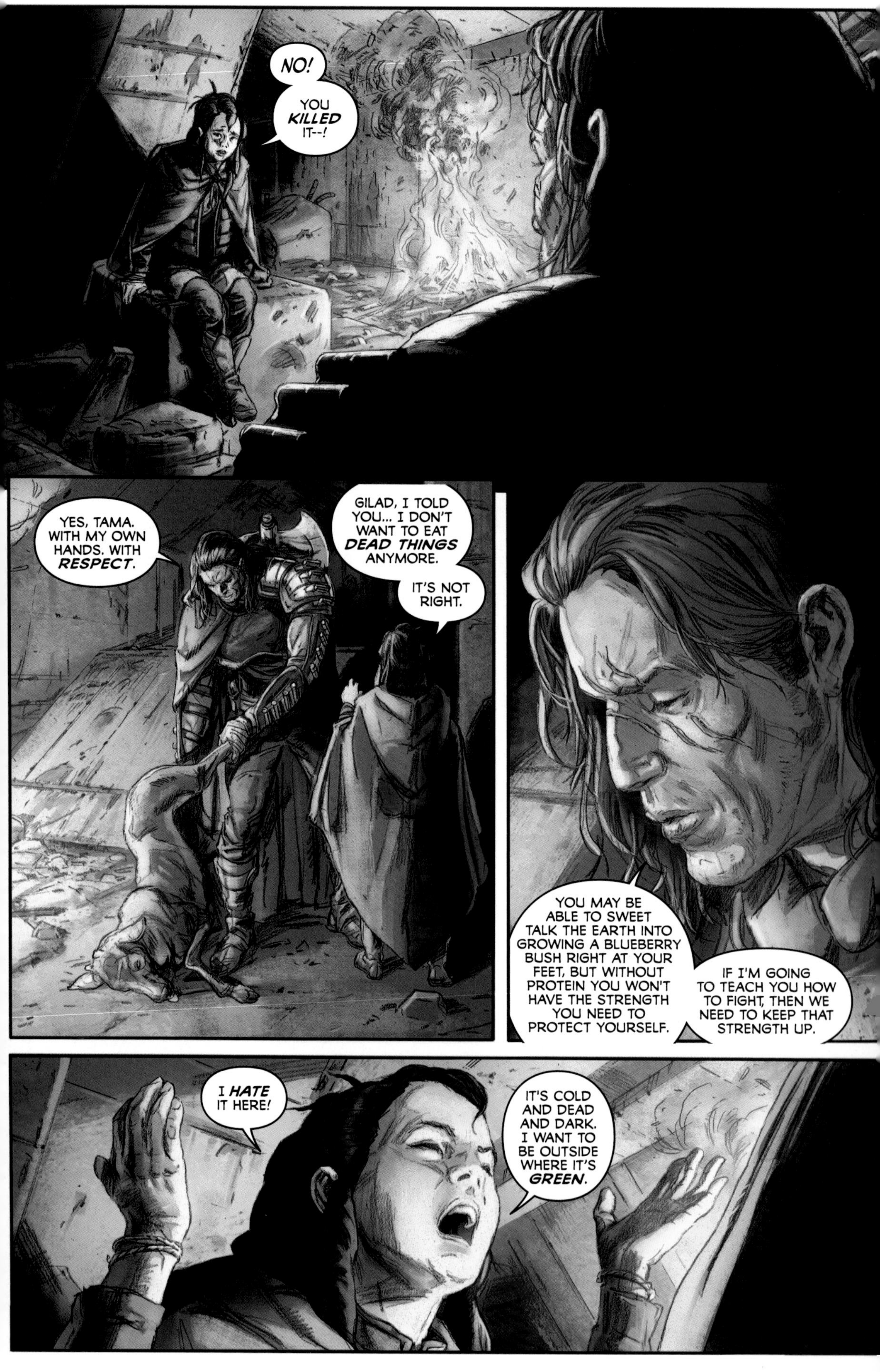
NO!
YOU KILLED IT--!
YES, TAMA. WITH MY OWN HANDS. WITH RESPECT.
GILAD, I TOLD YOU... I DON'T WANT TO EAT DEAD THINGS ANYMORE.
IT'S NOT RIGHT.
YOU MAY BE ABLE TO SWEET TALK THE EARTH INTO GROWING A BLUEBERRY BUSH RIGHT AT YOUR FEET, BUT WITHOUT PROTEIN YOU WON'T HAVE THE STRENGTH YOU NEED TO PROTECT YOURSELF.
IF I'M GOING TO TEACH YOU HOW TO FIGHT, THEN WE NEED TO KEEP THAT STRENGTH UP.
I HATE IT HERE!
IT'S COLD AND DEAD AND DARK. I WANT TO BE OUTSIDE WHERE IT'S GREEN.

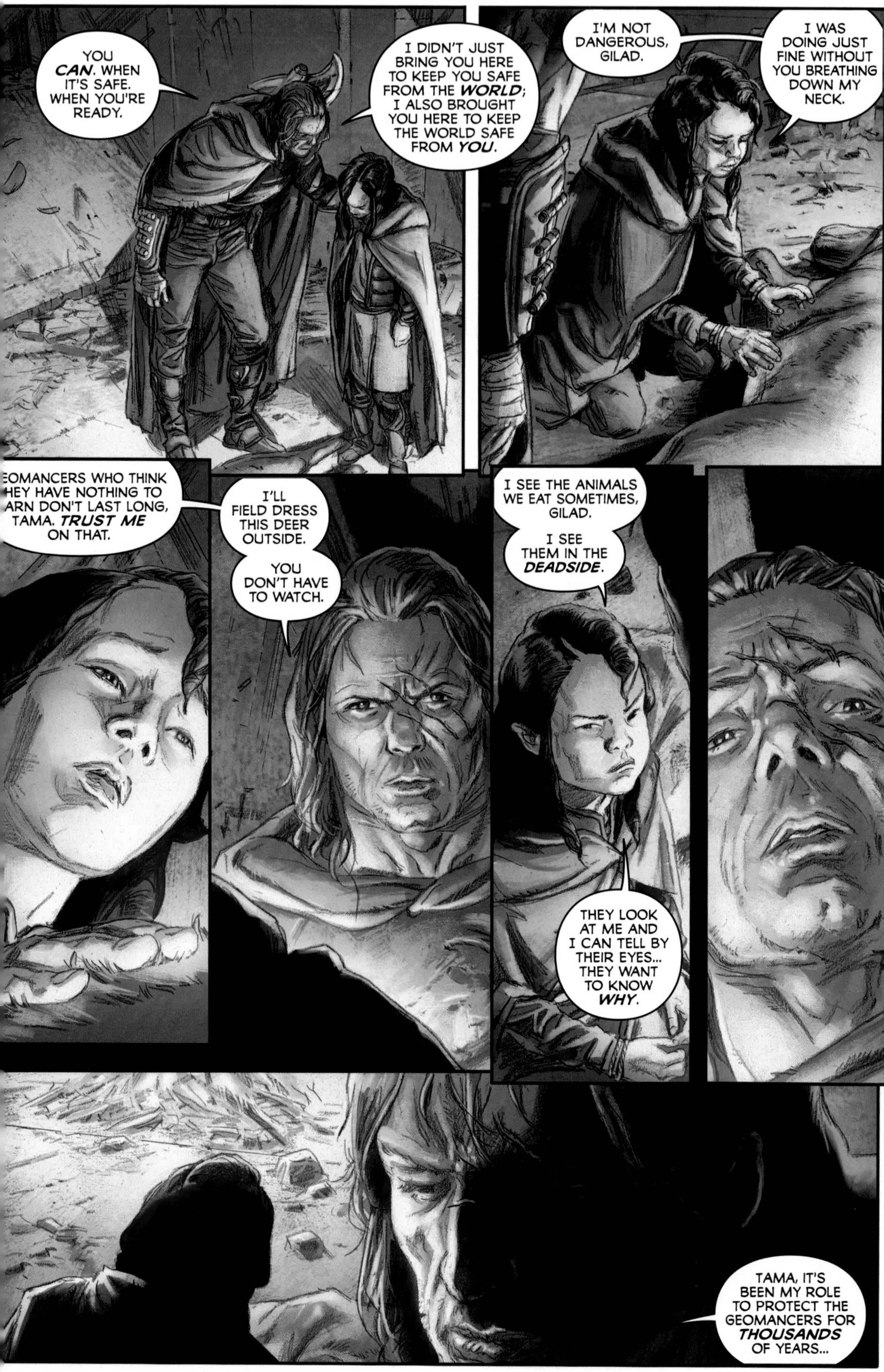
YOU **CAN**. WHEN IT'S SAFE. WHEN YOU'RE READY.
I DIDN'T JUST BRING YOU HERE TO KEEP YOU SAFE FROM THE **WORLD**; I ALSO BROUGHT YOU HERE TO KEEP THE WORLD SAFE FROM **YOU**.
I'M NOT DANGEROUS, GILAD.
I WAS DOING JUST FINE WITHOUT YOU BREATHING DOWN MY NECK.
EOMANCERS WHO THINK HEY HAVE NOTHING TO ARN DON'T LAST LONG, TAMA. **TRUST ME** ON THAT.
I'LL FIELD DRESS THIS DEER OUTSIDE.
YOU DON'T HAVE TO WATCH.
I SEE THE ANIMALS WE EAT SOMETIMES, GILAD.
I SEE THEM IN THE **DEADSIDE**.
THEY LOOK AT ME AND I CAN TELL BY THEIR EYES... THEY WANT TO KNOW **WHY**.
TAMA, IT'S BEEN MY ROLE TO PROTECT THE GEOMANCERS FOR **THOUSANDS** OF YEARS...

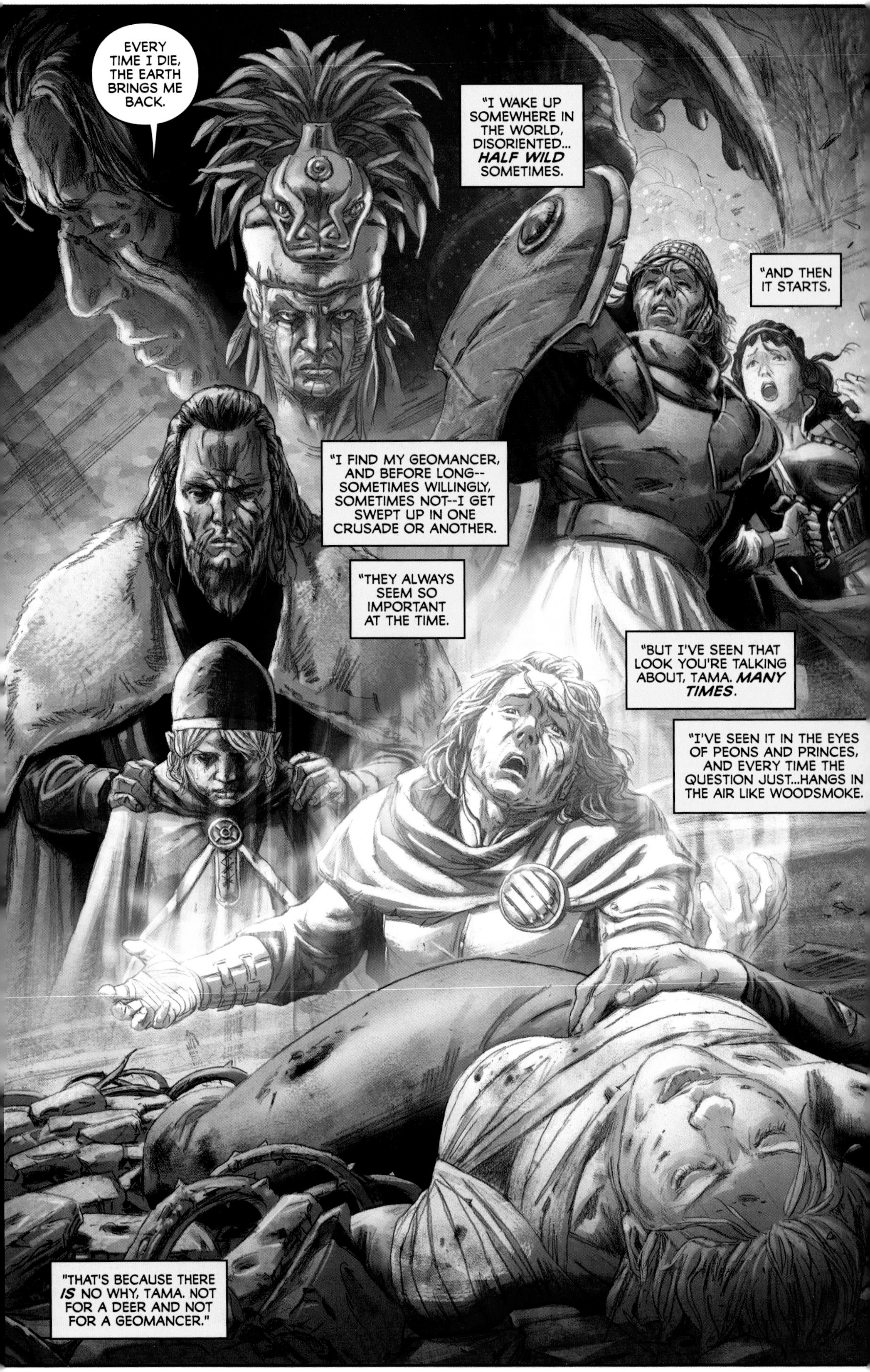
EVERY TIME I DIE, THE EARTH BRINGS ME BACK.
"I WAKE UP SOMEWHERE IN THE WORLD, DISORIENTED... *HALF WILD* SOMETIMES.
"AND THEN IT STARTS.
"I FIND MY GEOMANCER, AND BEFORE LONG--SOMETIMES WILLINGLY, SOMETIMES NOT--I GET SWEPT UP IN ONE CRUSADE OR ANOTHER.
"THEY ALWAYS SEEM SO IMPORTANT AT THE TIME.
"BUT I'VE SEEN THAT LOOK YOU'RE TALKING ABOUT, TAMA. *MANY TIMES*.
"I'VE SEEN IT IN THE EYES OF PEONS AND PRINCES, AND EVERY TIME THE QUESTION JUST...HANGS IN THE AIR LIKE WOODSMOKE.
"THAT'S BECAUSE THERE *IS* NO WHY, TAMA. NOT FOR A DEER AND NOT FOR A GEOMANCER."

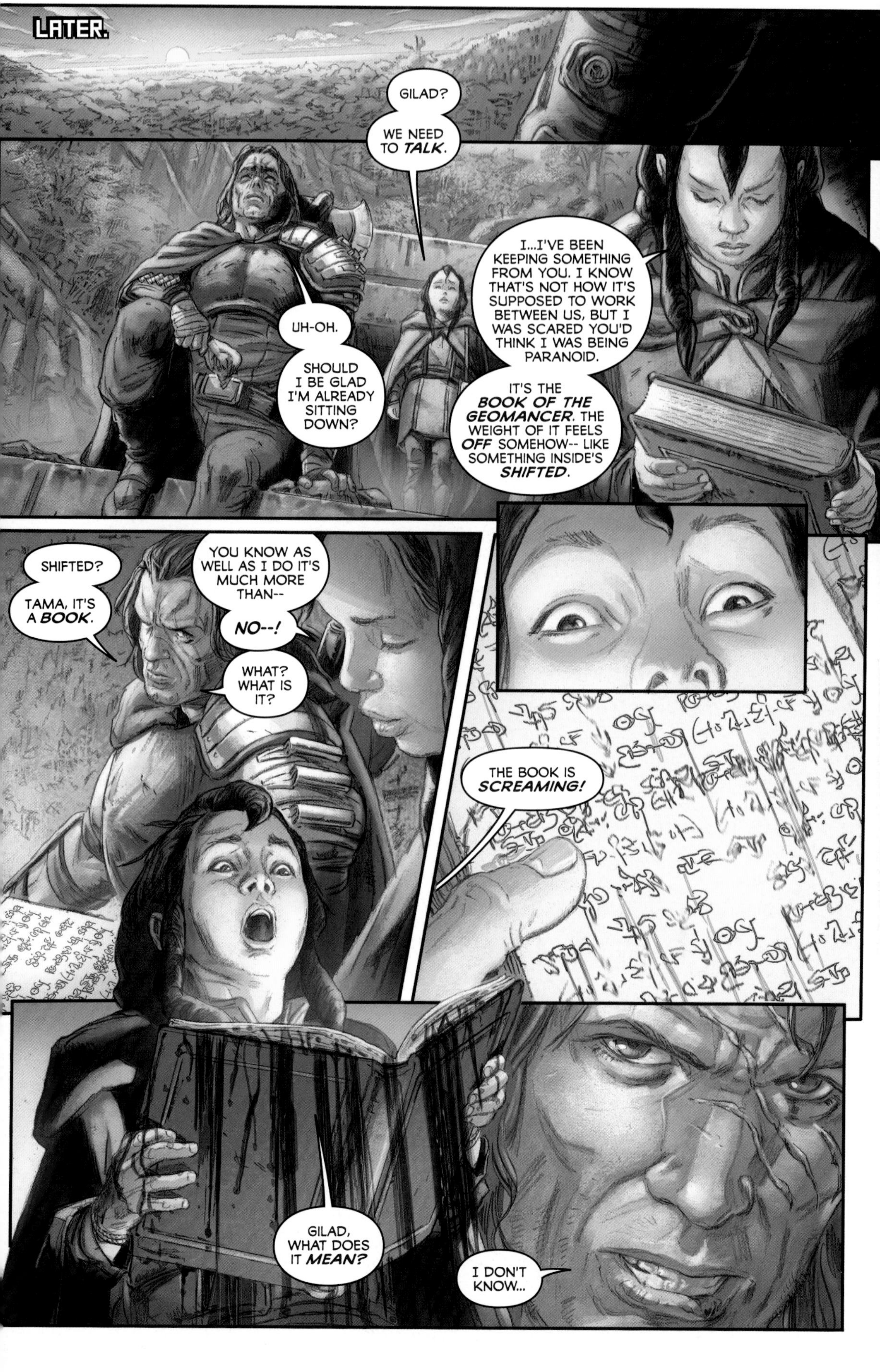
LATER.
GILAD?
WE NEED TO TALK.
UH-OH.
SHOULD I BE GLAD I'M ALREADY SITTING DOWN?
I...I'VE BEEN KEEPING SOMETHING FROM YOU. I KNOW THAT'S NOT HOW IT'S SUPPOSED TO WORK BETWEEN US, BUT I WAS SCARED YOU'D THINK I WAS BEING PARANOID.
IT'S THE BOOK OF THE GEOMANCER. THE WEIGHT OF IT FEELS OFF SOMEHOW-- LIKE SOMETHING INSIDE'S SHIFTED.
SHIFTED?
TAMA, IT'S A BOOK.
YOU KNOW AS WELL AS I DO IT'S MUCH MORE THAN--
NO--!
WHAT? WHAT IS IT?
THE BOOK IS SCREAMING!
GILAD, WHAT DOES IT MEAN?
I DON'T KNOW...

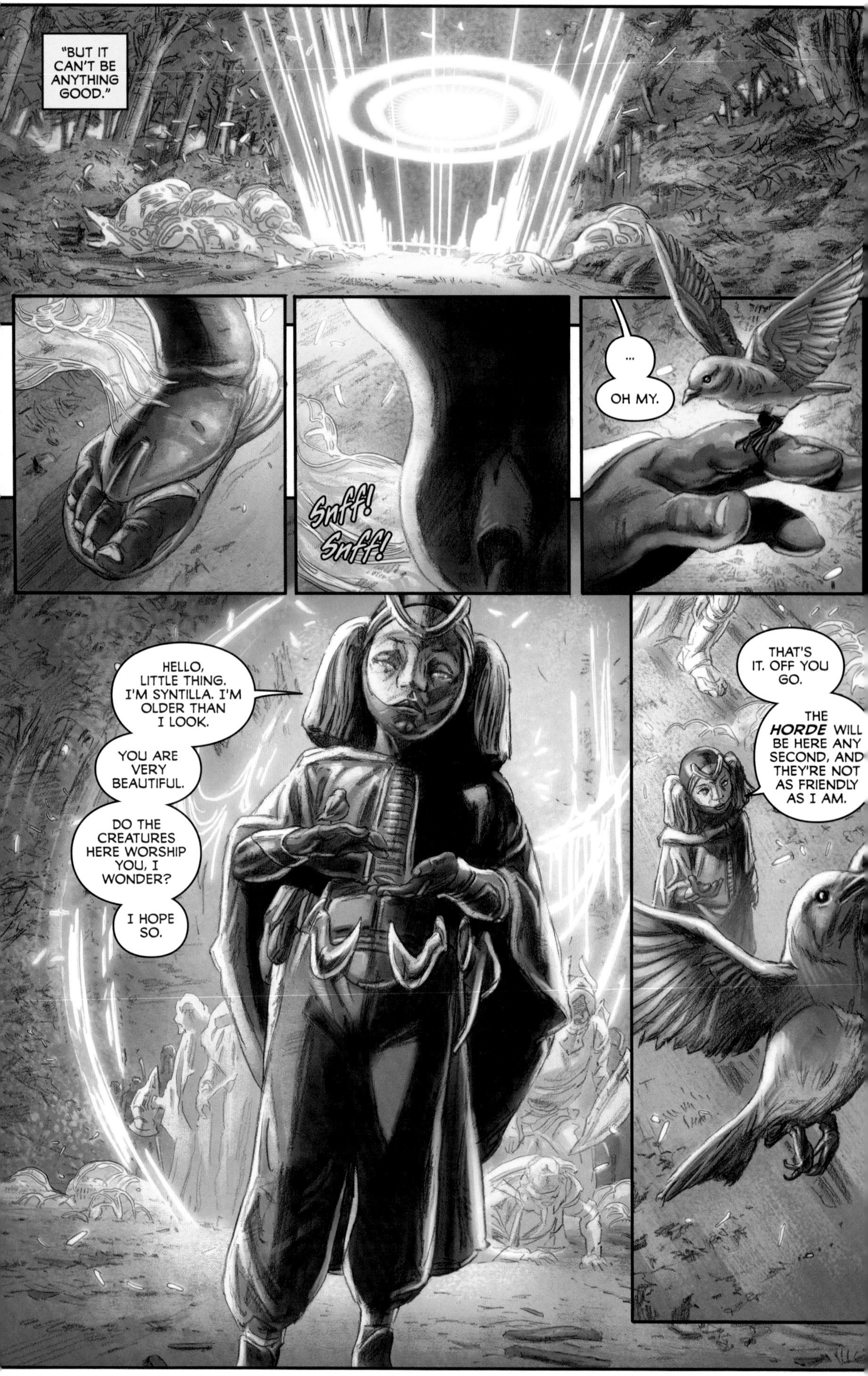
"BUT IT CAN'T BE ANYTHING GOOD."
Snff! Snff!
...
OH MY.
HELLO, LITTLE THING. I'M SYNTILLA. I'M OLDER THAN I LOOK.
YOU ARE VERY BEAUTIFUL.
DO THE CREATURES HERE WORSHIP YOU, I WONDER?
I HOPE SO.
THAT'S IT. OFF YOU GO.
THE *HORDE* WILL BE HERE ANY SECOND, AND THEY'RE NOT AS FRIENDLY AS I AM.

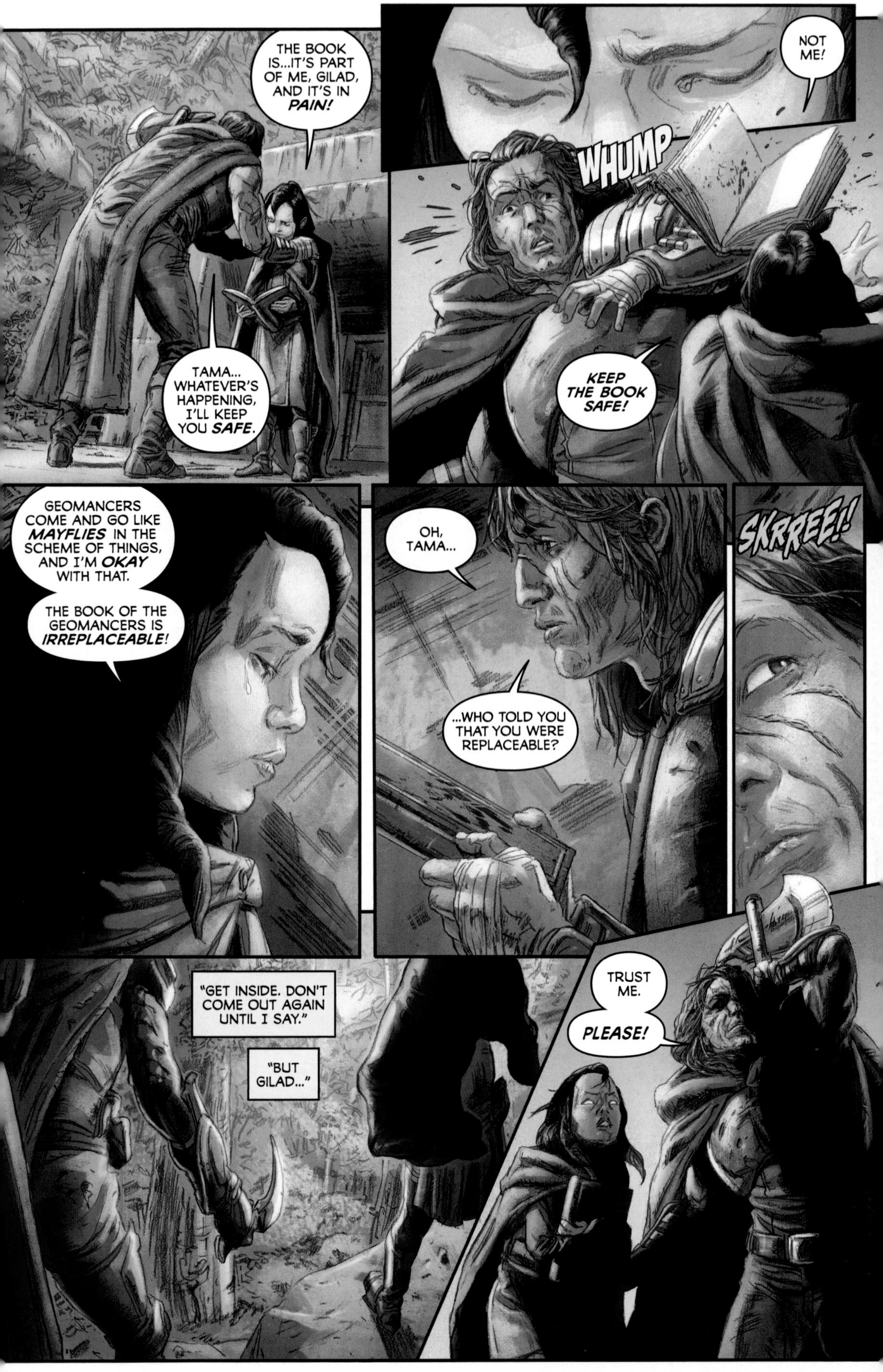
THE BOOK IS...IT'S PART OF ME, GILAD, AND IT'S IN *PAIN!*
TAMA... WHATEVER'S HAPPENING, I'LL KEEP YOU *SAFE*.
NOT ME!
WHUMP
KEEP THE BOOK SAFE!
GEOMANCERS COME AND GO LIKE *MAYFLIES* IN THE SCHEME OF THINGS, AND I'M *OKAY* WITH THAT.
THE BOOK OF THE GEOMANCERS IS *IRREPLACEABLE!*
OH, TAMA...
...WHO TOLD YOU THAT YOU WERE REPLACEABLE?
SKRREE!!
"GET INSIDE. DON'T COME OUT AGAIN UNTIL I SAY."
"BUT GILAD..."
TRUST ME.
PLEASE!

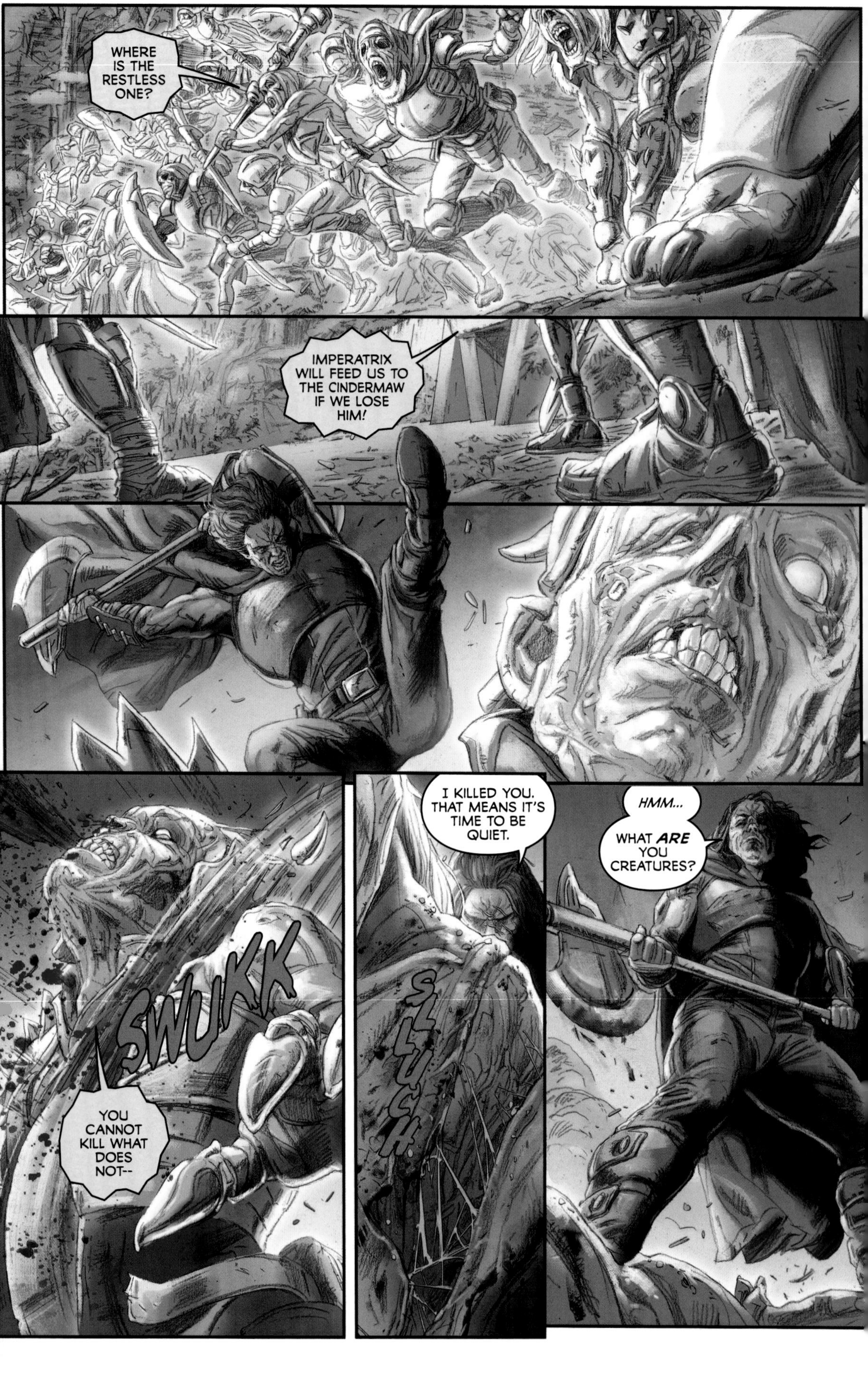
WHERE IS THE RESTLESS ONE?
IMPERATRIX WILL FEED US TO THE CINDERMAW IF WE LOSE HIM!
SWUKK
YOU CANNOT KILL WHAT DOES NOT--
SLUCH
I KILLED YOU. THAT MEANS IT'S TIME TO BE QUIET.
HMM...
WHAT *ARE* YOU CREATURES?

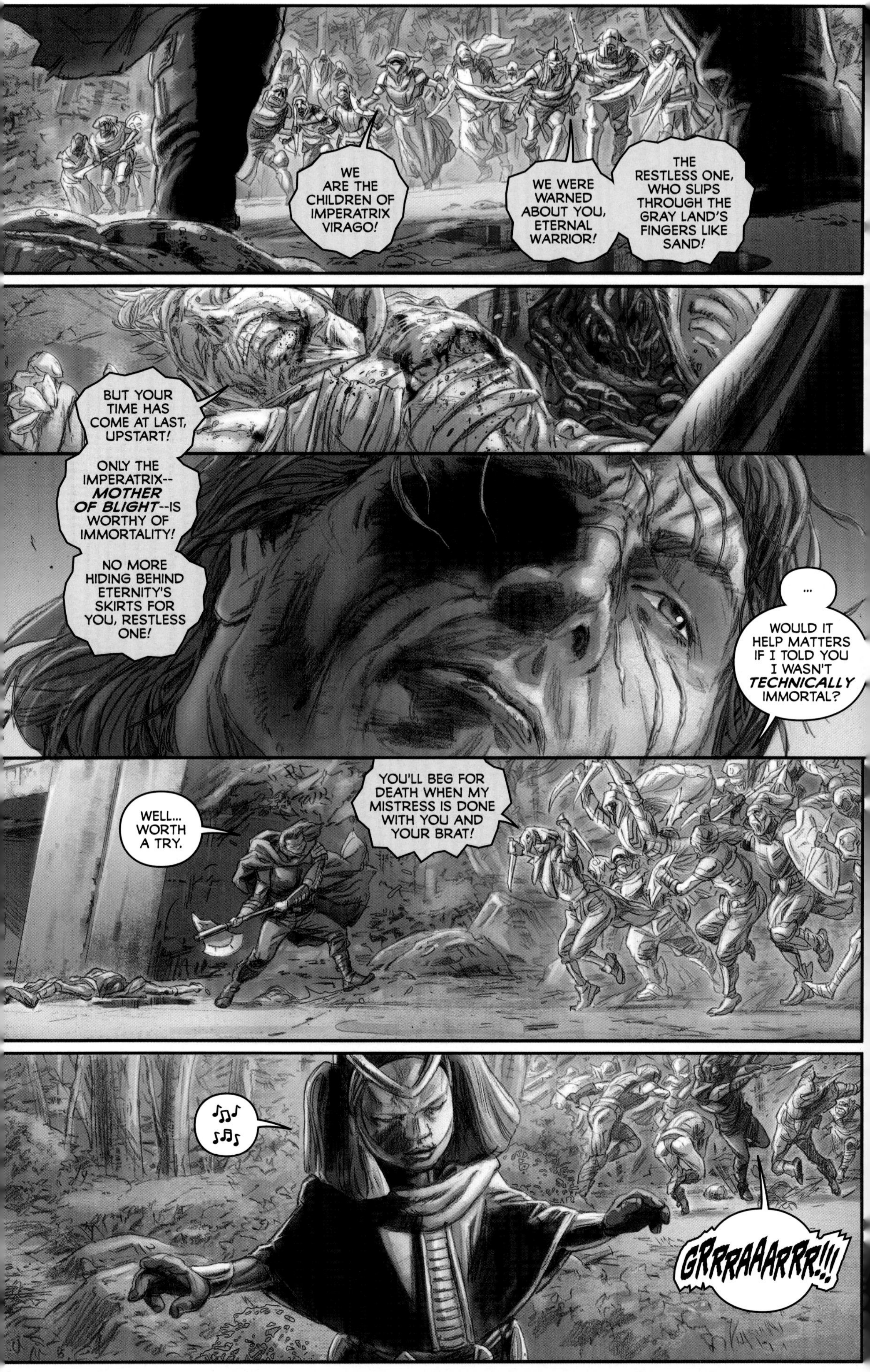
WE ARE THE CHILDREN OF IMPERATRIX VIRAGO!
WE WERE WARNED ABOUT YOU, ETERNAL WARRIOR!
THE RESTLESS ONE, WHO SLIPS THROUGH THE GRAY LAND'S FINGERS LIKE SAND!
BUT YOUR TIME HAS COME AT LAST, UPSTART!
ONLY THE IMPERATRIX--*MOTHER OF BLIGHT*--IS WORTHY OF IMMORTALITY!
NO MORE HIDING BEHIND ETERNITY'S SKIRTS FOR YOU, RESTLESS ONE!
...
WOULD IT HELP MATTERS IF I TOLD YOU I WASN'T *TECHNICALLY* IMMORTAL?
WELL... WORTH A TRY.
YOU'LL BEG FOR DEATH WHEN MY MISTRESS IS DONE WITH YOU AND YOUR BRAT!
GRRRAAARRR!!!

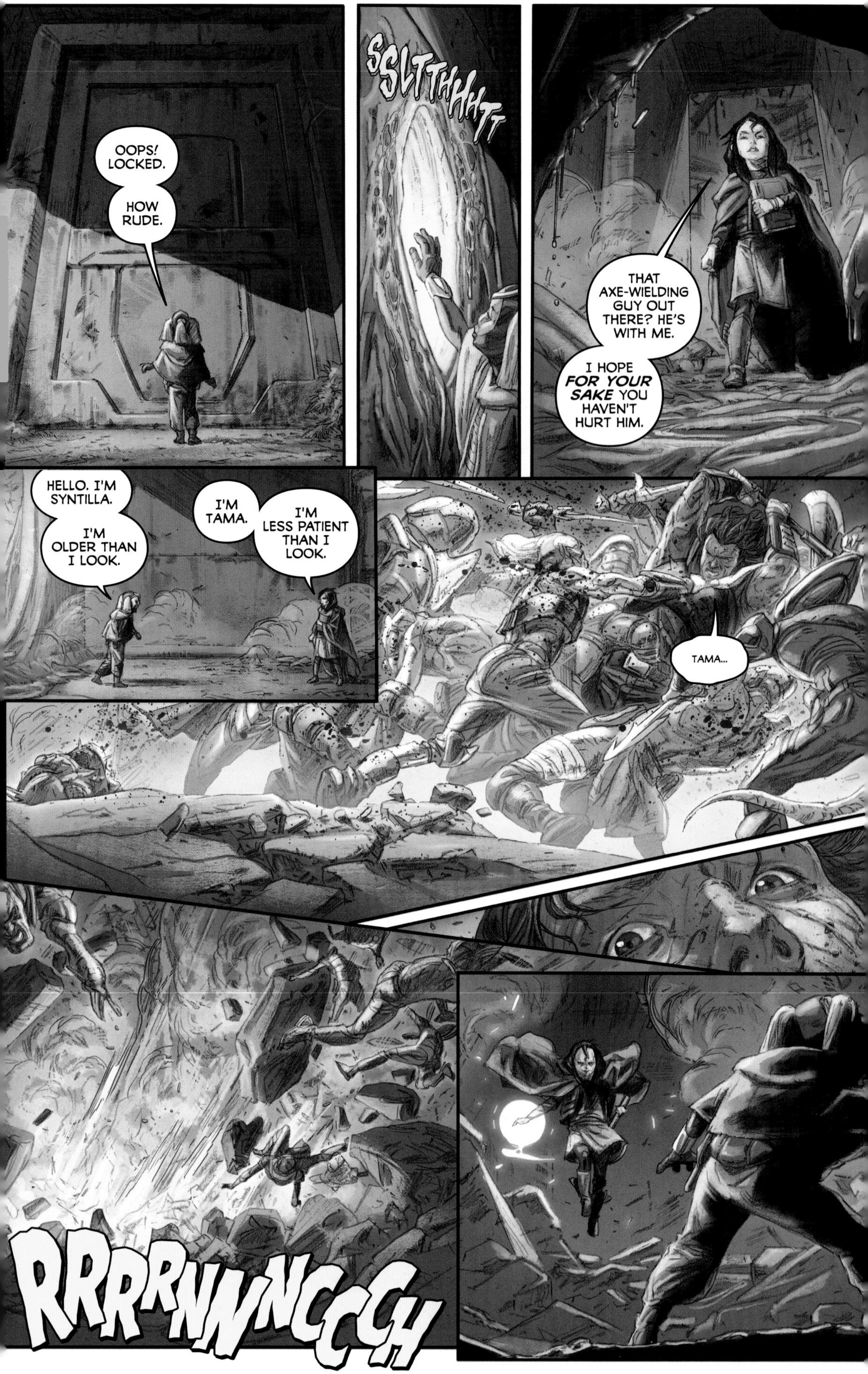
OOPS! LOCKED.
HOW RUDE.
SSLTTHHHTT
THAT AXE-WIELDING GUY OUT THERE? HE'S WITH ME.
I HOPE **FOR YOUR SAKE** YOU HAVEN'T HURT HIM.
HELLO. I'M SYNTILLA.
I'M OLDER THAN I LOOK.
I'M TAMA.
I'M LESS PATIENT THAN I LOOK.
TAMA...
RRRRNNNCCCH

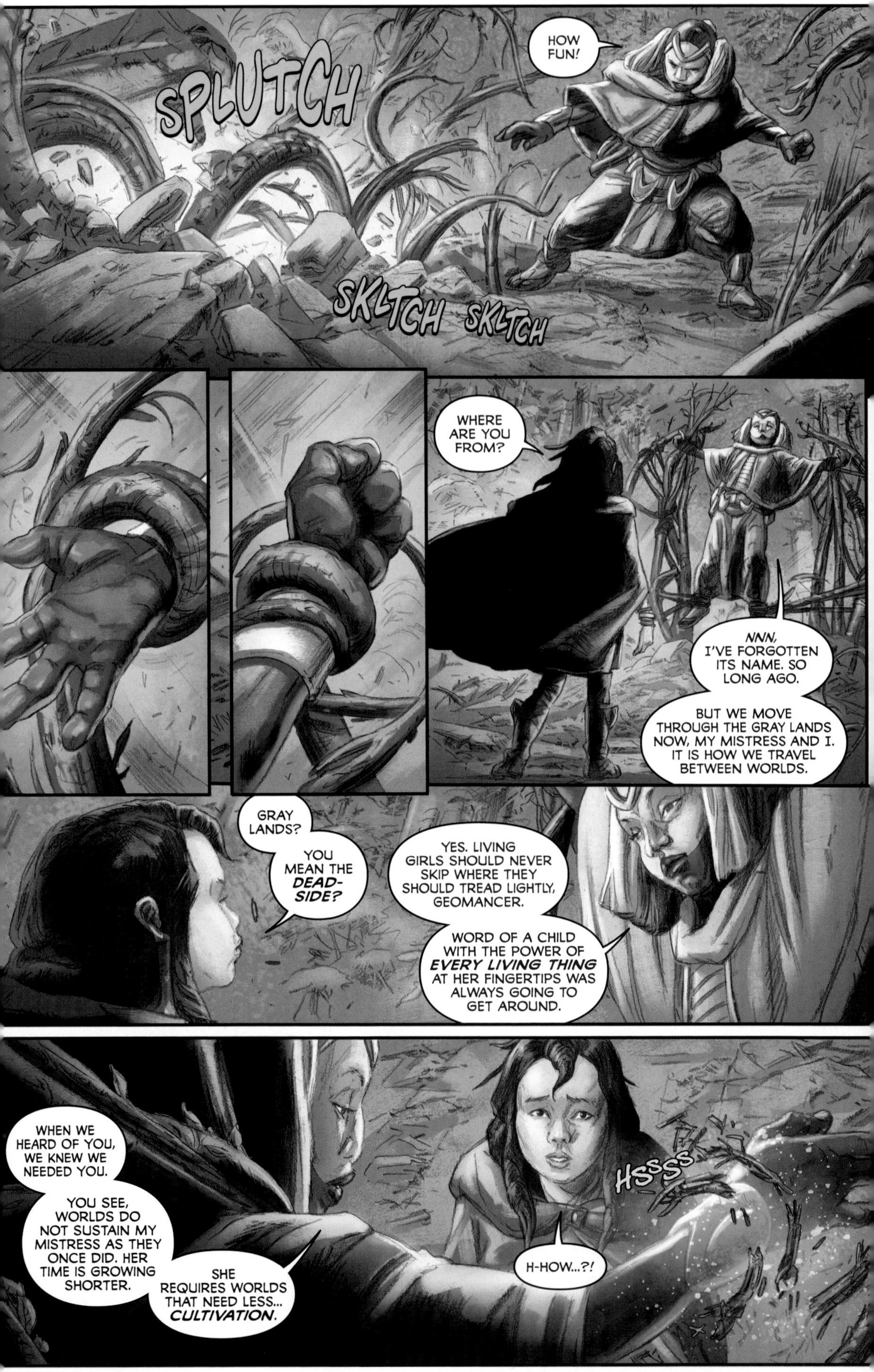
HOW FUN!
SPLUTCH
SKLTCH SKLTCH
WHERE ARE YOU FROM?
NNN, I'VE FORGOTTEN ITS NAME. SO LONG AGO.
BUT WE MOVE THROUGH THE GRAY LANDS NOW, MY MISTRESS AND I. IT IS HOW WE TRAVEL BETWEEN WORLDS.
GRAY LANDS?
YOU MEAN THE *DEAD-SIDE?*
YES. LIVING GIRLS SHOULD NEVER SKIP WHERE THEY SHOULD TREAD LIGHTLY, GEOMANCER.
WORD OF A CHILD WITH THE POWER OF ***EVERY LIVING THING*** AT HER FINGERTIPS WAS ALWAYS GOING TO GET AROUND.
WHEN WE HEARD OF YOU, WE KNEW WE NEEDED YOU.
YOU SEE, WORLDS DO NOT SUSTAIN MY MISTRESS AS THEY ONCE DID. HER TIME IS GROWING SHORTER.
SHE REQUIRES WORLDS THAT NEED LESS... ***CULTIVATION.***
HSSSS
H-HOW...?!

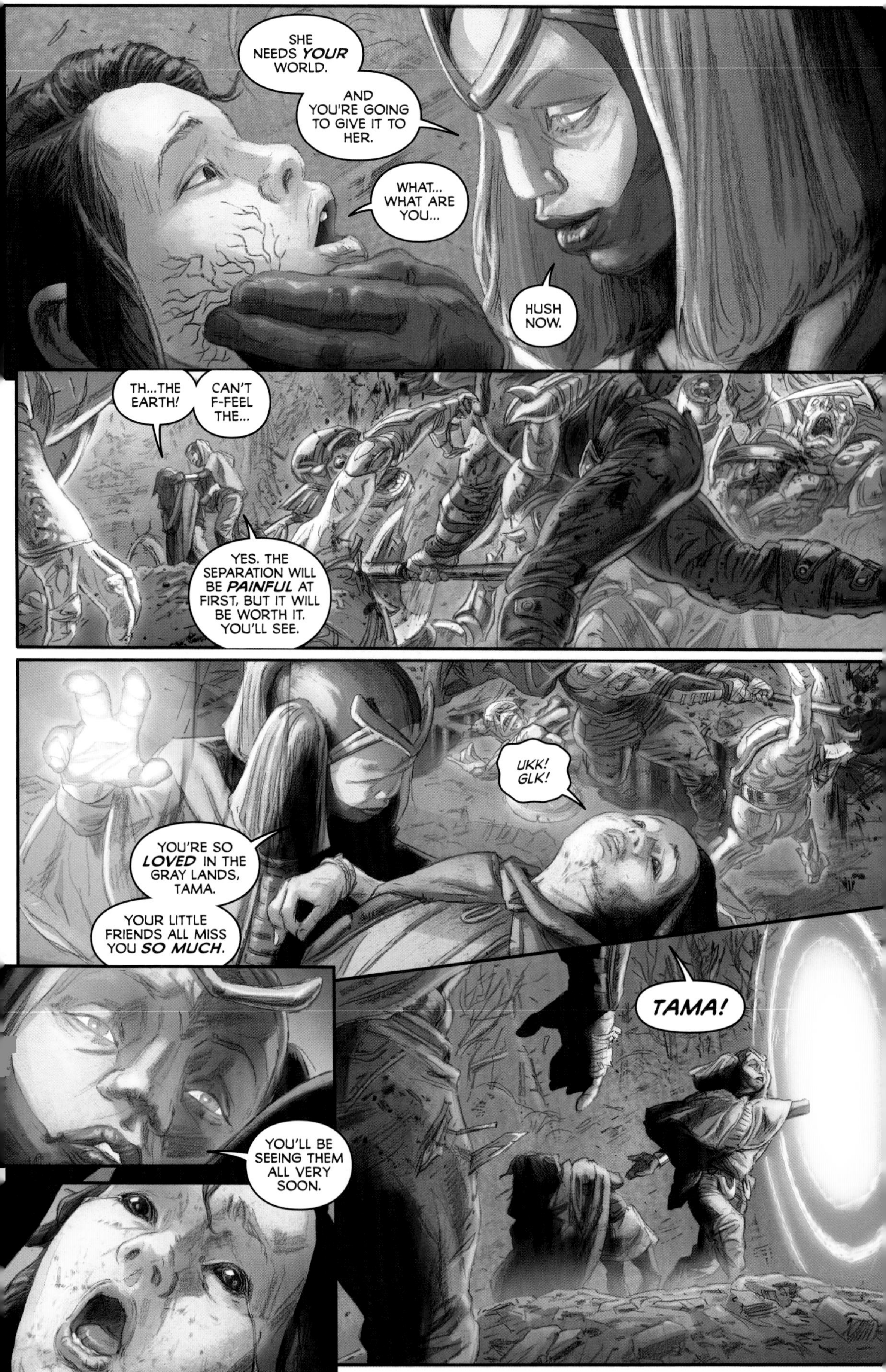
SHE NEEDS *YOUR* WORLD.
AND YOU'RE GOING TO GIVE IT TO HER.
WHAT... WHAT ARE YOU...
HUSH NOW.
TH...THE EARTH!
CAN'T F-FEEL THE...
YES. THE SEPARATION WILL BE *PAINFUL* AT FIRST, BUT IT WILL BE WORTH IT. YOU'LL SEE.
UKK! GLK!
YOU'RE SO *LOVED* IN THE GRAY LANDS, TAMA.
YOUR LITTLE FRIENDS ALL MISS YOU *SO MUCH*.
TAMA!
YOU'LL BE SEEING THEM ALL VERY SOON.

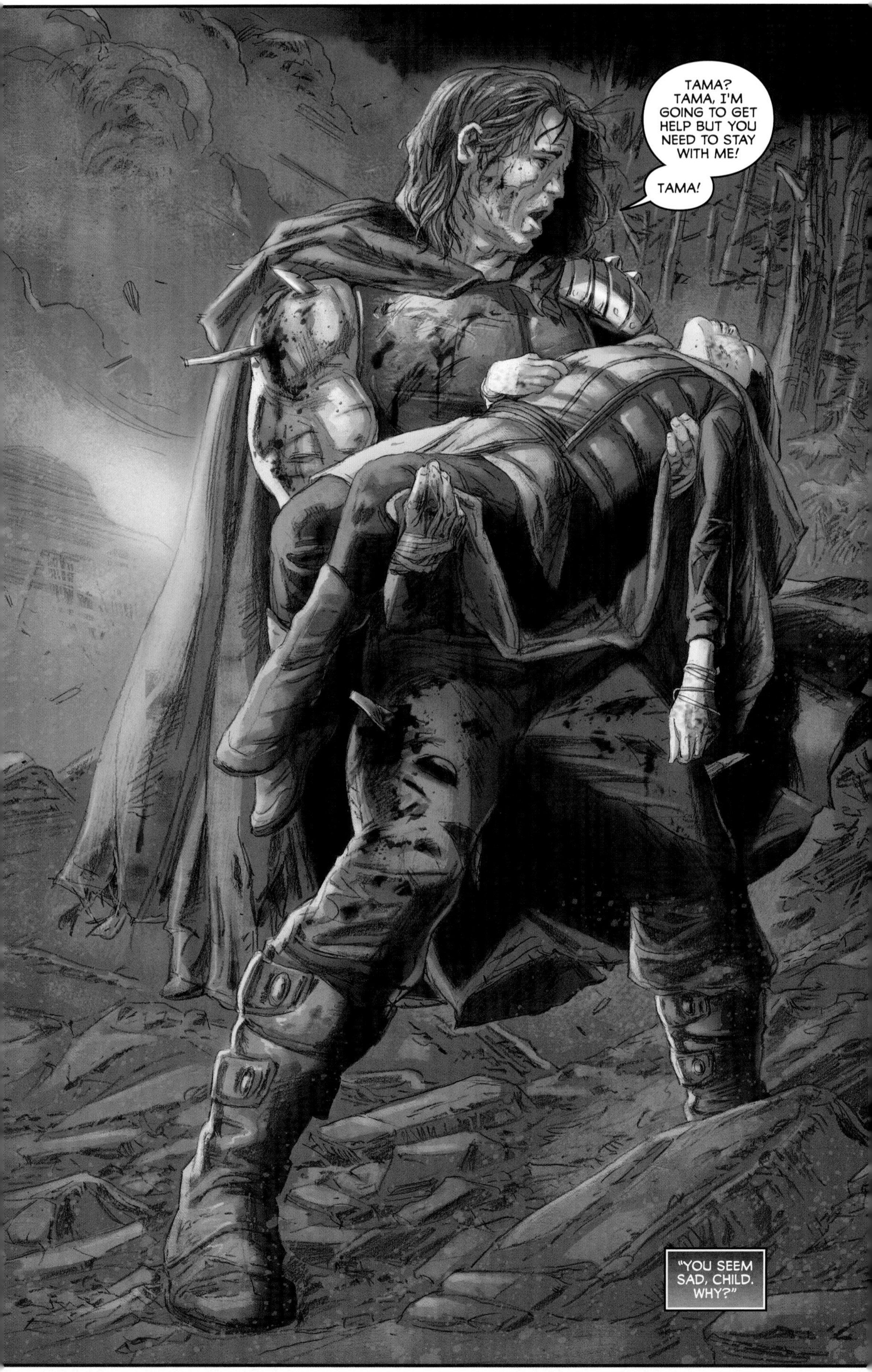
TAMA? TAMA, I'M GOING TO GET HELP BUT YOU NEED TO STAY WITH ME!
TAMA!
"YOU SEEM SAD, CHILD. WHY?"

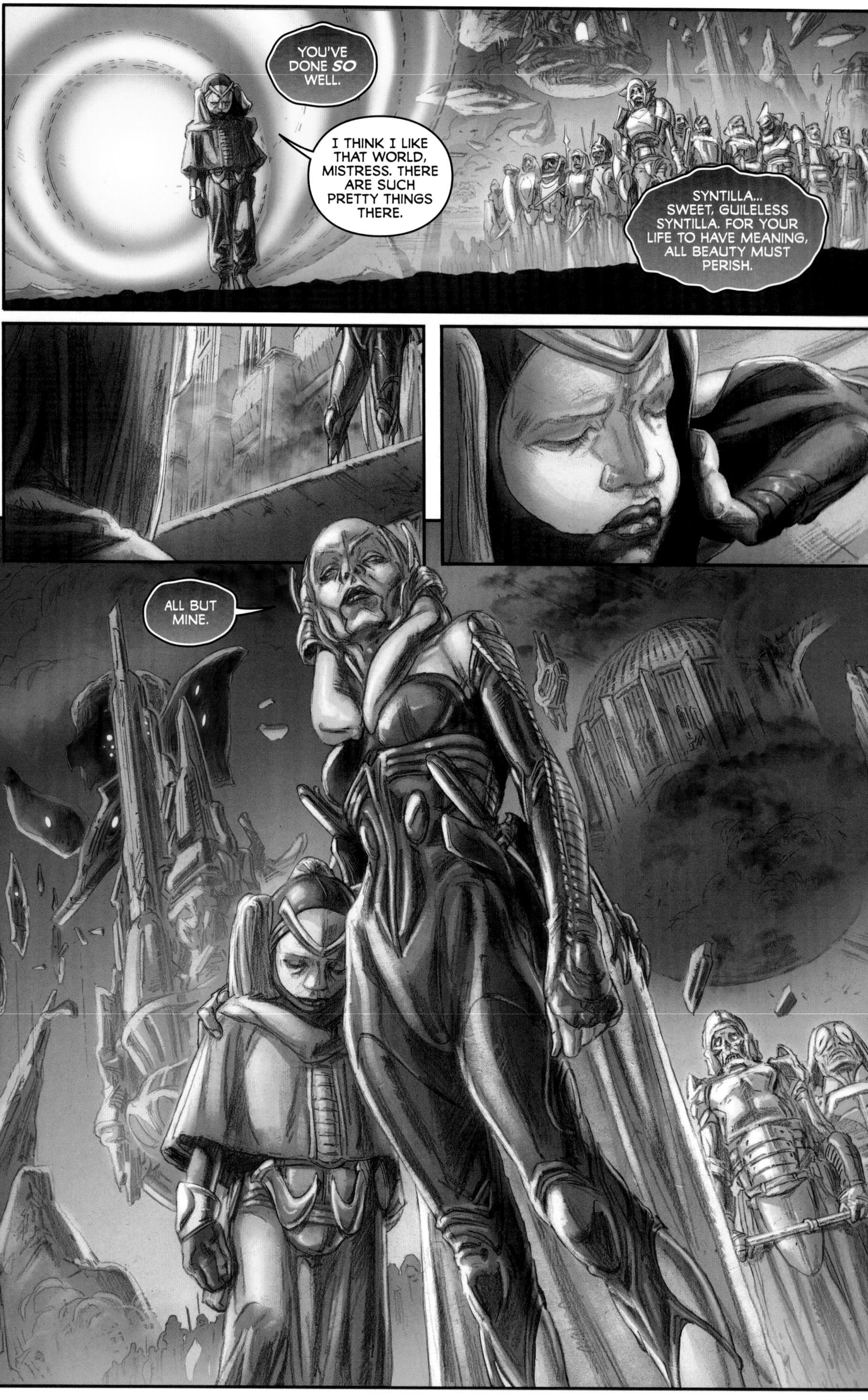
YOU'VE DONE SO WELL.
I THINK I LIKE THAT WORLD, MISTRESS. THERE ARE SUCH PRETTY THINGS THERE.
SYNTILLA... SWEET, GUILELESS SYNTILLA. FOR YOUR LIFE TO HAVE MEANING, ALL BEAUTY MUST PERISH.
ALL BUT MINE.

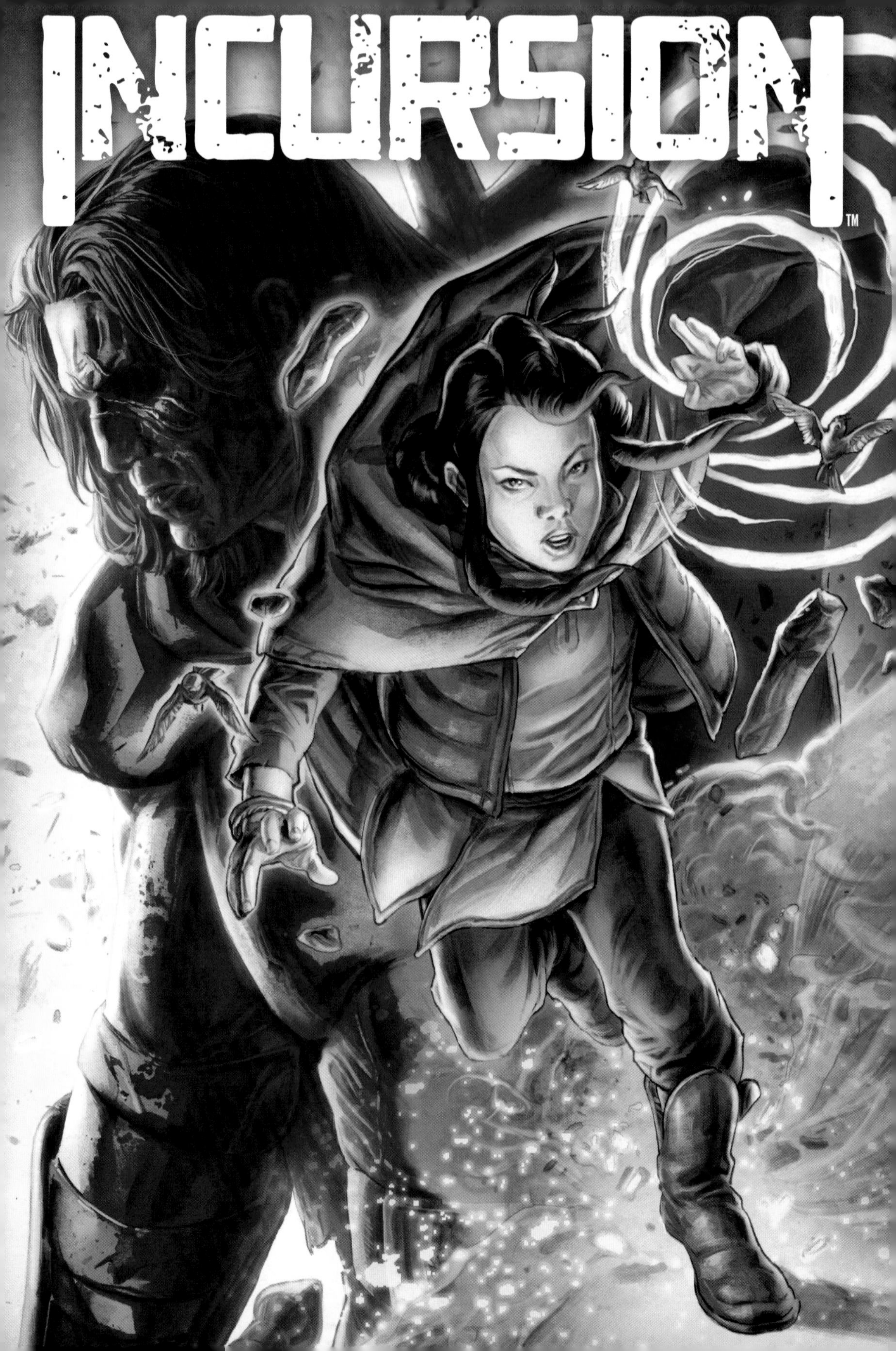
INCURSION™

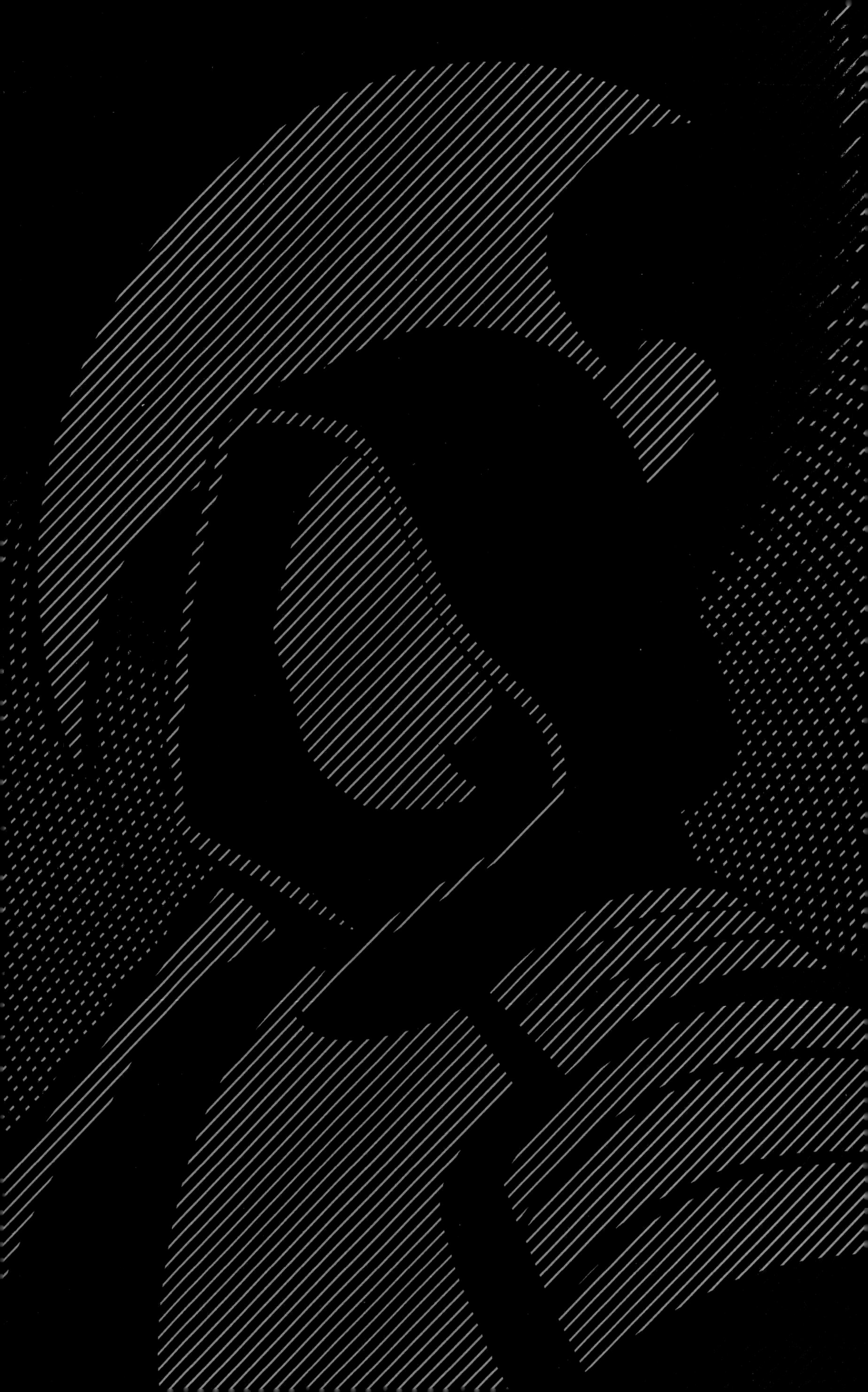

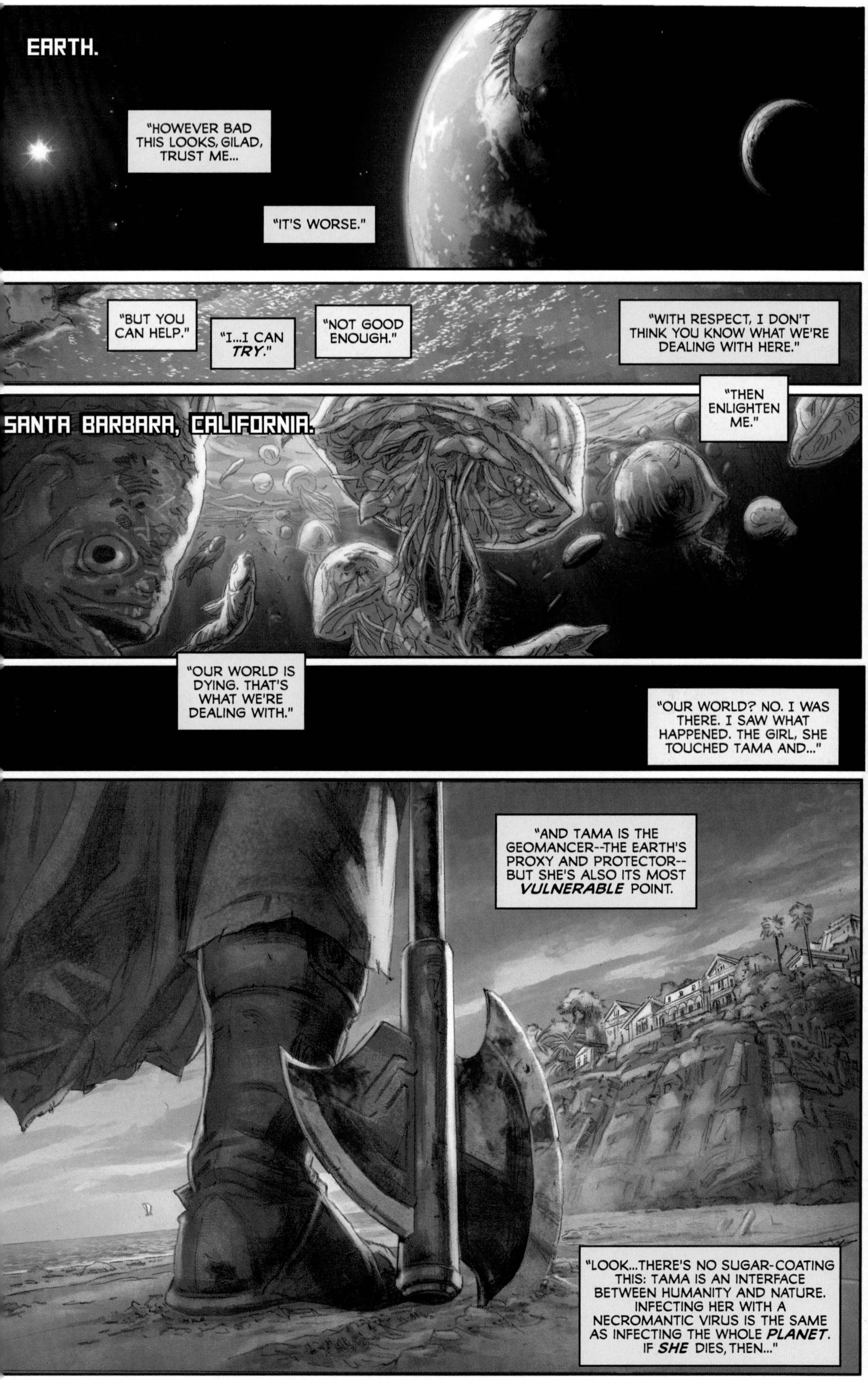
EARTH.
"HOWEVER BAD THIS LOOKS, GILAD, TRUST ME...
"IT'S WORSE."
"BUT YOU CAN HELP."
"I...I CAN *TRY*."
"NOT GOOD ENOUGH."
"WITH RESPECT, I DON'T THINK YOU KNOW WHAT WE'RE DEALING WITH HERE."
"THEN ENLIGHTEN ME."
SANTA BARBARA, CALIFORNIA.
"OUR WORLD IS DYING. THAT'S WHAT WE'RE DEALING WITH."
"OUR WORLD? NO. I WAS THERE. I SAW WHAT HAPPENED. THE GIRL, SHE TOUCHED TAMA AND..."
"AND TAMA IS THE GEOMANCER--THE EARTH'S PROXY AND PROTECTOR--BUT SHE'S ALSO ITS MOST ***VULNERABLE*** POINT.
"LOOK...THERE'S NO SUGAR-COATING THIS: TAMA IS AN INTERFACE BETWEEN HUMANITY AND NATURE. INFECTING HER WITH A NECROMANTIC VIRUS IS THE SAME AS INFECTING THE WHOLE ***PLANET***. IF ***SHE*** DIES, THEN..."

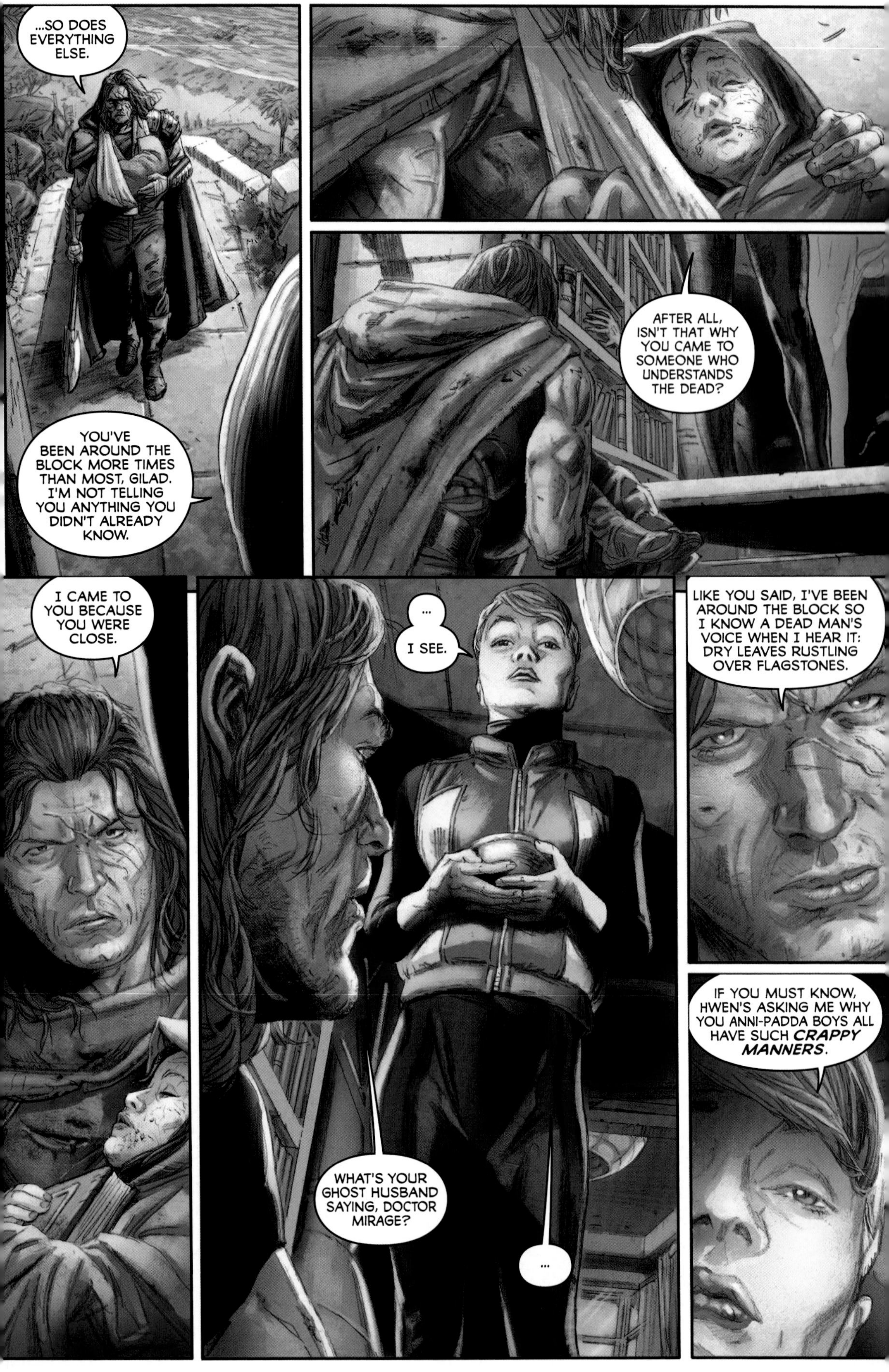
...SO DOES EVERYTHING ELSE.
YOU'VE BEEN AROUND THE BLOCK MORE TIMES THAN MOST, GILAD. I'M NOT TELLING YOU ANYTHING YOU DIDN'T ALREADY KNOW.
AFTER ALL, ISN'T THAT WHY YOU CAME TO SOMEONE WHO UNDERSTANDS THE DEAD?
I CAME TO YOU BECAUSE YOU WERE CLOSE.
...
I SEE.
WHAT'S YOUR GHOST HUSBAND SAYING, DOCTOR MIRAGE?
...
LIKE YOU SAID, I'VE BEEN AROUND THE BLOCK SO I KNOW A DEAD MAN'S VOICE WHEN I HEAR IT: DRY LEAVES RUSTLING OVER FLAGSTONES.
IF YOU MUST KNOW, HWEN'S ASKING ME WHY YOU ANNI-PADDA BOYS ALL HAVE SUCH *CRAPPY MANNERS*.

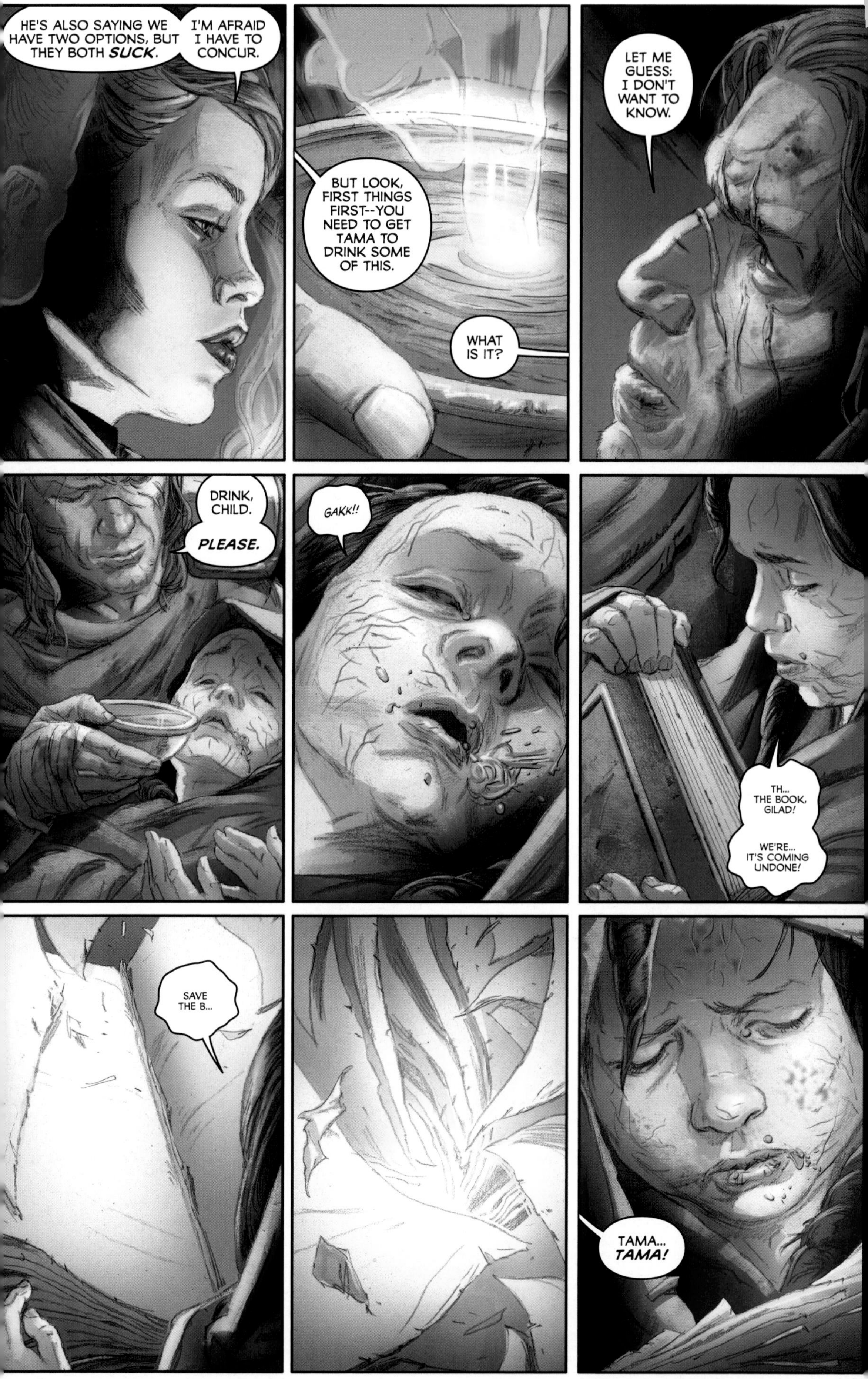
HE'S ALSO SAYING WE HAVE TWO OPTIONS, BUT THEY BOTH ***SUCK***.
I'M AFRAID I HAVE TO CONCUR.
BUT LOOK, FIRST THINGS FIRST--YOU NEED TO GET TAMA TO DRINK SOME OF THIS.
WHAT IS IT?
LET ME GUESS: I DON'T WANT TO KNOW.
DRINK, CHILD.
PLEASE.
GAKK!!
TH... THE BOOK, GILAD!
WE'RE... IT'S COMING UNDONE!
SAVE THE B...
TAMA... ***TAMA!***

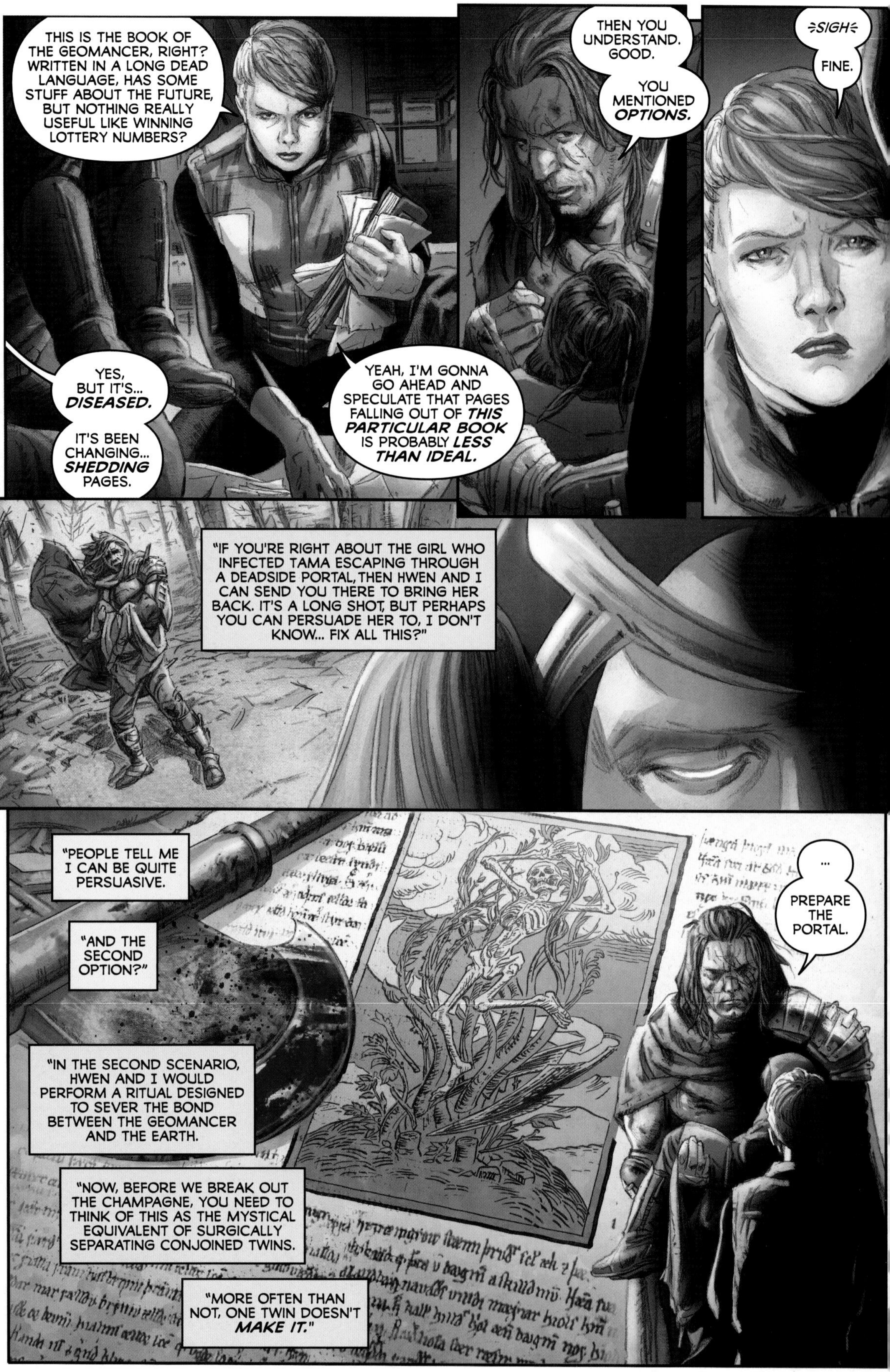
THIS IS THE BOOK OF THE GEOMANCER, RIGHT? WRITTEN IN A LONG DEAD LANGUAGE, HAS SOME STUFF ABOUT THE FUTURE, BUT NOTHING REALLY USEFUL LIKE WINNING LOTTERY NUMBERS?
YES, BUT IT'S... DISEASED.
IT'S BEEN CHANGING... SHEDDING PAGES.
YEAH, I'M GONNA GO AHEAD AND SPECULATE THAT PAGES FALLING OUT OF THIS PARTICULAR BOOK IS PROBABLY LESS THAN IDEAL.
THEN YOU UNDERSTAND. GOOD.
YOU MENTIONED OPTIONS.
SIGH
FINE.
"IF YOU'RE RIGHT ABOUT THE GIRL WHO INFECTED TAMA ESCAPING THROUGH A DEADSIDE PORTAL, THEN HWEN AND I CAN SEND YOU THERE TO BRING HER BACK. IT'S A LONG SHOT, BUT PERHAPS YOU CAN PERSUADE HER TO, I DON'T KNOW... FIX ALL THIS?"
"PEOPLE TELL ME I CAN BE QUITE PERSUASIVE.
"AND THE SECOND OPTION?"
"IN THE SECOND SCENARIO, HWEN AND I WOULD PERFORM A RITUAL DESIGNED TO SEVER THE BOND BETWEEN THE GEOMANCER AND THE EARTH.
"NOW, BEFORE WE BREAK OUT THE CHAMPAGNE, YOU NEED TO THINK OF THIS AS THE MYSTICAL EQUIVALENT OF SURGICALLY SEPARATING CONJOINED TWINS.
"MORE OFTEN THAN NOT, ONE TWIN DOESN'T MAKE IT."
...
PREPARE THE PORTAL.

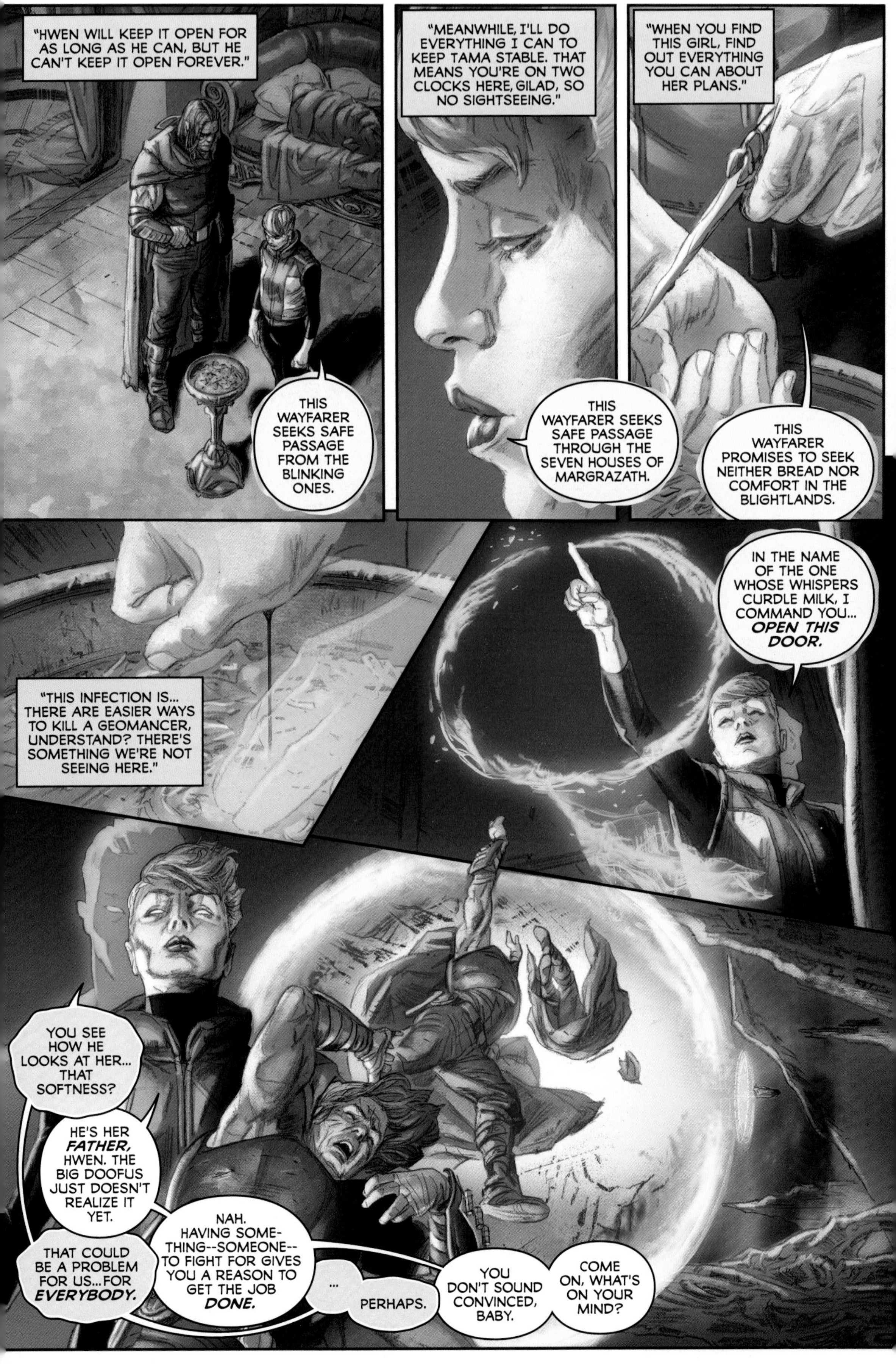
"HWEN WILL KEEP IT OPEN FOR AS LONG AS HE CAN, BUT HE CAN'T KEEP IT OPEN FOREVER."
THIS WAYFARER SEEKS SAFE PASSAGE FROM THE BLINKING ONES.
"MEANWHILE, I'LL DO EVERYTHING I CAN TO KEEP TAMA STABLE. THAT MEANS YOU'RE ON TWO CLOCKS HERE, GILAD, SO NO SIGHTSEEING."
THIS WAYFARER SEEKS SAFE PASSAGE THROUGH THE SEVEN HOUSES OF MARGRAZATH.
"WHEN YOU FIND THIS GIRL, FIND OUT EVERYTHING YOU CAN ABOUT HER PLANS."
THIS WAYFARER PROMISES TO SEEK NEITHER BREAD NOR COMFORT IN THE BLIGHTLANDS.
"THIS INFECTION IS... THERE ARE EASIER WAYS TO KILL A GEOMANCER, UNDERSTAND? THERE'S SOMETHING WE'RE NOT SEEING HERE."
IN THE NAME OF THE ONE WHOSE WHISPERS CURDLE MILK, I COMMAND YOU... ***OPEN THIS DOOR.***
YOU SEE HOW HE LOOKS AT HER... THAT SOFTNESS?
HE'S HER ***FATHER,*** HWEN. THE BIG DOOFUS JUST DOESN'T REALIZE IT YET.
THAT COULD BE A PROBLEM FOR US...FOR ***EVERYBODY.***
NAH. HAVING SOME-THING--SOMEONE--TO FIGHT FOR GIVES YOU A REASON TO GET THE JOB ***DONE.***
...
PERHAPS.
YOU DON'T SOUND CONVINCED, BABY.
COME ON, WHAT'S ON YOUR MIND?

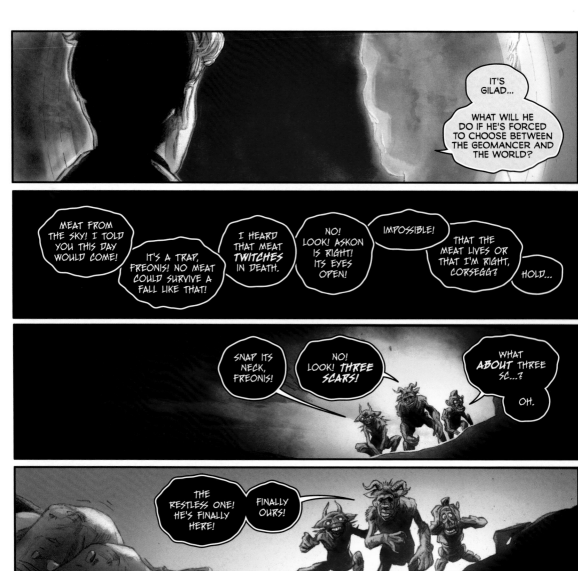

IT'S GILAD...

WHAT WILL HE DO IF HE'S FORCED TO CHOOSE BETWEEN THE GEOMANCER AND THE WORLD?

MEAT FROM THE SKY! I TOLD YOU THIS DAY WOULD COME!

IT'S A TRAP, FREONIS! NO MEAT COULD SURVIVE A FALL LIKE THAT!

I HEARD THAT MEAT TWITCHES IN DEATH.

NO! LOOK! ASKON IS RIGHT! ITS EYES OPEN!

IMPOSSIBLE!

THAT THE MEAT LIVES OR THAT I'M RIGHT, CORSEGG?

HOLD...

SNAP ITS NECK, FREONIS!

NO! LOOK! THREE SCARS!

WHAT ABOUT THREE SC...?

OH.

THE RESTLESS ONE! HE'S FINALLY HERE!

FINALLY OURS!

I WANT HIS TEETH! IMAGINE WHAT THOSE UPPER CASTE TURDS WILL PAY FOR THEM!

CARVE OUT HIS EYES, FREONIS! JUST IMAGINE WHAT THEY'VE SEEN...!

SHUKK

UTT!

SKLCH

GLLGGLL

?

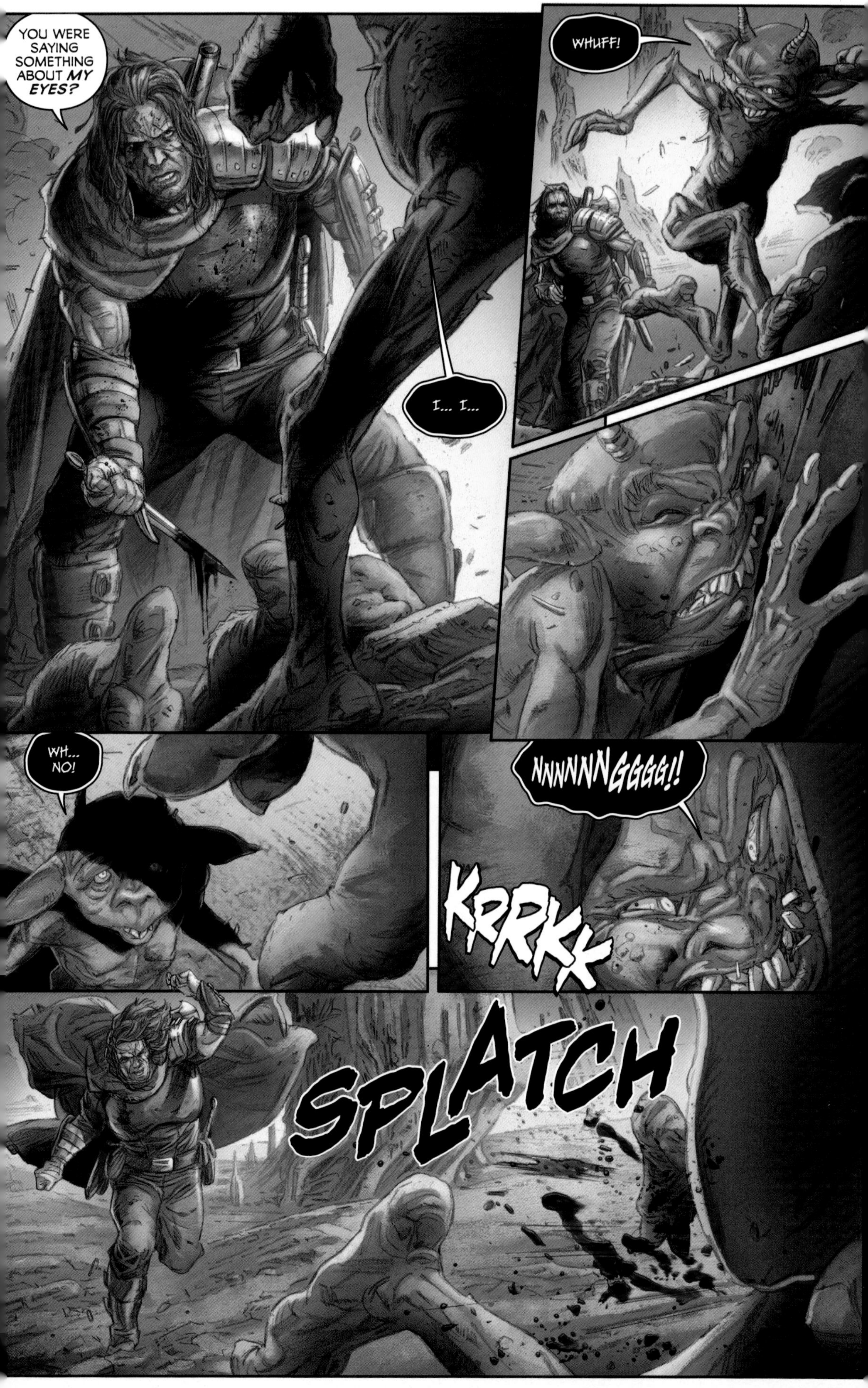
YOU WERE SAYING SOMETHING ABOUT *MY EYES?*
I... I...
WHUFF!
WH... NO!
NNNNNNGGGG!!
KRRKK
SPLATCH

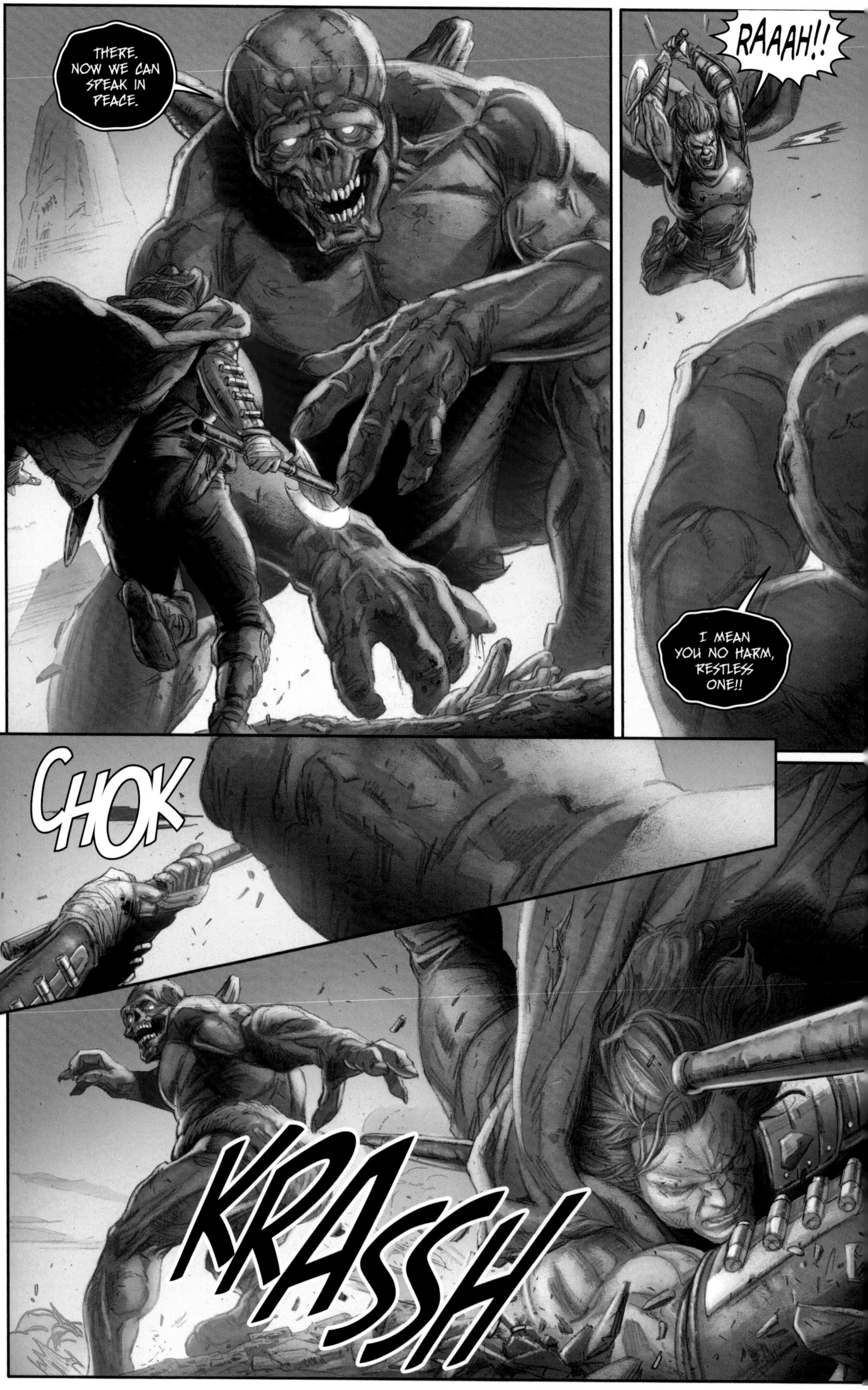
THERE. NOW WE CAN SPEAK IN PEACE.
RAAAH!!
I MEAN YOU NO HARM, RESTLESS ONE!!
CHOK
KRASSH

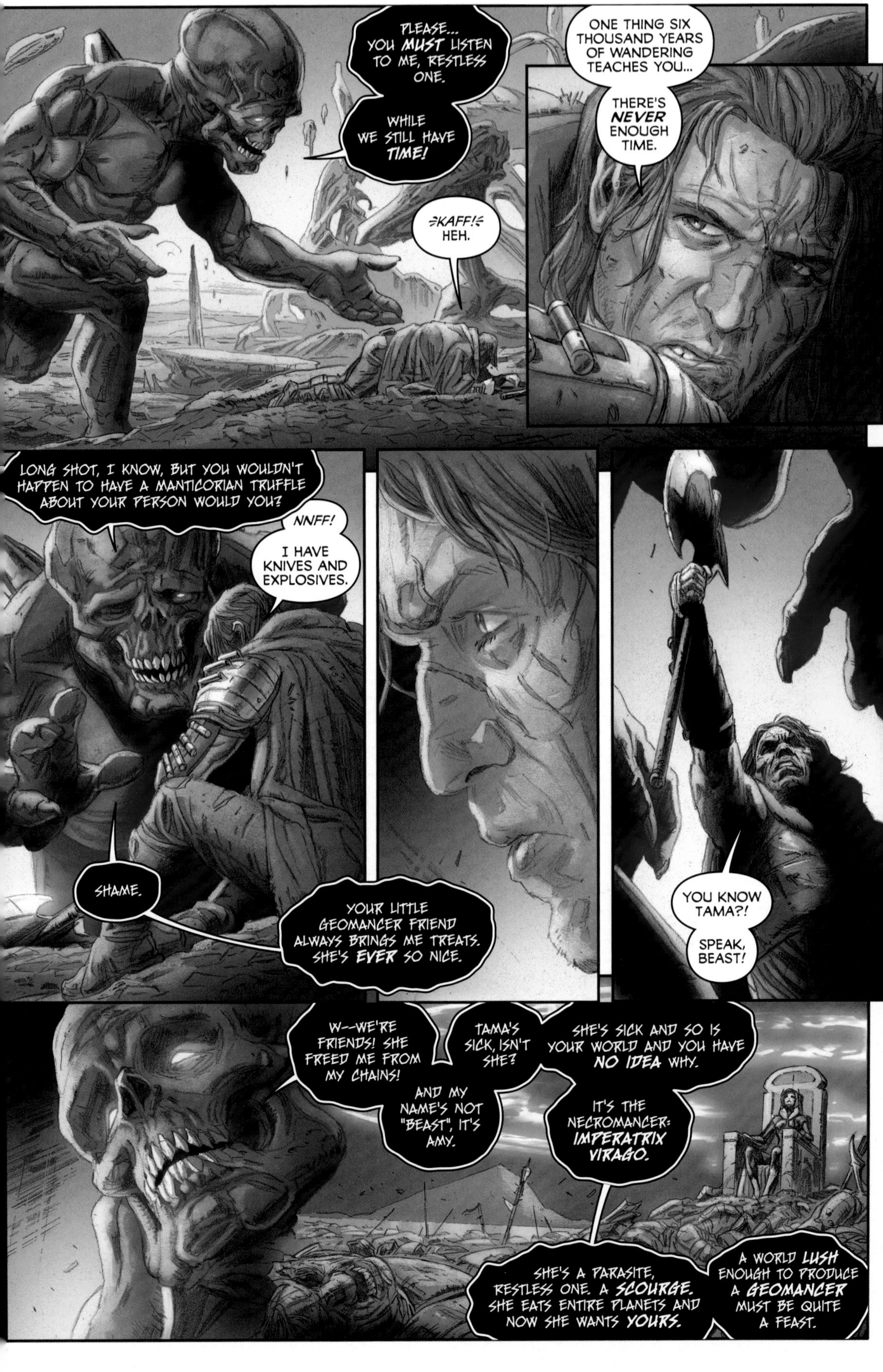
PLEASE... YOU MUST LISTEN TO ME, RESTLESS ONE.
WHILE WE STILL HAVE TIME!
≈KAFF!≈ HEH.
ONE THING SIX THOUSAND YEARS OF WANDERING TEACHES YOU...
THERE'S NEVER ENOUGH TIME.
LONG SHOT, I KNOW, BUT YOU WOULDN'T HAPPEN TO HAVE A MANTICORIAN TRUFFLE ABOUT YOUR PERSON WOULD YOU?
NNFF!
I HAVE KNIVES AND EXPLOSIVES.
SHAME.
YOUR LITTLE GEOMANCER FRIEND ALWAYS BRINGS ME TREATS. SHE'S EVER SO NICE.
YOU KNOW TAMA?!
SPEAK, BEAST!
W--WE'RE FRIENDS! SHE FREED ME FROM MY CHAINS!
AND MY NAME'S NOT "BEAST", IT'S AMY.
TAMA'S SICK, ISN'T SHE?
SHE'S SICK AND SO IS YOUR WORLD AND YOU HAVE NO IDEA WHY.
IT'S THE NECROMANCER: IMPERATRIX VIRAGO.
SHE'S A PARASITE, RESTLESS ONE. A SCOURGE. SHE EATS ENTIRE PLANETS AND NOW SHE WANTS YOURS.
A WORLD LUSH ENOUGH TO PRODUCE A GEOMANCER MUST BE QUITE A FEAST.

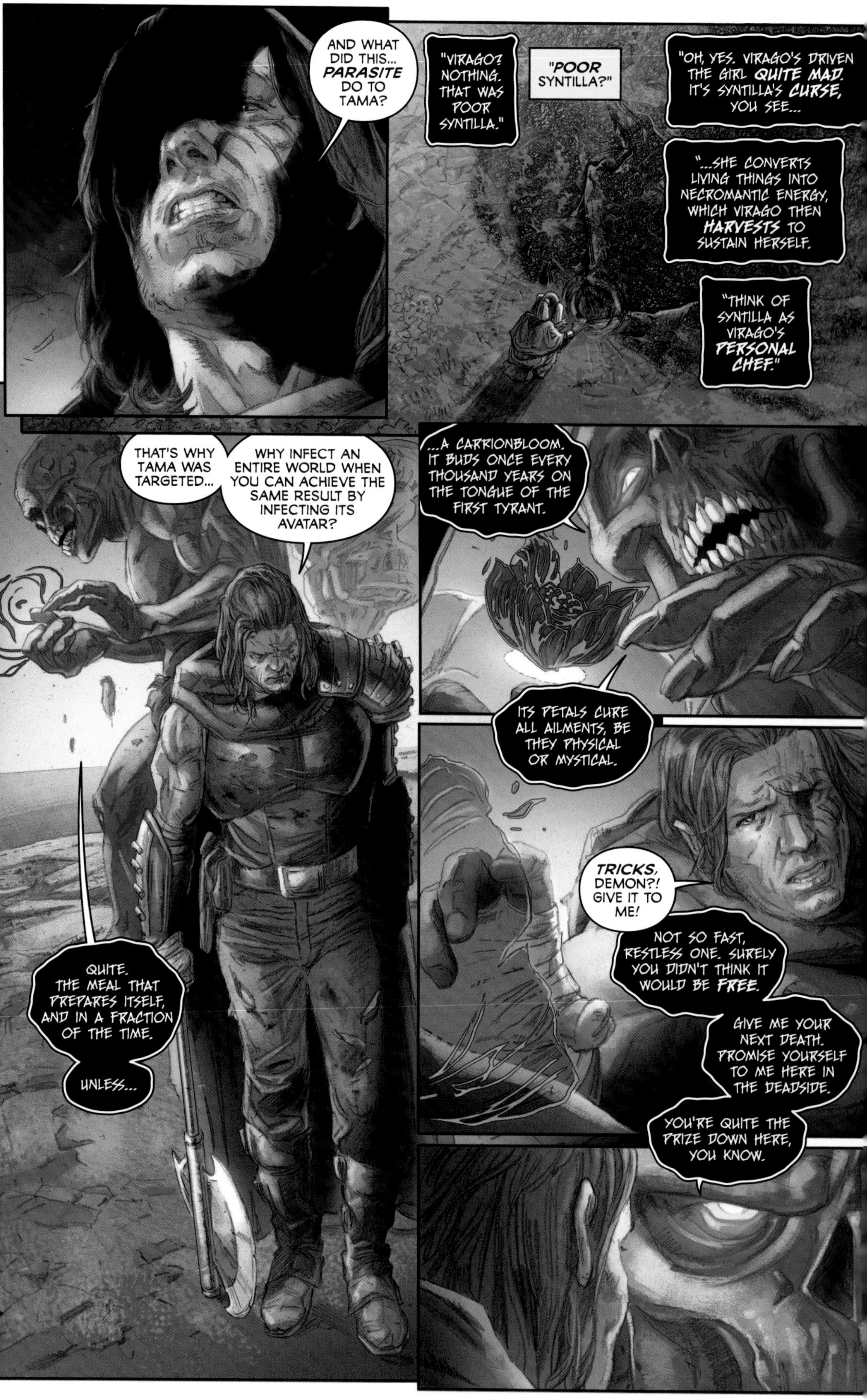

AND WHAT DID THIS... *PARASITE* DO TO TAMA?
"VIRAGO? NOTHING. THAT WAS POOR SYNTILLA."
"*POOR* SYNTILLA?"
"OH, YES. VIRAGO'S DRIVEN THE GIRL *QUITE MAD.* IT'S SYNTILLA'S *CURSE,* YOU SEE...
"...SHE CONVERTS LIVING THINGS INTO NECROMANTIC ENERGY, WHICH VIRAGO THEN *HARVESTS* TO SUSTAIN HERSELF.
"THINK OF SYNTILLA AS VIRAGO'S *PERSONAL CHEF.*"
THAT'S WHY TAMA WAS TARGETED...
WHY INFECT AN ENTIRE WORLD WHEN YOU CAN ACHIEVE THE SAME RESULT BY INFECTING ITS AVATAR?
QUITE. THE MEAL THAT PREPARES ITSELF, AND IN A FRACTION OF THE TIME.
UNLESS...
...A CARRIONBLOOM. IT BUDS ONCE EVERY THOUSAND YEARS ON THE TONGUE OF THE FIRST TYRANT.
ITS PETALS CURE ALL AILMENTS, BE THEY PHYSICAL OR MYSTICAL.
TRICKS, DEMON?! GIVE IT TO ME!
NOT SO FAST, RESTLESS ONE. SURELY YOU DIDN'T THINK IT WOULD BE *FREE.*
GIVE ME YOUR NEXT DEATH. PROMISE YOURSELF TO ME HERE IN THE DEADSIDE.
YOU'RE QUITE THE PRIZE DOWN HERE, YOU KNOW.

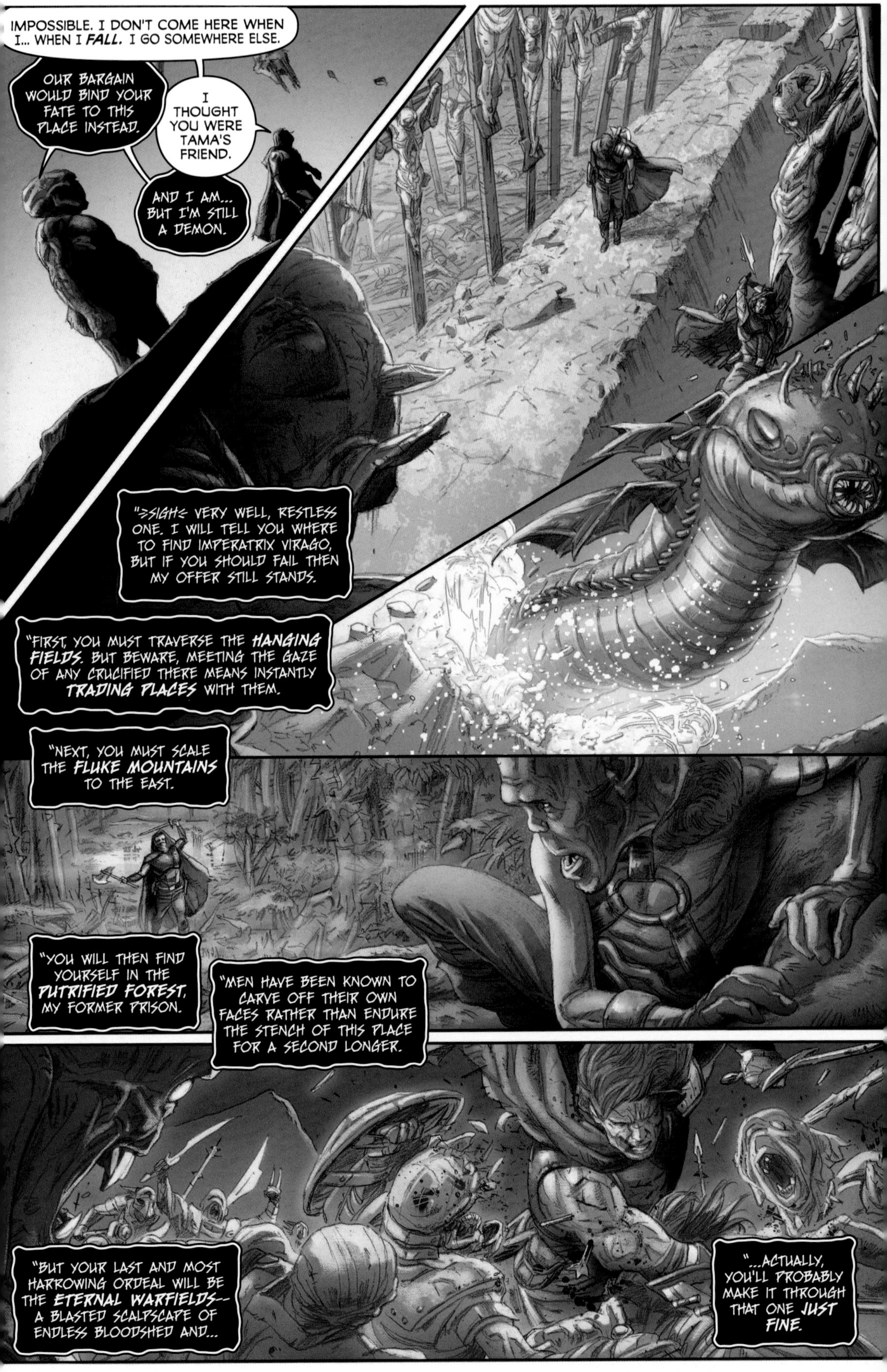
IMPOSSIBLE. I DON'T COME HERE WHEN I... WHEN I FALL. I GO SOMEWHERE ELSE.
OUR BARGAIN WOULD BIND YOUR FATE TO THIS PLACE INSTEAD.
I THOUGHT YOU WERE TAMA'S FRIEND.
AND I AM... BUT I'M STILL A DEMON.
">SIGH< VERY WELL, RESTLESS ONE. I WILL TELL YOU WHERE TO FIND IMPERATRIX VIRAGO, BUT IF YOU SHOULD FAIL THEN MY OFFER STILL STANDS.
"FIRST, YOU MUST TRAVERSE THE HANGING FIELDS. BUT BEWARE, MEETING THE GAZE OF ANY CRUCIFIED THERE MEANS INSTANTLY TRADING PLACES WITH THEM.
"NEXT, YOU MUST SCALE THE FLUKE MOUNTAINS TO THE EAST.
"YOU WILL THEN FIND YOURSELF IN THE PUTRIFIED FOREST, MY FORMER PRISON.
"MEN HAVE BEEN KNOWN TO CARVE OFF THEIR OWN FACES RATHER THAN ENDURE THE STENCH OF THIS PLACE FOR A SECOND LONGER.
"BUT YOUR LAST AND MOST HARROWING ORDEAL WILL BE THE ETERNAL WARFIELDS-- A BLASTED SCALPSCAPE OF ENDLESS BLOODSHED AND...
"...ACTUALLY, YOU'LL PROBABLY MAKE IT THROUGH THAT ONE JUST FINE.

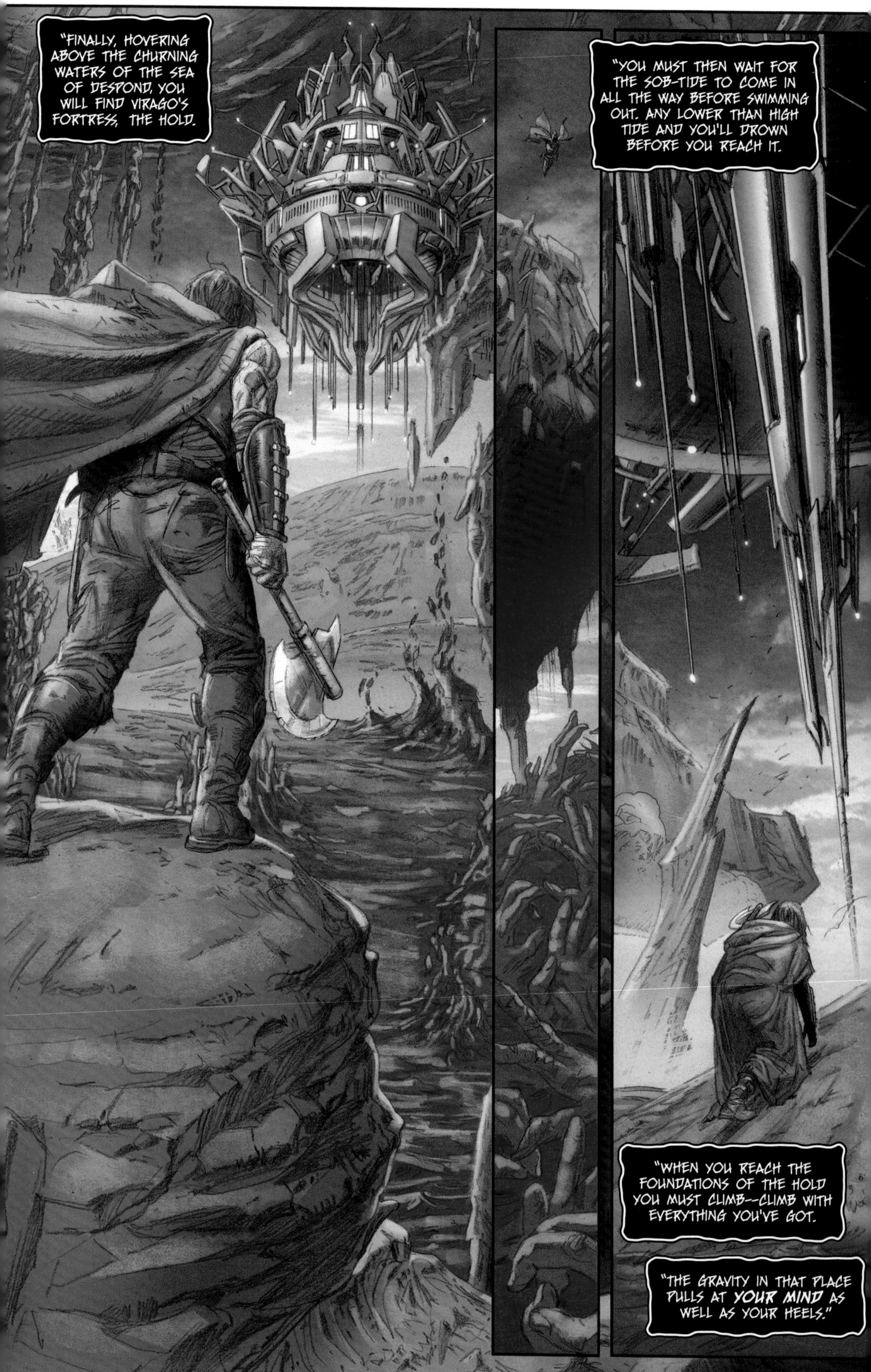
"FINALLY, HOVERING ABOVE THE CHURNING WATERS OF THE SEA OF DESPOND, YOU WILL FIND VIRAGO'S FORTRESS, THE HOLD.
"YOU MUST THEN WAIT FOR THE SOB-TIDE TO COME IN ALL THE WAY BEFORE SWIMMING OUT. ANY LOWER THAN HIGH TIDE AND YOU'LL DROWN BEFORE YOU REACH IT.
"WHEN YOU REACH THE FOUNDATIONS OF THE HOLD YOU MUST CLIMB--CLIMB WITH EVERYTHING YOU'VE GOT.
"THE GRAVITY IN THAT PLACE PULLS AT *YOUR MIND* AS WELL AS YOUR HEELS."

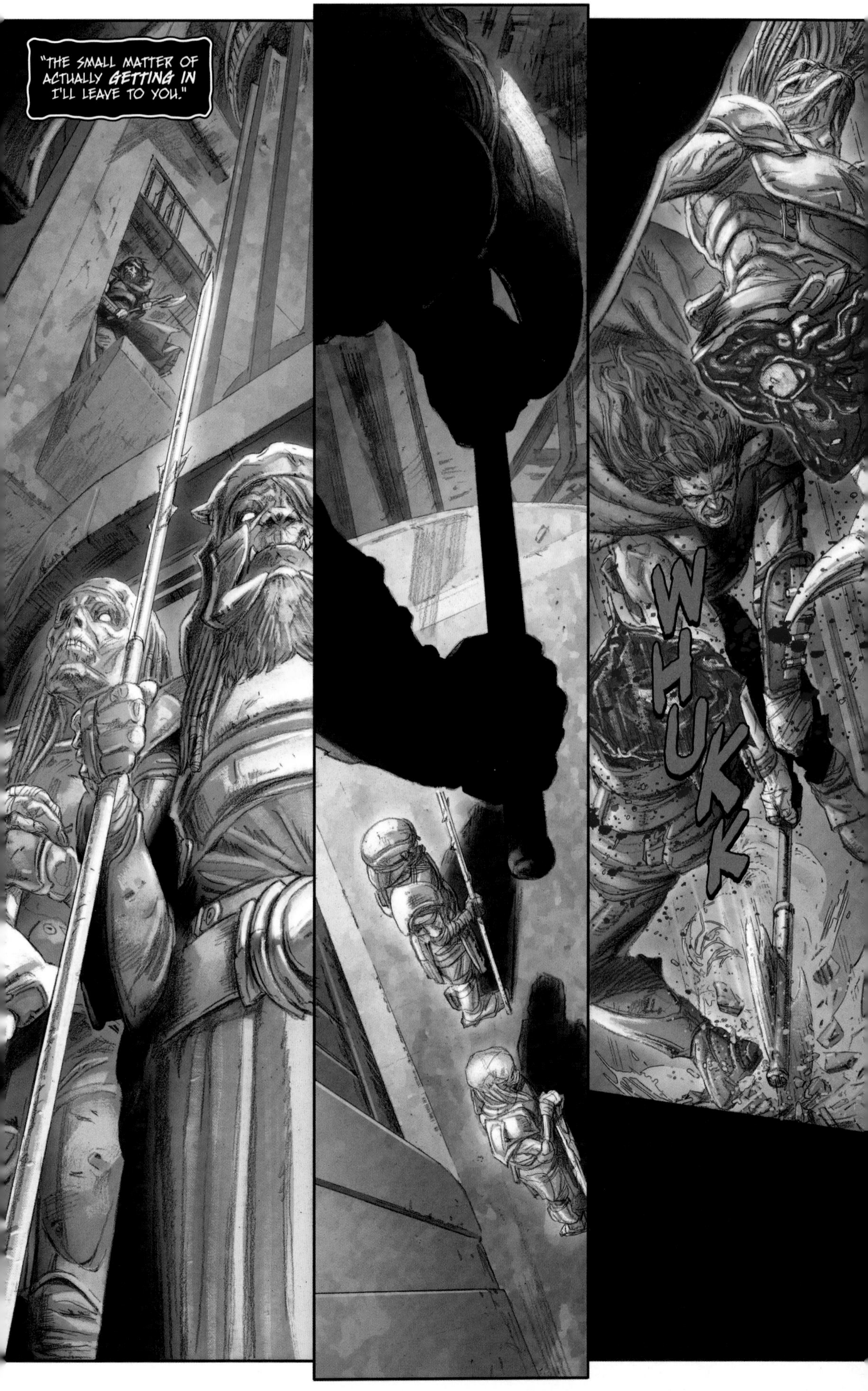
"THE SMALL MATTER OF ACTUALLY GETTING IN I'LL LEAVE TO YOU."
WHUKK

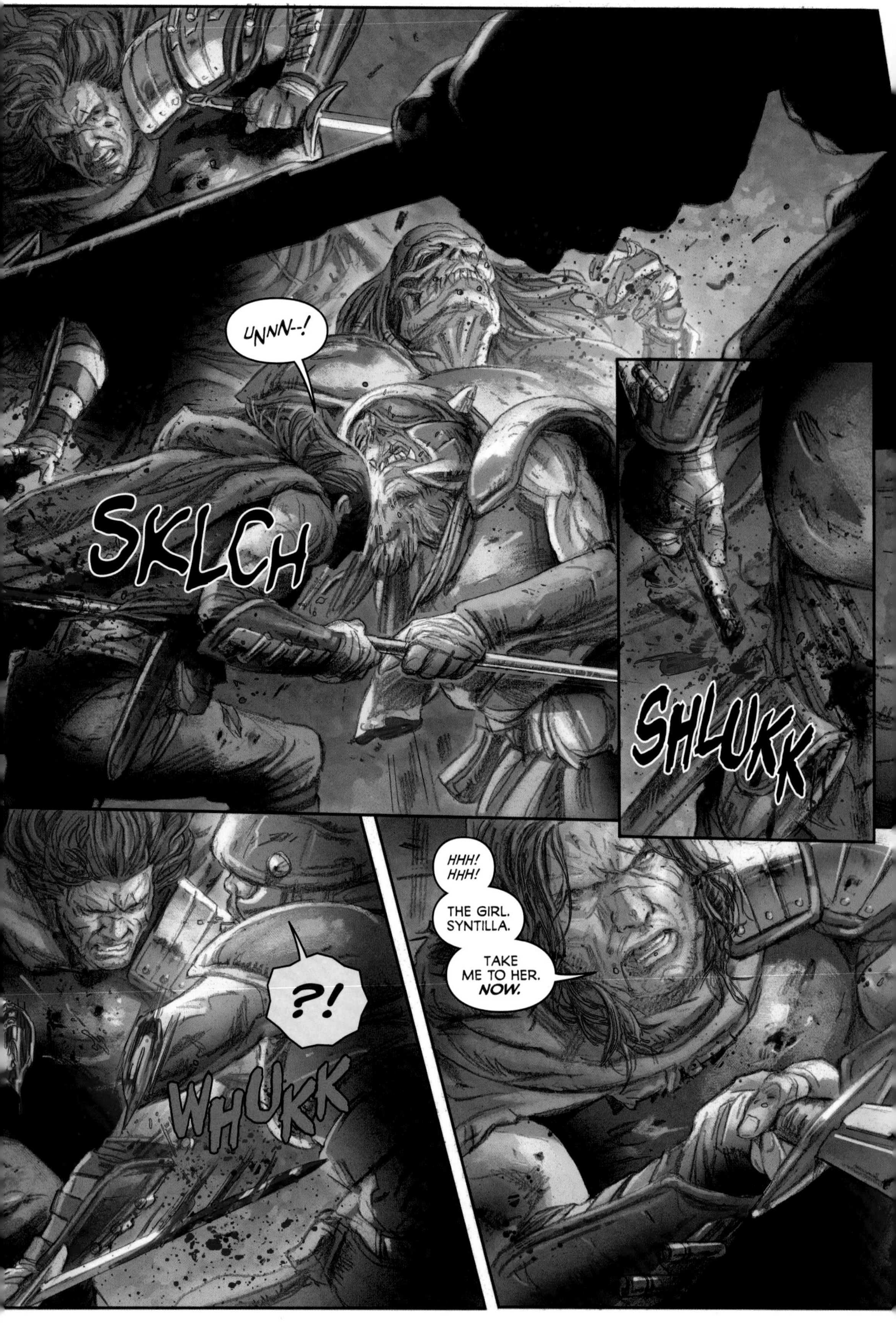
UNNN--!
SKLCH
SHLUKK
?!
WHUKK
HHH! HHH!
THE GIRL. SYNTILLA.
TAKE ME TO HER. NOW.

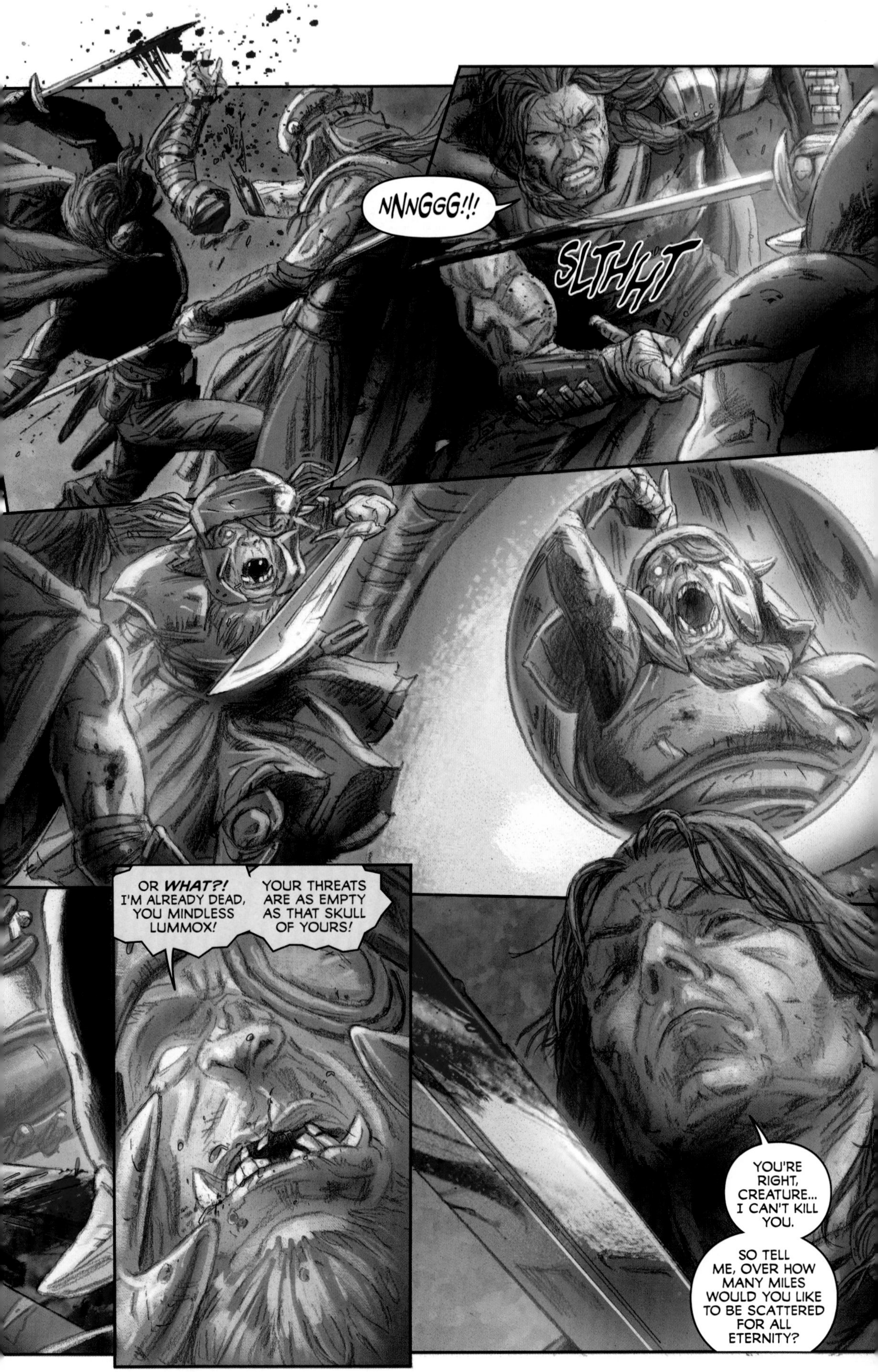
NNNGGG!!!
SLTHHT
OR WHAT?! I'M ALREADY DEAD, YOU MINDLESS LUMMOX!
YOUR THREATS ARE AS EMPTY AS THAT SKULL OF YOURS!
YOU'RE RIGHT, CREATURE... I CAN'T KILL YOU.
SO TELL ME, OVER HOW MANY MILES WOULD YOU LIKE TO BE SCATTERED FOR ALL ETERNITY?

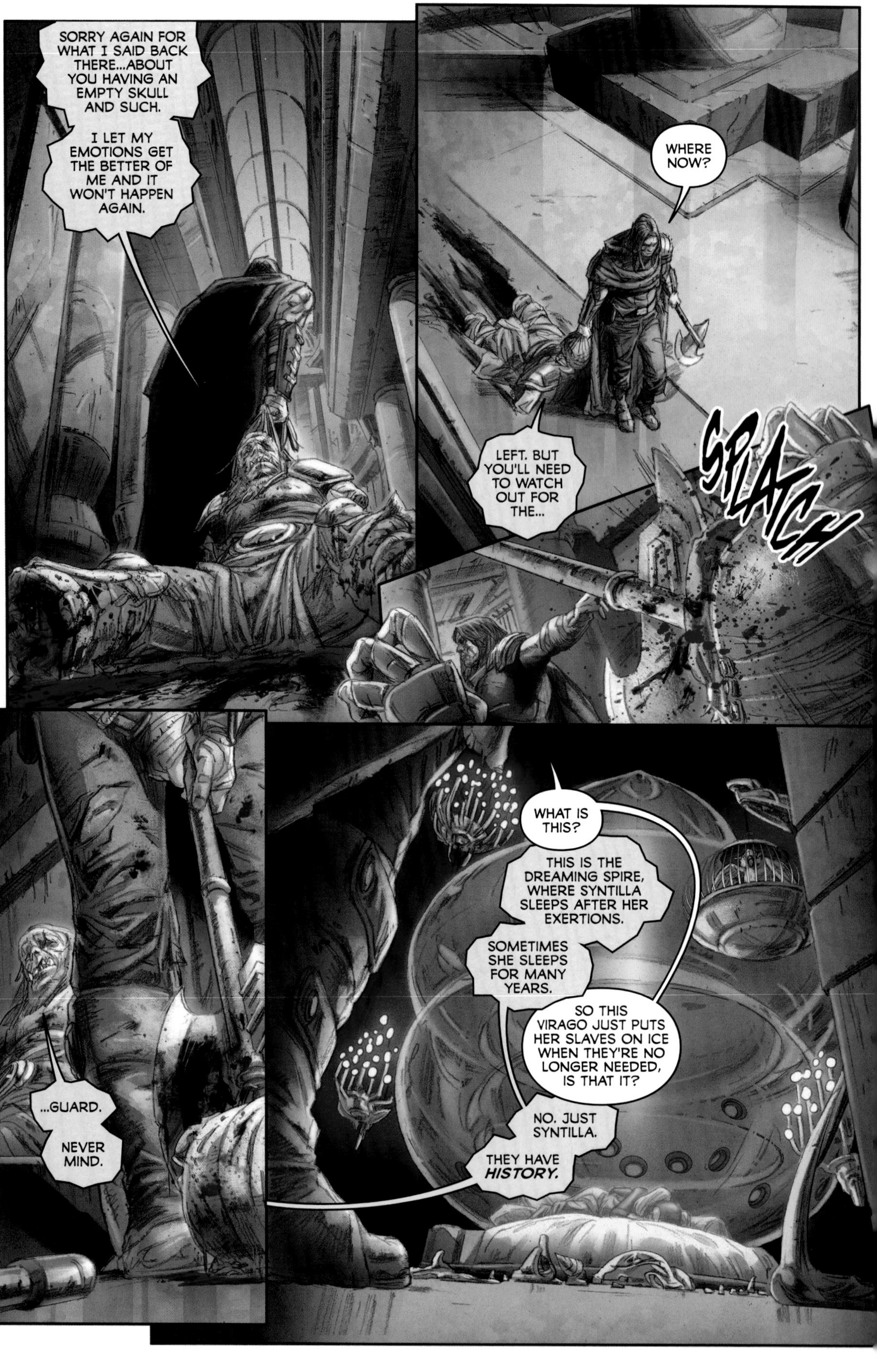
SORRY AGAIN FOR WHAT I SAID BACK THERE...ABOUT YOU HAVING AN EMPTY SKULL AND SUCH.
I LET MY EMOTIONS GET THE BETTER OF ME AND IT WON'T HAPPEN AGAIN.
WHERE NOW?
LEFT. BUT YOU'LL NEED TO WATCH OUT FOR THE...
SPLATCH
...GUARD.
NEVER MIND.
WHAT IS THIS?
THIS IS THE DREAMING SPIRE, WHERE SYNTILLA SLEEPS AFTER HER EXERTIONS.
SOMETIMES SHE SLEEPS FOR MANY YEARS.
SO THIS VIRAGO JUST PUTS HER SLAVES ON ICE WHEN THEY'RE NO LONGER NEEDED, IS THAT IT?
NO. JUST SYNTILLA.
THEY HAVE *HISTORY.*

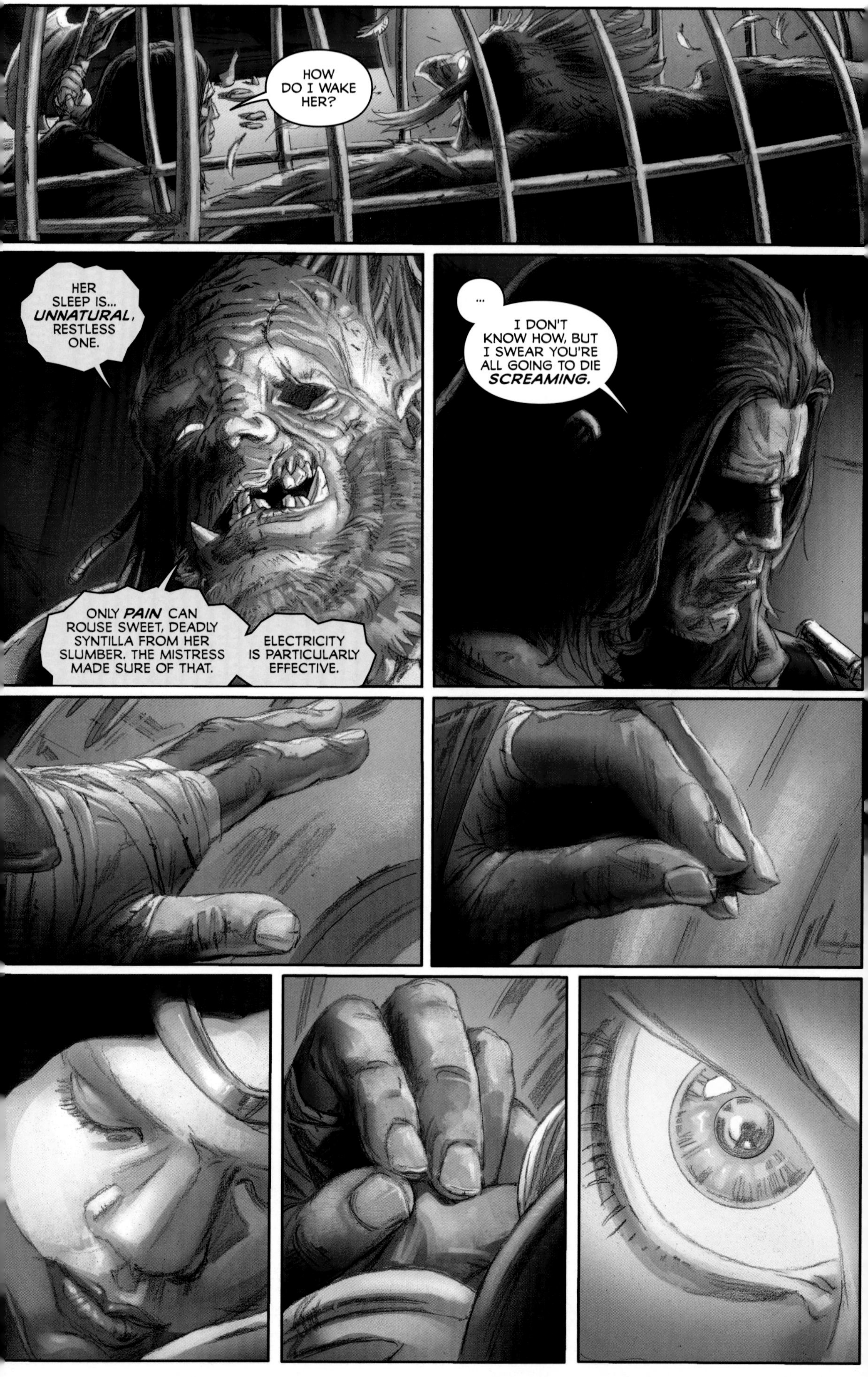
HOW DO I WAKE HER?
HER SLEEP IS... UNNATURAL, RESTLESS ONE.
ONLY PAIN CAN ROUSE SWEET, DEADLY SYNTILLA FROM HER SLUMBER. THE MISTRESS MADE SURE OF THAT.
ELECTRICITY IS PARTICULARLY EFFECTIVE.
...
I DON'T KNOW HOW, BUT I SWEAR YOU'RE ALL GOING TO DIE SCREAMING.

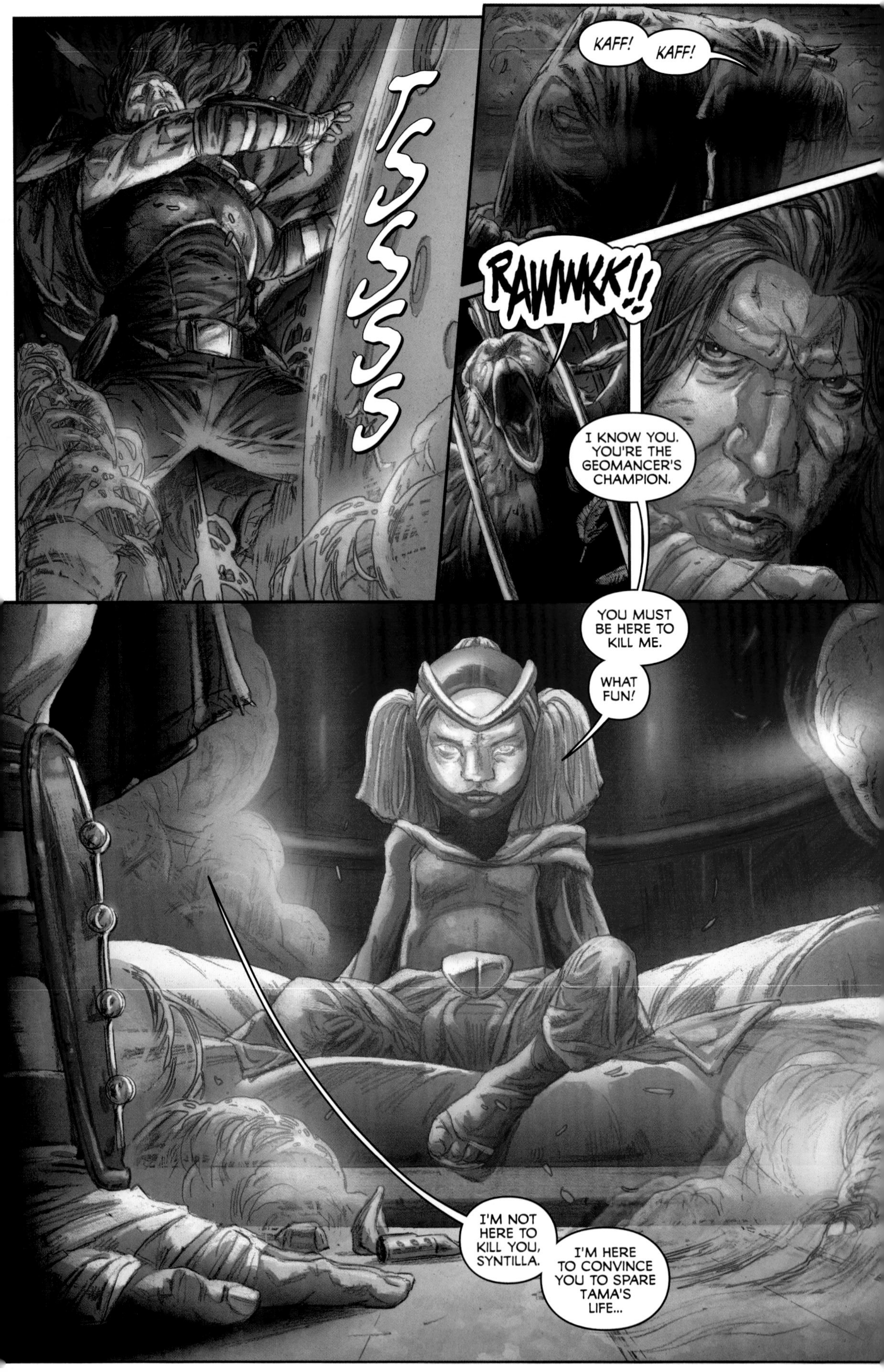
TSSSSSS
KAFF!
KAFF!
RAWWKK!!
I KNOW YOU. YOU'RE THE GEOMANCER'S CHAMPION.
YOU MUST BE HERE TO KILL ME.
WHAT FUN!
I'M NOT HERE TO KILL YOU, SYNTILLA.
I'M HERE TO CONVINCE YOU TO SPARE TAMA'S LIFE...

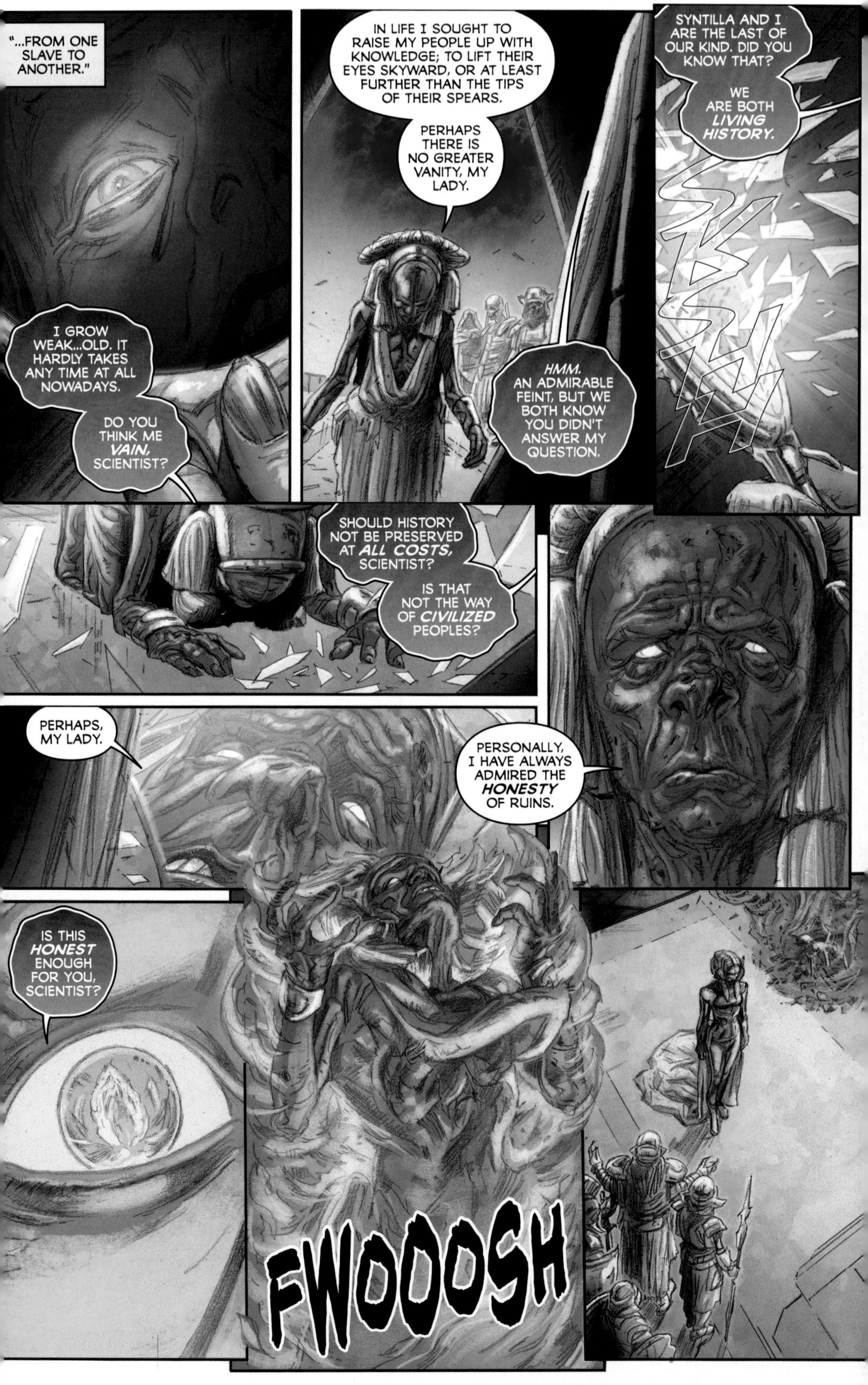

"...FROM ONE SLAVE TO ANOTHER."
I GROW WEAK...OLD. IT HARDLY TAKES ANY TIME AT ALL NOWADAYS.
DO YOU THINK ME *VAIN,* SCIENTIST?
IN LIFE I SOUGHT TO RAISE MY PEOPLE UP WITH KNOWLEDGE; TO LIFT THEIR EYES SKYWARD, OR AT LEAST FURTHER THAN THE TIPS OF THEIR SPEARS.
PERHAPS THERE IS NO GREATER VANITY, MY LADY.
HMM. AN ADMIRABLE FEINT, BUT WE BOTH KNOW YOU DIDN'T ANSWER MY QUESTION.
SYNTILLA AND I ARE THE LAST OF OUR KIND. DID YOU KNOW THAT?
WE ARE BOTH *LIVING HISTORY.*
SHOULD HISTORY NOT BE PRESERVED AT *ALL COSTS,* SCIENTIST?
IS THAT NOT THE WAY OF *CIVILIZED* PEOPLES?
PERHAPS, MY LADY.
PERSONALLY, I HAVE ALWAYS ADMIRED THE *HONESTY* OF RUINS.
IS THIS *HONEST* ENOUGH FOR YOU, SCIENTIST?
FWOOOSH

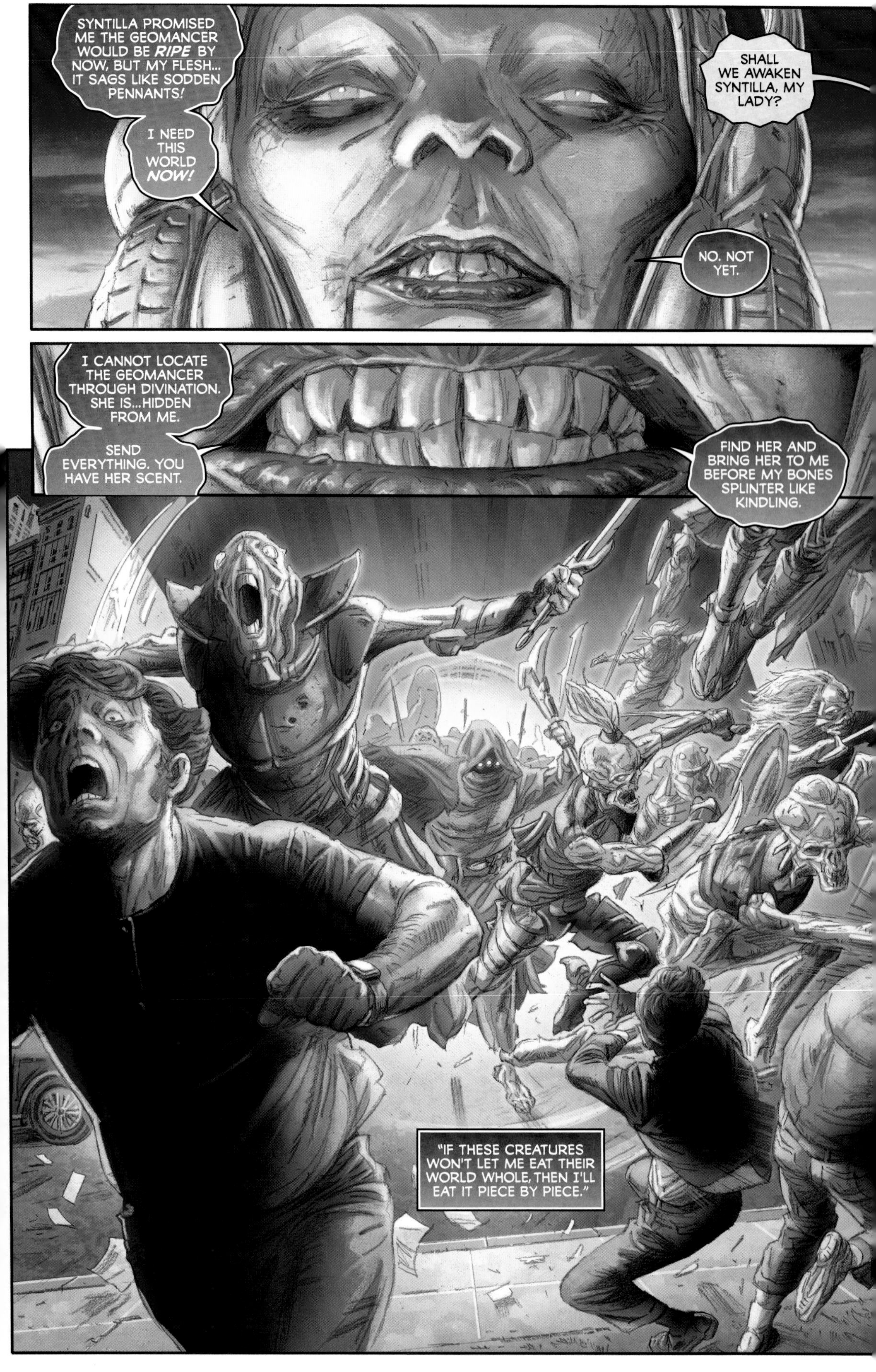
SYNTILLA PROMISED ME THE GEOMANCER WOULD BE *RIPE* BY NOW, BUT MY FLESH... IT SAGS LIKE SODDEN PENNANTS!
I NEED THIS WORLD *NOW!*
SHALL WE AWAKEN SYNTILLA, MY LADY?
NO. NOT YET.
I CANNOT LOCATE THE GEOMANCER THROUGH DIVINATION. SHE IS...HIDDEN FROM ME.
SEND EVERYTHING. YOU HAVE HER SCENT.
FIND HER AND BRING HER TO ME BEFORE MY BONES SPLINTER LIKE KINDLING.
"IF THESE CREATURES WON'T LET ME EAT THEIR WORLD WHOLE, THEN I'LL EAT IT PIECE BY PIECE."

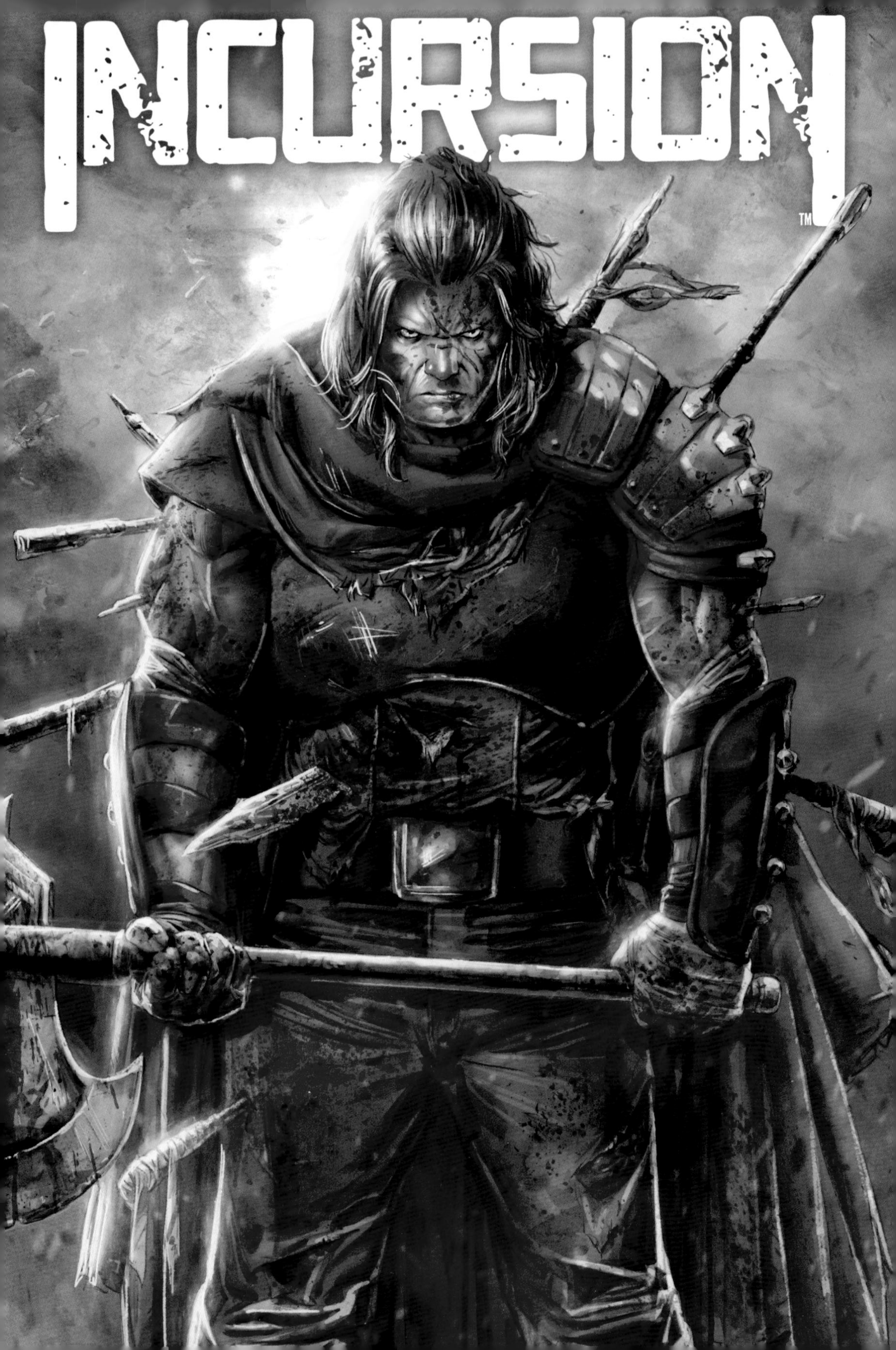
INCURSION
TM

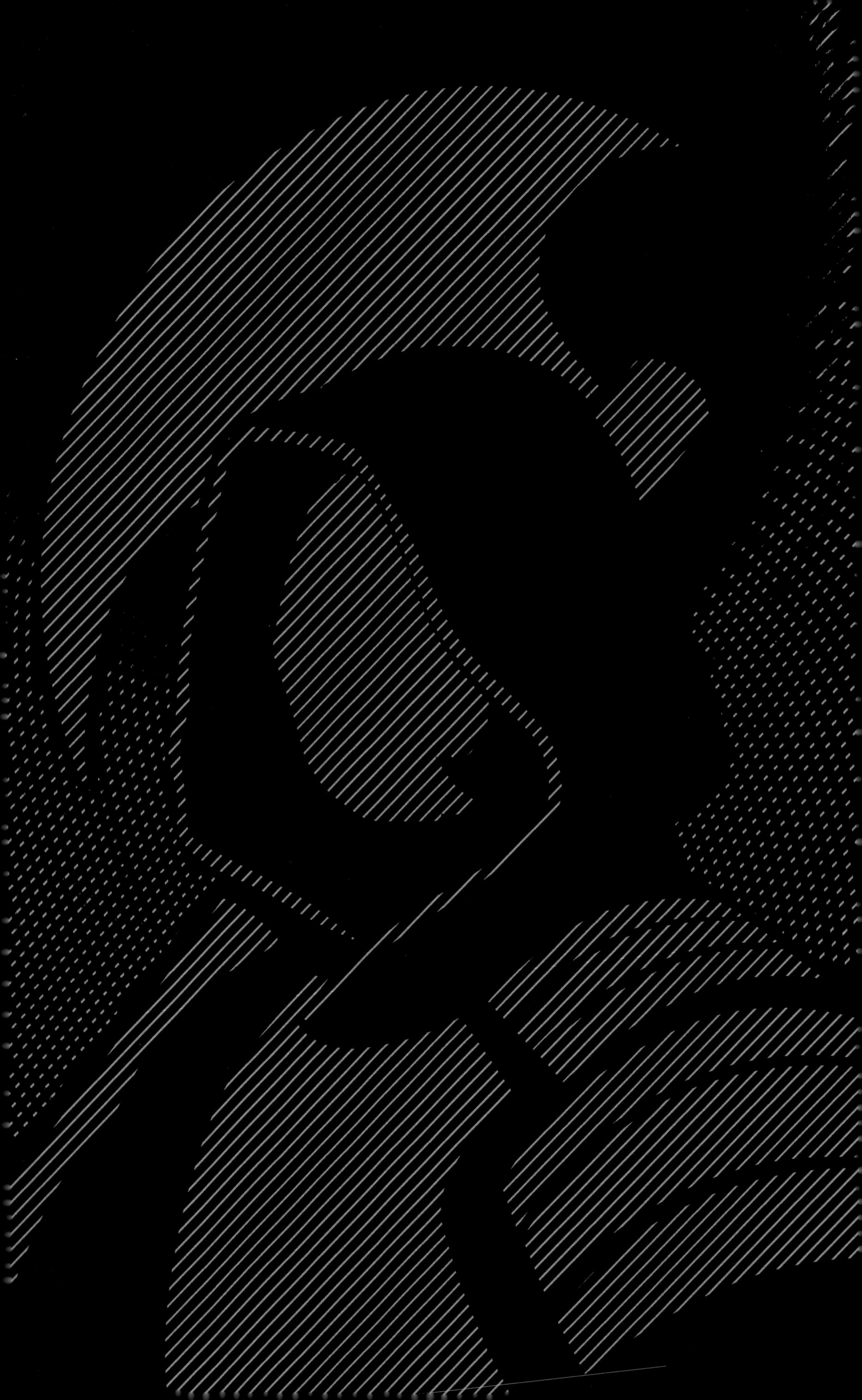

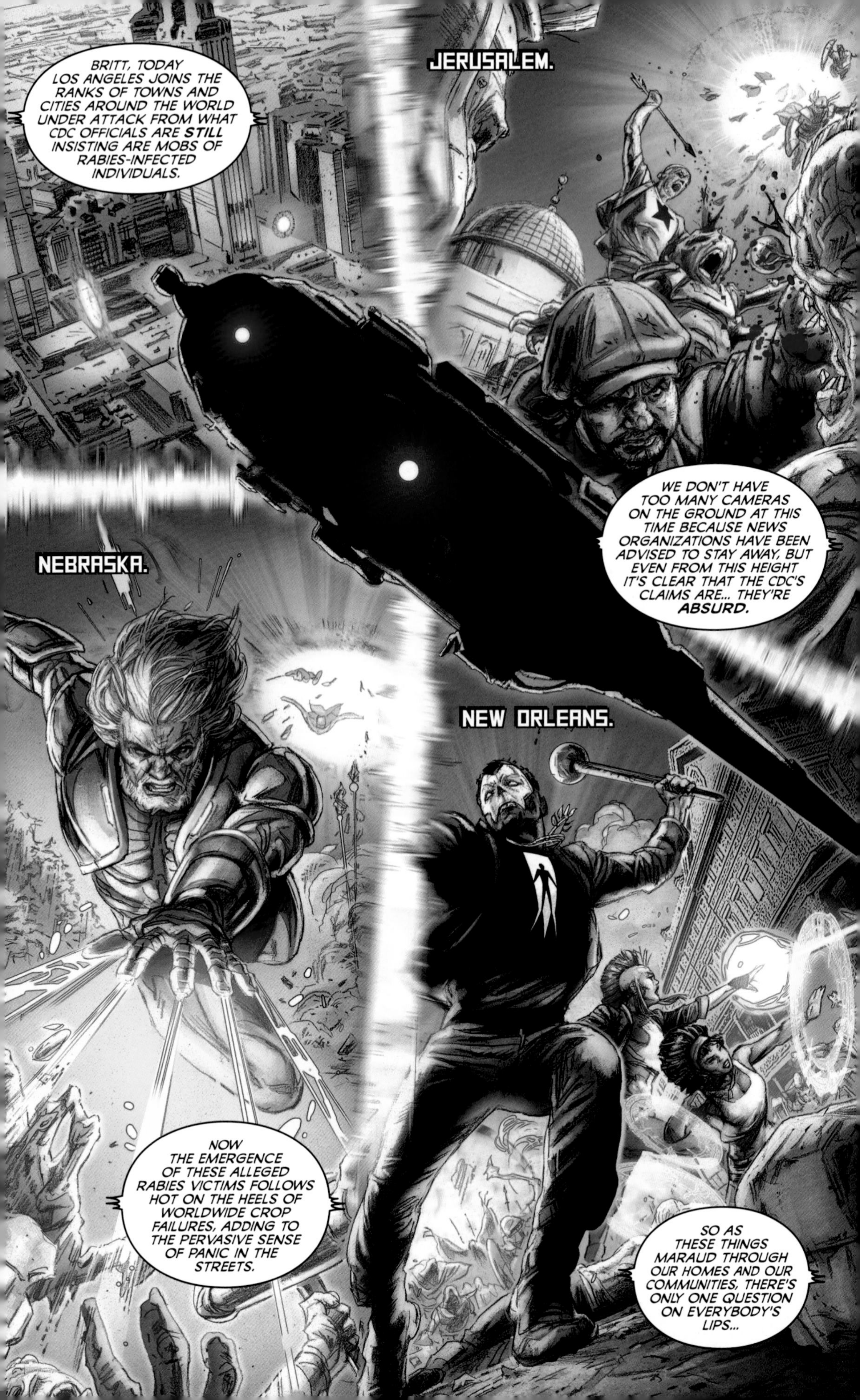
BRITT, TODAY LOS ANGELES JOINS THE RANKS OF TOWNS AND CITIES AROUND THE WORLD UNDER ATTACK FROM WHAT CDC OFFICIALS ARE STILL INSISTING ARE MOBS OF RABIES-INFECTED INDIVIDUALS.
JERUSALEM.
WE DON'T HAVE TOO MANY CAMERAS ON THE GROUND AT THIS TIME BECAUSE NEWS ORGANIZATIONS HAVE BEEN ADVISED TO STAY AWAY, BUT EVEN FROM THIS HEIGHT IT'S CLEAR THAT THE CDC'S CLAIMS ARE... THEY'RE ABSURD.
NEBRASKA.
NEW ORLEANS.
NOW THE EMERGENCE OF THESE ALLEGED RABIES VICTIMS FOLLOWS HOT ON THE HEELS OF WORLDWIDE CROP FAILURES, ADDING TO THE PERVASIVE SENSE OF PANIC IN THE STREETS.
SO AS THESE THINGS MARAUD THROUGH OUR HOMES AND OUR COMMUNITIES, THERE'S ONLY ONE QUESTION ON EVERYBODY'S LIPS...

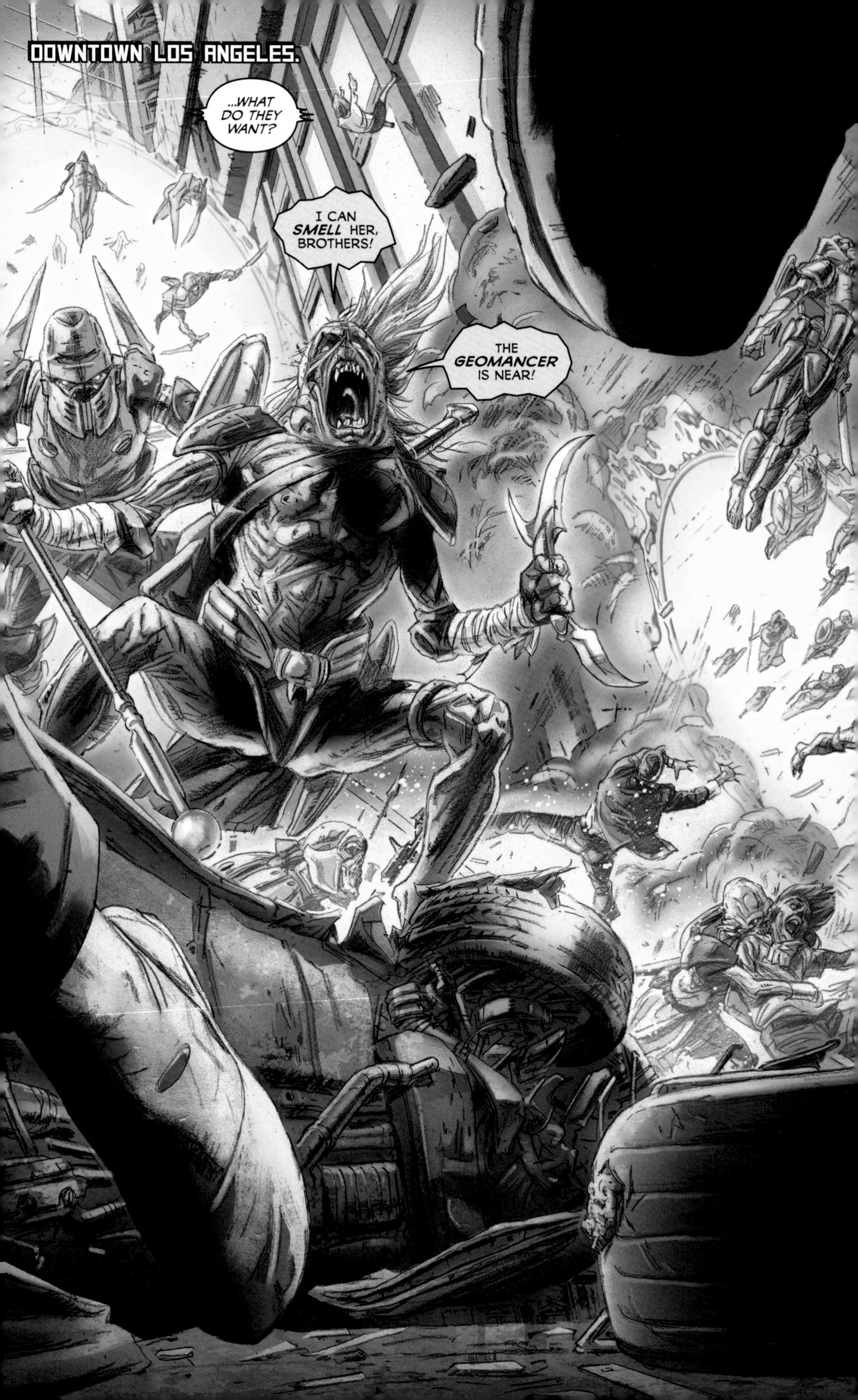
DOWNTOWN LOS ANGELES.
...WHAT DO THEY WANT?
I CAN SMELL HER, BROTHERS!
THE GEOMANCER IS NEAR!

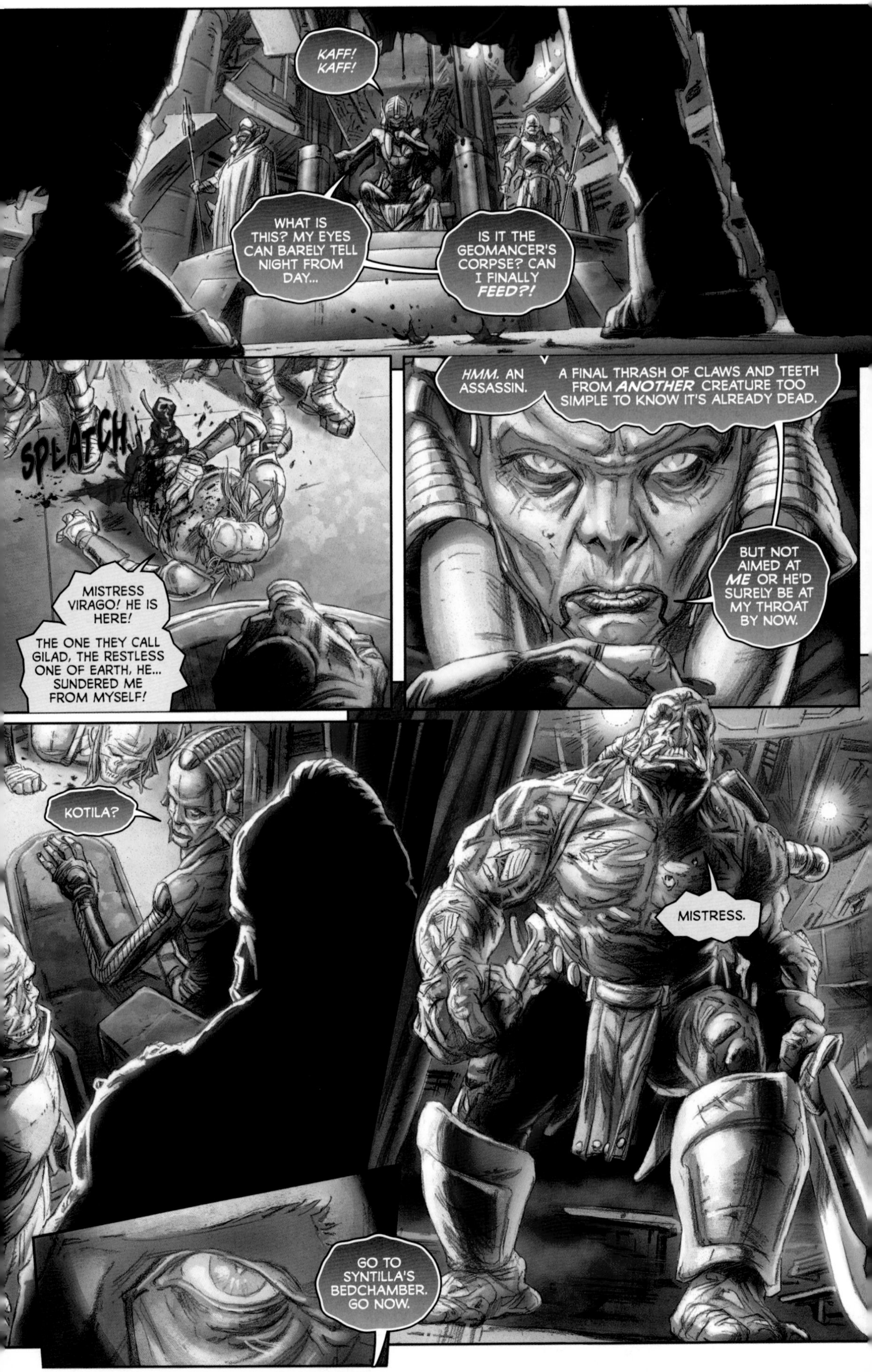
KAFF! KAFF!
WHAT IS THIS? MY EYES CAN BARELY TELL NIGHT FROM DAY...
IS IT THE GEOMANCER'S CORPSE? CAN I FINALLY FEED?!
SPLATCH
MISTRESS VIRAGO! HE IS HERE!
THE ONE THEY CALL GILAD, THE RESTLESS ONE OF EARTH, HE... SUNDERED ME FROM MYSELF!
HMM. AN ASSASSIN.
A FINAL THRASH OF CLAWS AND TEETH FROM ANOTHER CREATURE TOO SIMPLE TO KNOW IT'S ALREADY DEAD.
BUT NOT AIMED AT ME OR HE'D SURELY BE AT MY THROAT BY NOW.
KOTILA?
MISTRESS.
GO TO SYNTILLA'S BEDCHAMBER. GO NOW.

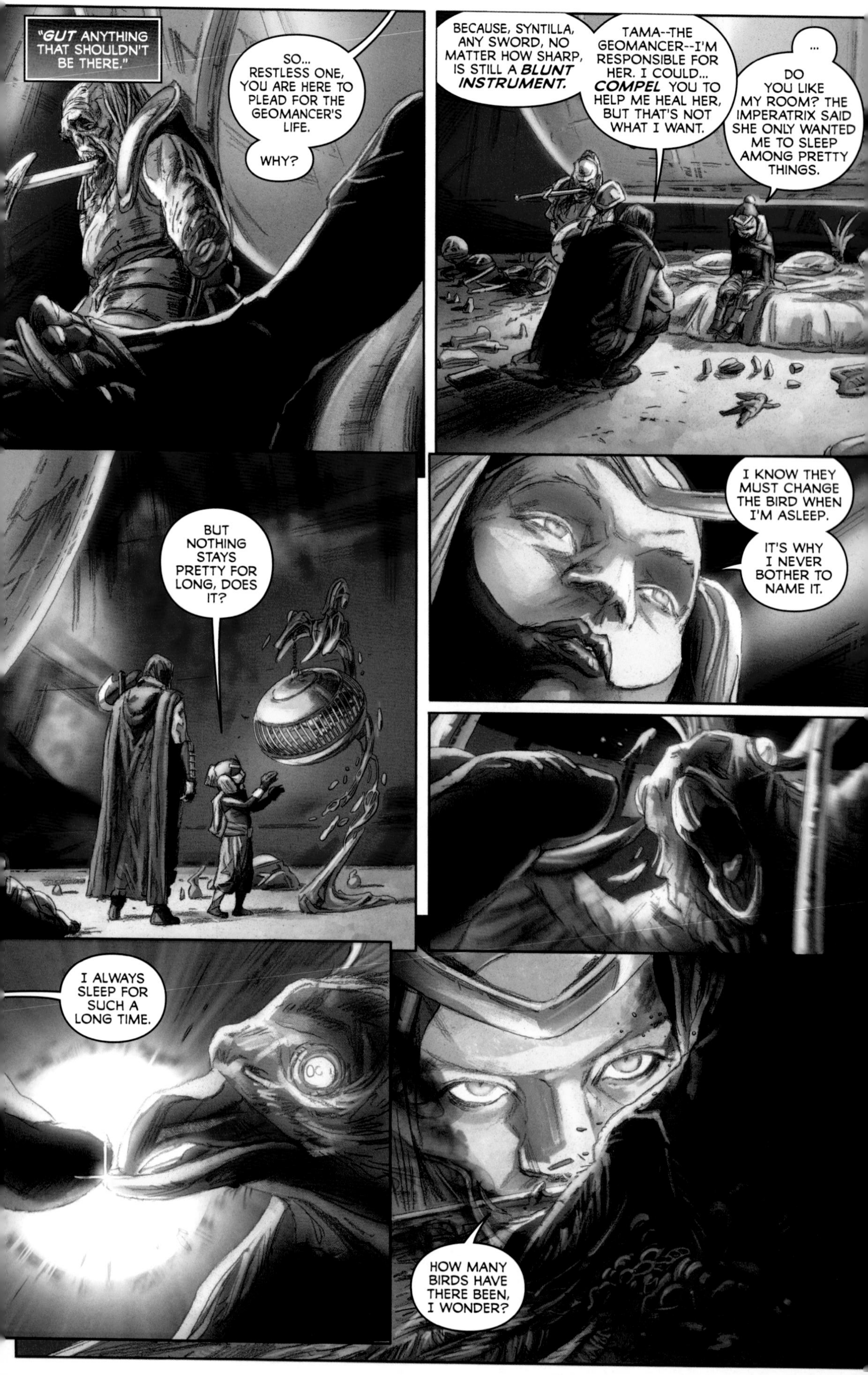
"GUT ANYTHING THAT SHOULDN'T BE THERE."
SO... RESTLESS ONE, YOU ARE HERE TO PLEAD FOR THE GEOMANCER'S LIFE.
WHY?
BECAUSE, SYNTILLA, ANY SWORD, NO MATTER HOW SHARP, IS STILL A BLUNT INSTRUMENT.
TAMA--THE GEOMANCER--I'M RESPONSIBLE FOR HER. I COULD... COMPEL YOU TO HELP ME HEAL HER, BUT THAT'S NOT WHAT I WANT.
...
DO YOU LIKE MY ROOM? THE IMPERATRIX SAID SHE ONLY WANTED ME TO SLEEP AMONG PRETTY THINGS.
BUT NOTHING STAYS PRETTY FOR LONG, DOES IT?
I KNOW THEY MUST CHANGE THE BIRD WHEN I'M ASLEEP.
IT'S WHY I NEVER BOTHER TO NAME IT.
I ALWAYS SLEEP FOR SUCH A LONG TIME.
HOW MANY BIRDS HAVE THERE BEEN, I WONDER?

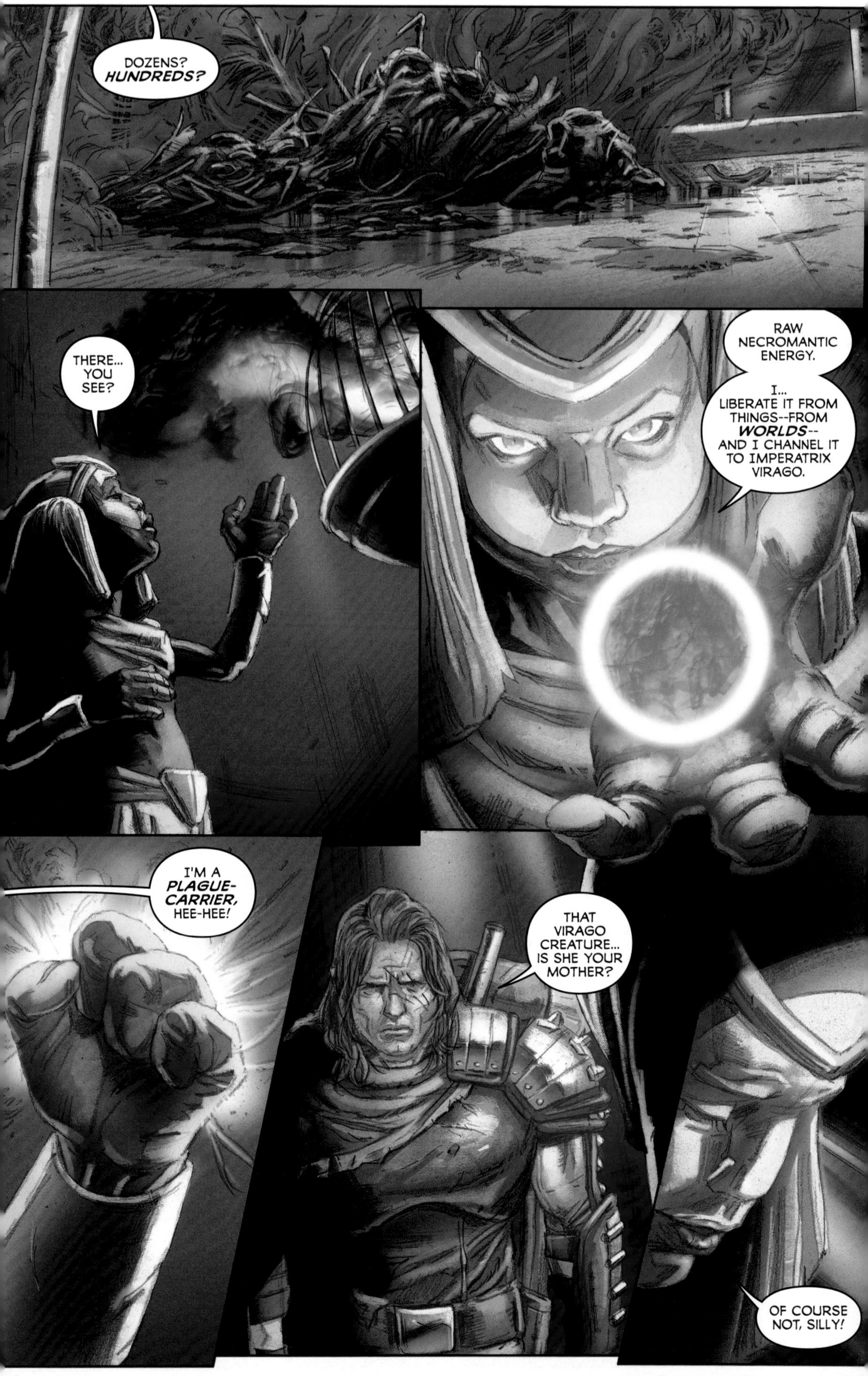
DOZENS? ***HUNDREDS?***
THERE... YOU SEE?
RAW NECROMANTIC ENERGY.
I... LIBERATE IT FROM THINGS--FROM ***WORLDS***-- AND I CHANNEL IT TO IMPERATRIX VIRAGO.
I'M A ***PLAGUE-CARRIER,*** HEE-HEE!
THAT VIRAGO CREATURE... IS SHE YOUR MOTHER?
OF COURSE NOT, SILLY!

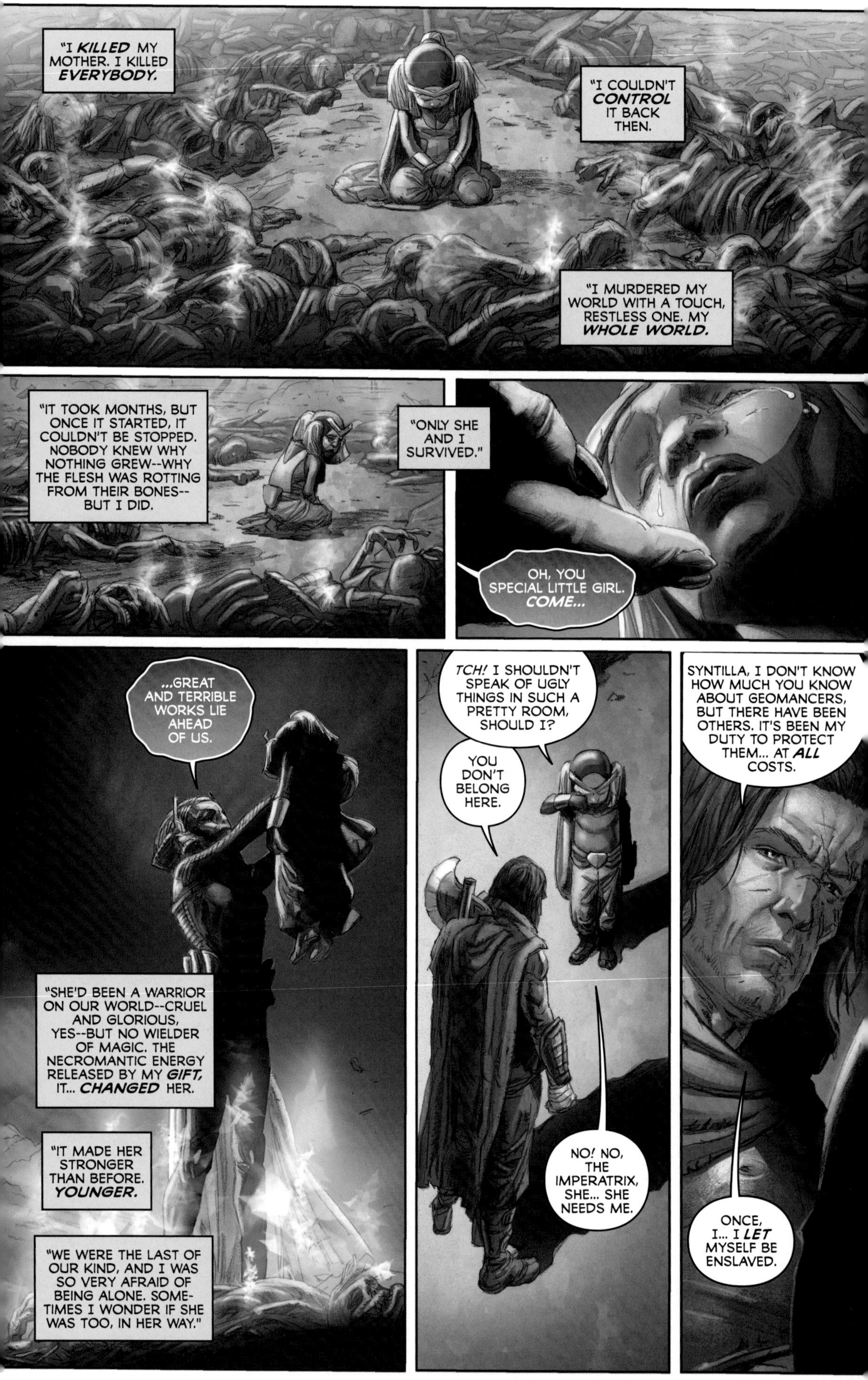
"I KILLED MY MOTHER. I KILLED EVERYBODY.
"I COULDN'T CONTROL IT BACK THEN.
"I MURDERED MY WORLD WITH A TOUCH, RESTLESS ONE. MY WHOLE WORLD.
"IT TOOK MONTHS, BUT ONCE IT STARTED, IT COULDN'T BE STOPPED. NOBODY KNEW WHY NOTHING GREW--WHY THE FLESH WAS ROTTING FROM THEIR BONES--BUT I DID.
"ONLY SHE AND I SURVIVED."
OH, YOU SPECIAL LITTLE GIRL. COME...
...GREAT AND TERRIBLE WORKS LIE AHEAD OF US.
"SHE'D BEEN A WARRIOR ON OUR WORLD--CRUEL AND GLORIOUS, YES--BUT NO WIELDER OF MAGIC. THE NECROMANTIC ENERGY RELEASED BY MY GIFT, IT... CHANGED HER.
"IT MADE HER STRONGER THAN BEFORE. YOUNGER.
"WE WERE THE LAST OF OUR KIND, AND I WAS SO VERY AFRAID OF BEING ALONE. SOMETIMES I WONDER IF SHE WAS TOO, IN HER WAY."
TCH! I SHOULDN'T SPEAK OF UGLY THINGS IN SUCH A PRETTY ROOM, SHOULD I?
YOU DON'T BELONG HERE.
NO! NO, THE IMPERATRIX, SHE... SHE NEEDS ME.
SYNTILLA, I DON'T KNOW HOW MUCH YOU KNOW ABOUT GEOMANCERS, BUT THERE HAVE BEEN OTHERS. IT'S BEEN MY DUTY TO PROTECT THEM... AT ALL COSTS.
ONCE, I... I LET MYSELF BE ENSLAVED.

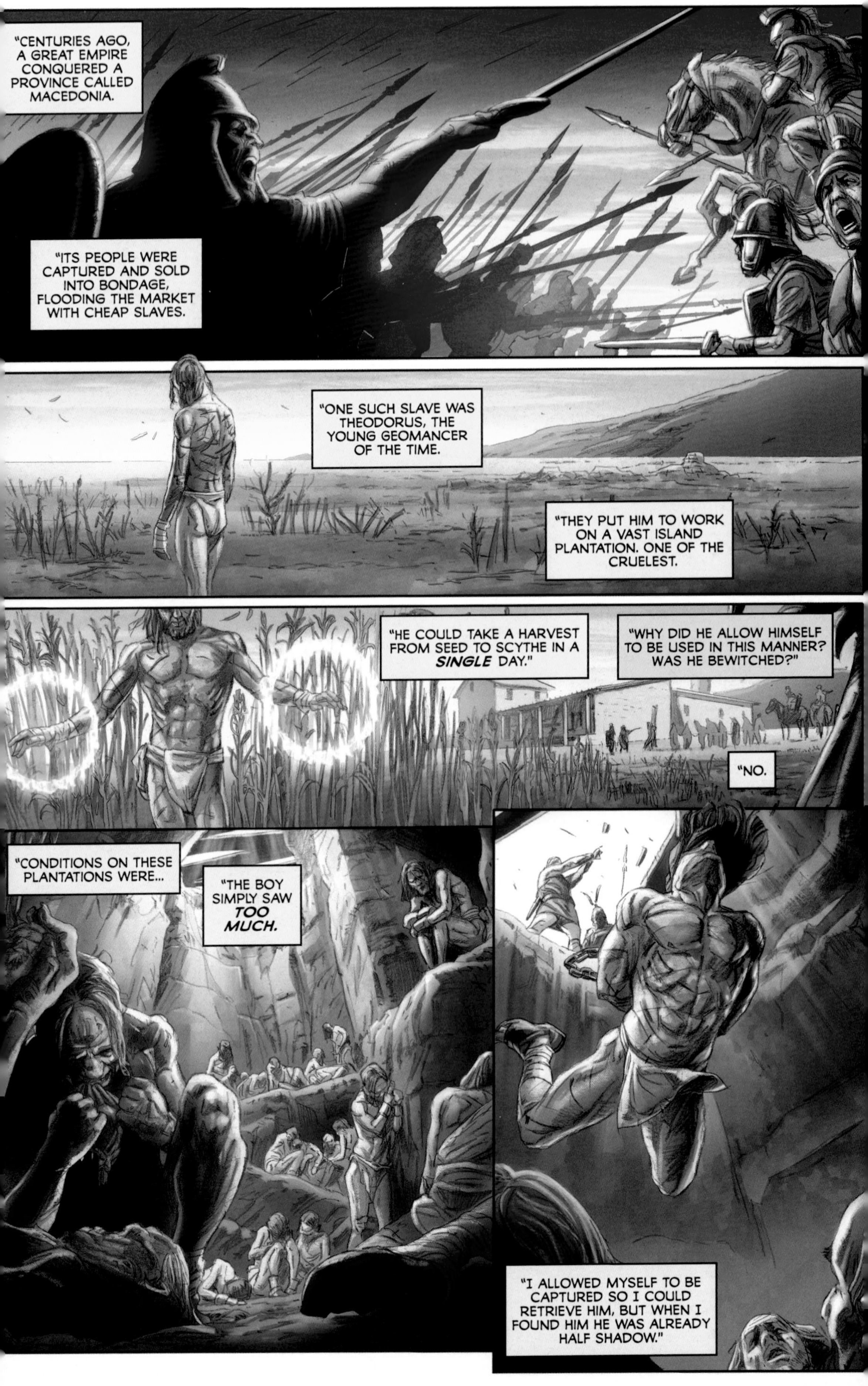
"CENTURIES AGO, A GREAT EMPIRE CONQUERED A PROVINCE CALLED MACEDONIA.
"ITS PEOPLE WERE CAPTURED AND SOLD INTO BONDAGE, FLOODING THE MARKET WITH CHEAP SLAVES.
"ONE SUCH SLAVE WAS THEODORUS, THE YOUNG GEOMANCER OF THE TIME.
"THEY PUT HIM TO WORK ON A VAST ISLAND PLANTATION. ONE OF THE CRUELEST.
"HE COULD TAKE A HARVEST FROM SEED TO SCYTHE IN A ***SINGLE*** DAY."
"WHY DID HE ALLOW HIMSELF TO BE USED IN THIS MANNER? WAS HE BEWITCHED?"
"NO.
"CONDITIONS ON THESE PLANTATIONS WERE...
"THE BOY SIMPLY SAW ***TOO MUCH.***
"I ALLOWED MYSELF TO BE CAPTURED SO I COULD RETRIEVE HIM, BUT WHEN I FOUND HIM HE WAS ALREADY HALF SHADOW."

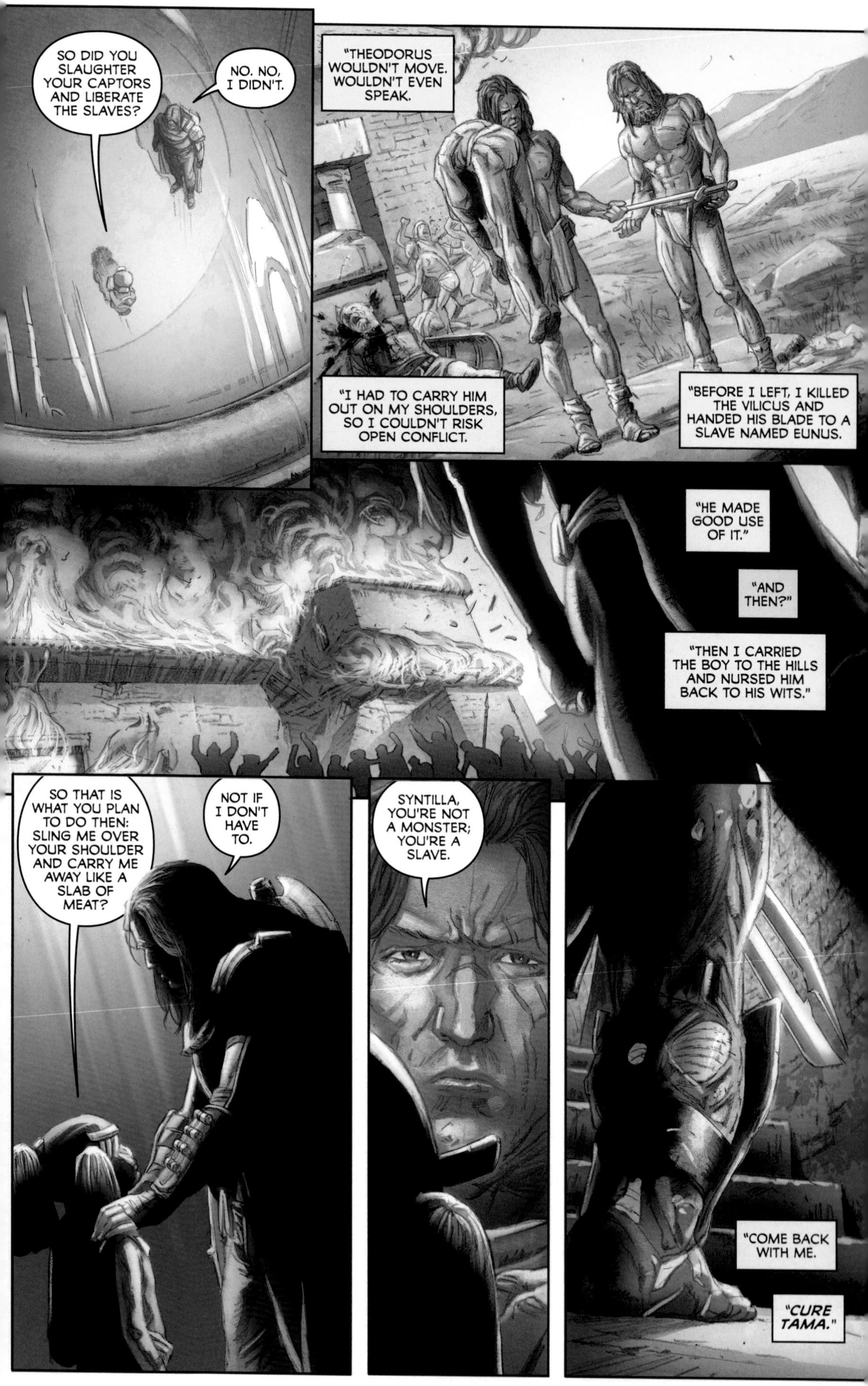
SO DID YOU SLAUGHTER YOUR CAPTORS AND LIBERATE THE SLAVES?
NO. NO, I DIDN'T.
"THEODORUS WOULDN'T MOVE. WOULDN'T EVEN SPEAK.
"I HAD TO CARRY HIM OUT ON MY SHOULDERS, SO I COULDN'T RISK OPEN CONFLICT.
"BEFORE I LEFT, I KILLED THE VILICUS AND HANDED HIS BLADE TO A SLAVE NAMED EUNUS.
"HE MADE GOOD USE OF IT."
"AND THEN?"
"THEN I CARRIED THE BOY TO THE HILLS AND NURSED HIM BACK TO HIS WITS."
SO THAT IS WHAT YOU PLAN TO DO THEN: SLING ME OVER YOUR SHOULDER AND CARRY ME AWAY LIKE A SLAB OF MEAT?
NOT IF I DON'T HAVE TO.
SYNTILLA, YOU'RE NOT A MONSTER; YOU'RE A SLAVE.
"COME BACK WITH ME.
"*CURE TAMA.*"

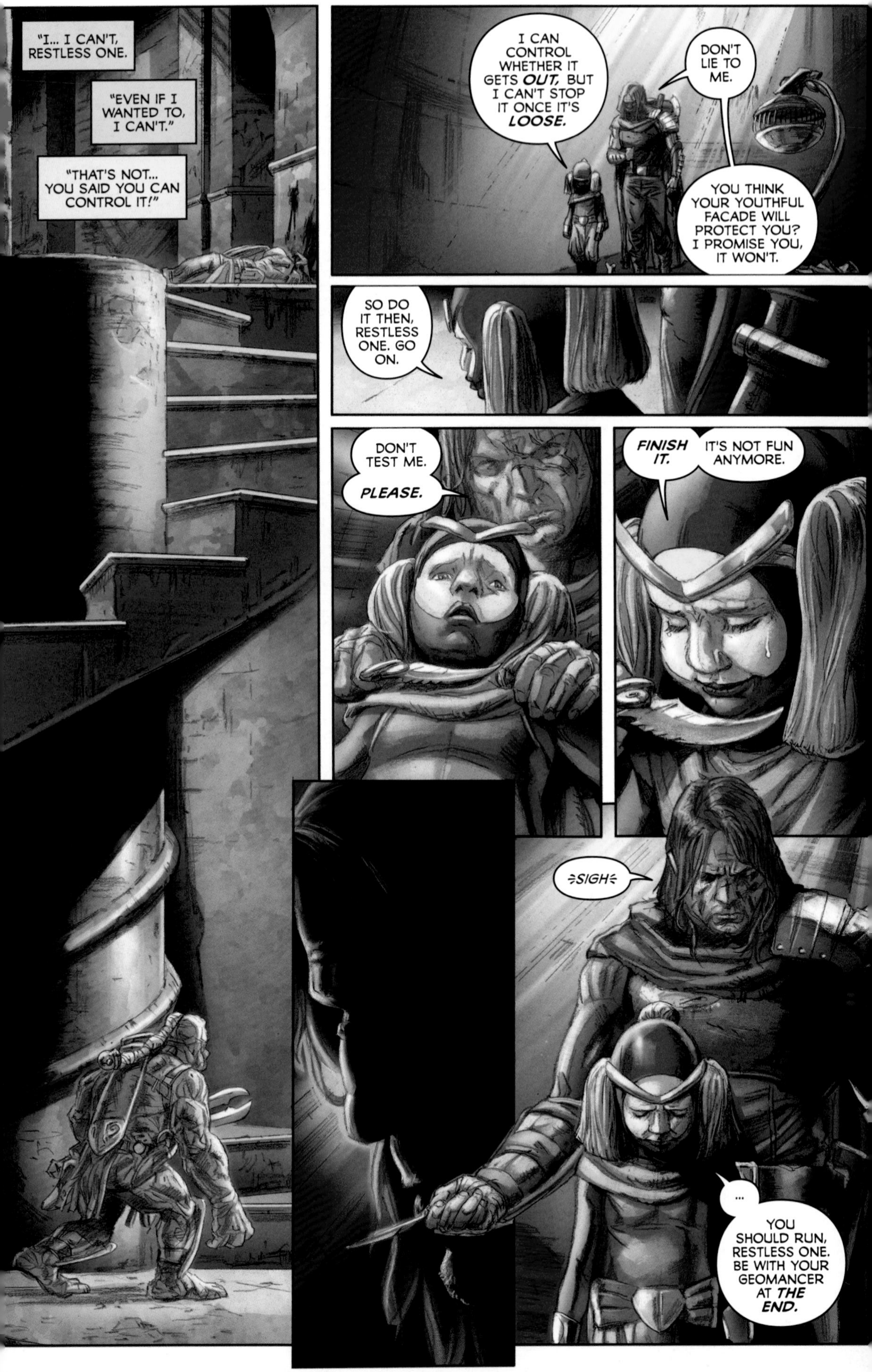
"I... I CAN'T, RESTLESS ONE.
"EVEN IF I WANTED TO, I CAN'T."
"THAT'S NOT... YOU SAID YOU CAN CONTROL IT!"
I CAN CONTROL WHETHER IT GETS OUT, BUT I CAN'T STOP IT ONCE IT'S LOOSE.
DON'T LIE TO ME.
YOU THINK YOUR YOUTHFUL FACADE WILL PROTECT YOU? I PROMISE YOU, IT WON'T.
SO DO IT THEN, RESTLESS ONE. GO ON.
DON'T TEST ME.
PLEASE.
FINISH IT.
IT'S NOT FUN ANYMORE.
SIGH
...
YOU SHOULD RUN, RESTLESS ONE. BE WITH YOUR GEOMANCER AT THE END.

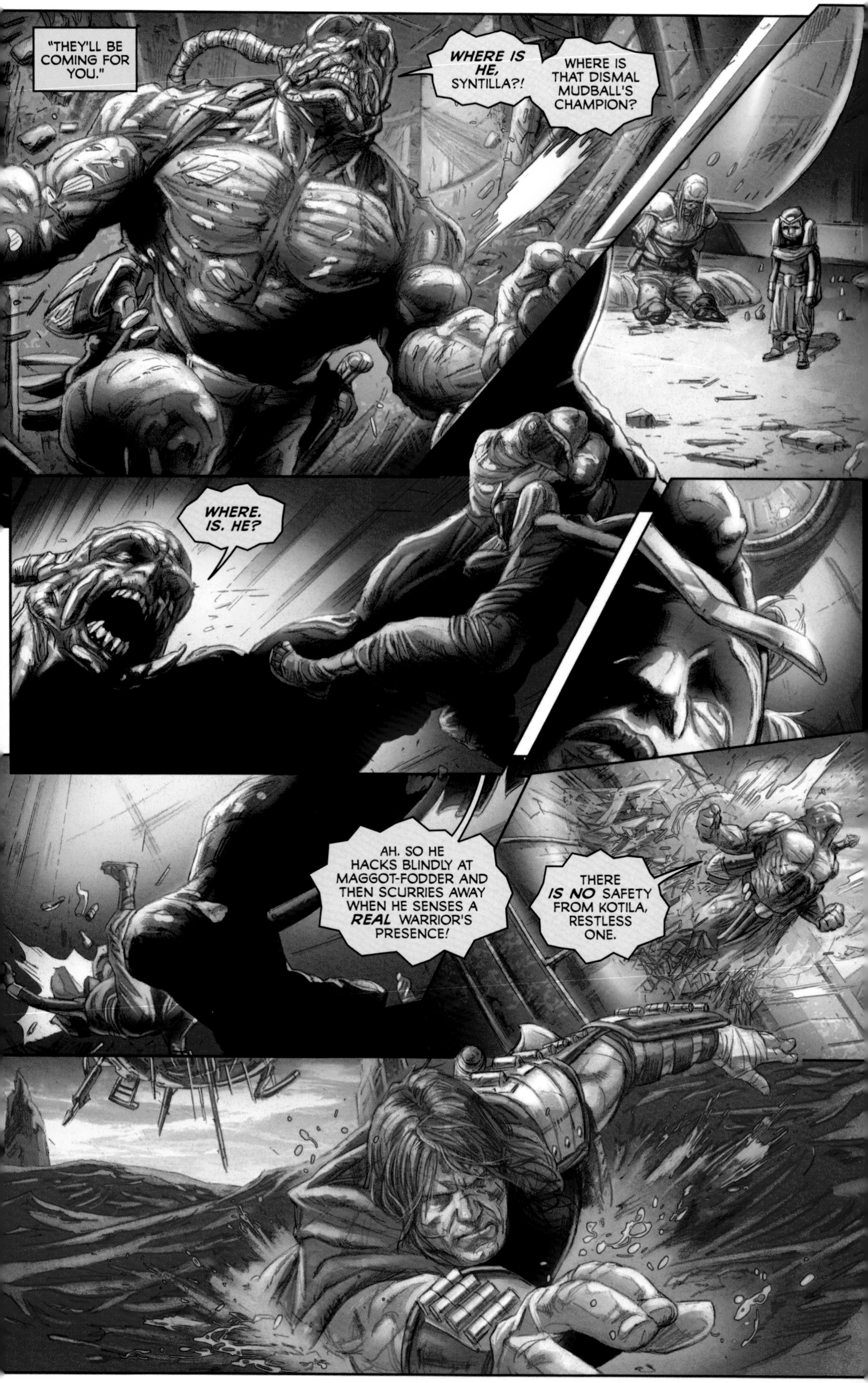
"THEY'LL BE COMING FOR YOU."
WHERE IS HE, SYNTILLA?!
WHERE IS THAT DISMAL MUDBALL'S CHAMPION?
WHERE. IS. HE?
AH. SO HE HACKS BLINDLY AT MAGGOT-FODDER AND THEN SCURRIES AWAY WHEN HE SENSES A REAL WARRIOR'S PRESENCE!
THERE IS NO SAFETY FROM KOTILA, RESTLESS ONE.

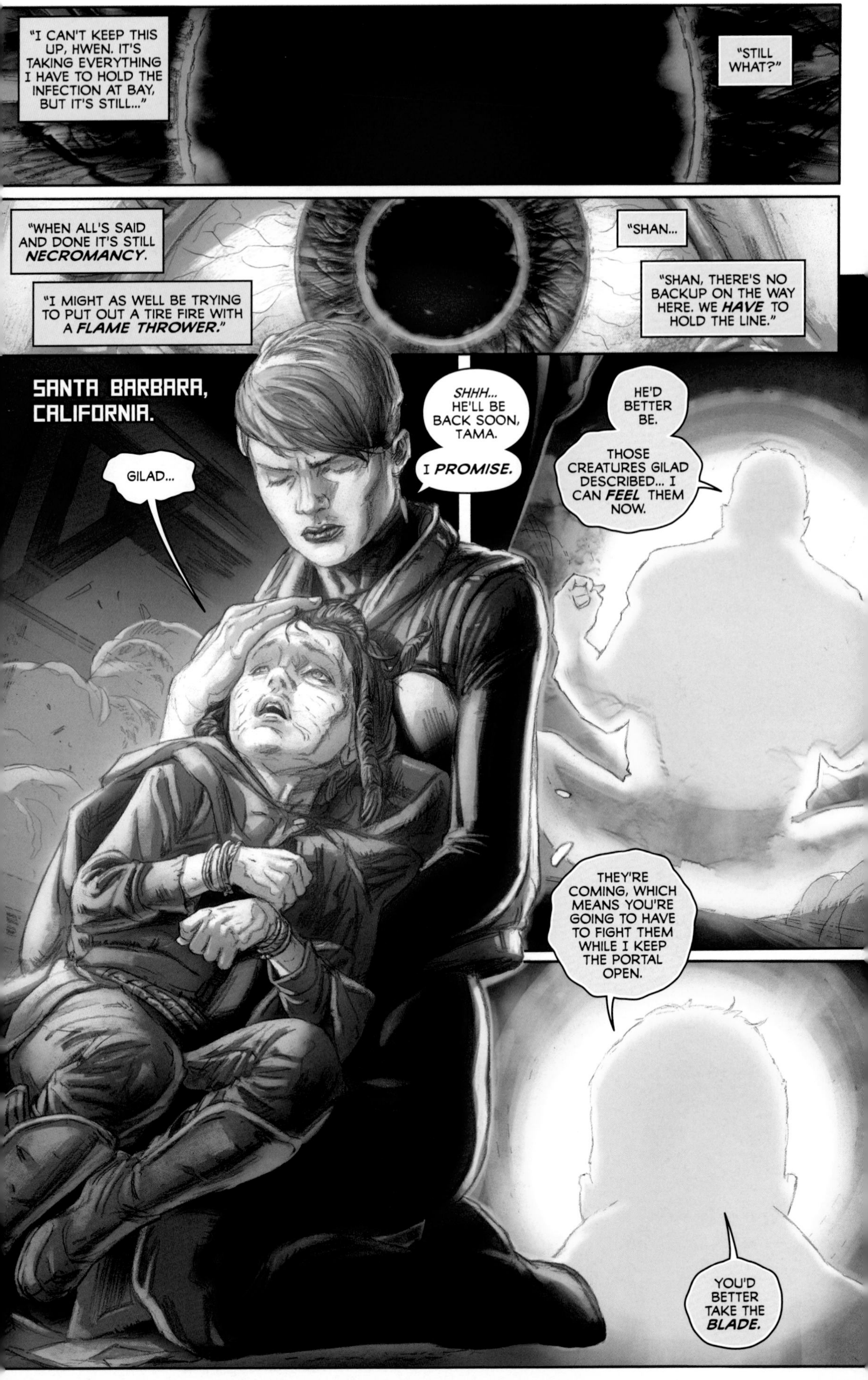
"I CAN'T KEEP THIS UP, HWEN. IT'S TAKING EVERYTHING I HAVE TO HOLD THE INFECTION AT BAY, BUT IT'S STILL..."
"STILL WHAT?"
"WHEN ALL'S SAID AND DONE IT'S STILL NECROMANCY.
"I MIGHT AS WELL BE TRYING TO PUT OUT A TIRE FIRE WITH A FLAME THROWER."
"SHAN...
"SHAN, THERE'S NO BACKUP ON THE WAY HERE. WE HAVE TO HOLD THE LINE."
SANTA BARBARA, CALIFORNIA.
GILAD...
SHHH... HE'LL BE BACK SOON, TAMA.
I PROMISE.
HE'D BETTER BE.
THOSE CREATURES GILAD DESCRIBED... I CAN FEEL THEM NOW.
THEY'RE COMING, WHICH MEANS YOU'RE GOING TO HAVE TO FIGHT THEM WHILE I KEEP THE PORTAL OPEN.
YOU'D BETTER TAKE THE BLADE.

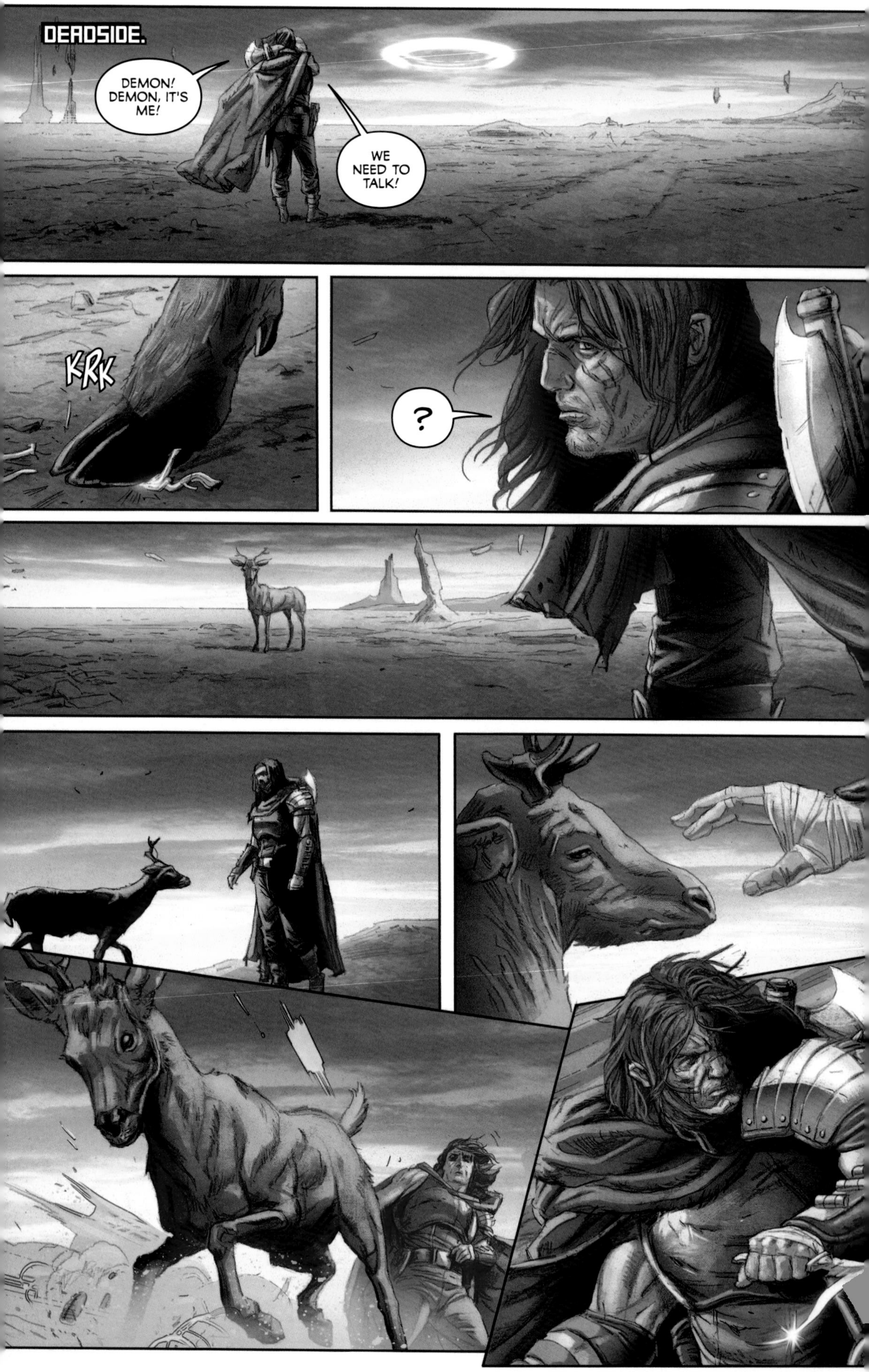
DEADSIDE.
DEMON! DEMON, IT'S ME!
WE NEED TO TALK!
KRK
?

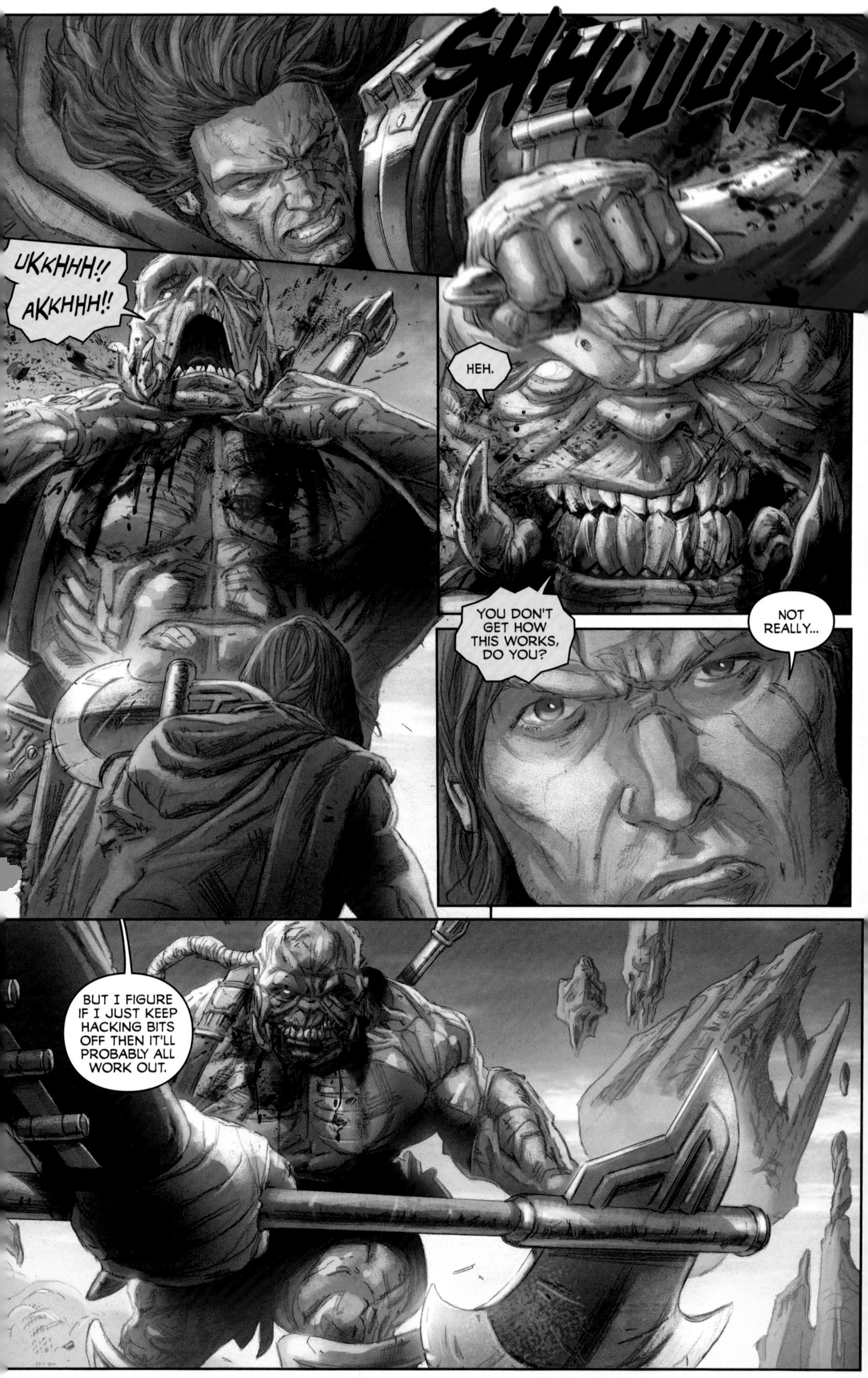
SHHLUUKK
UKKHHH!!
AKKHHH!!
HEH.
YOU DON'T GET HOW THIS WORKS, DO YOU?
NOT REALLY...
BUT I FIGURE IF I JUST KEEP HACKING BITS OFF THEN IT'LL PROBABLY ALL WORK OUT.

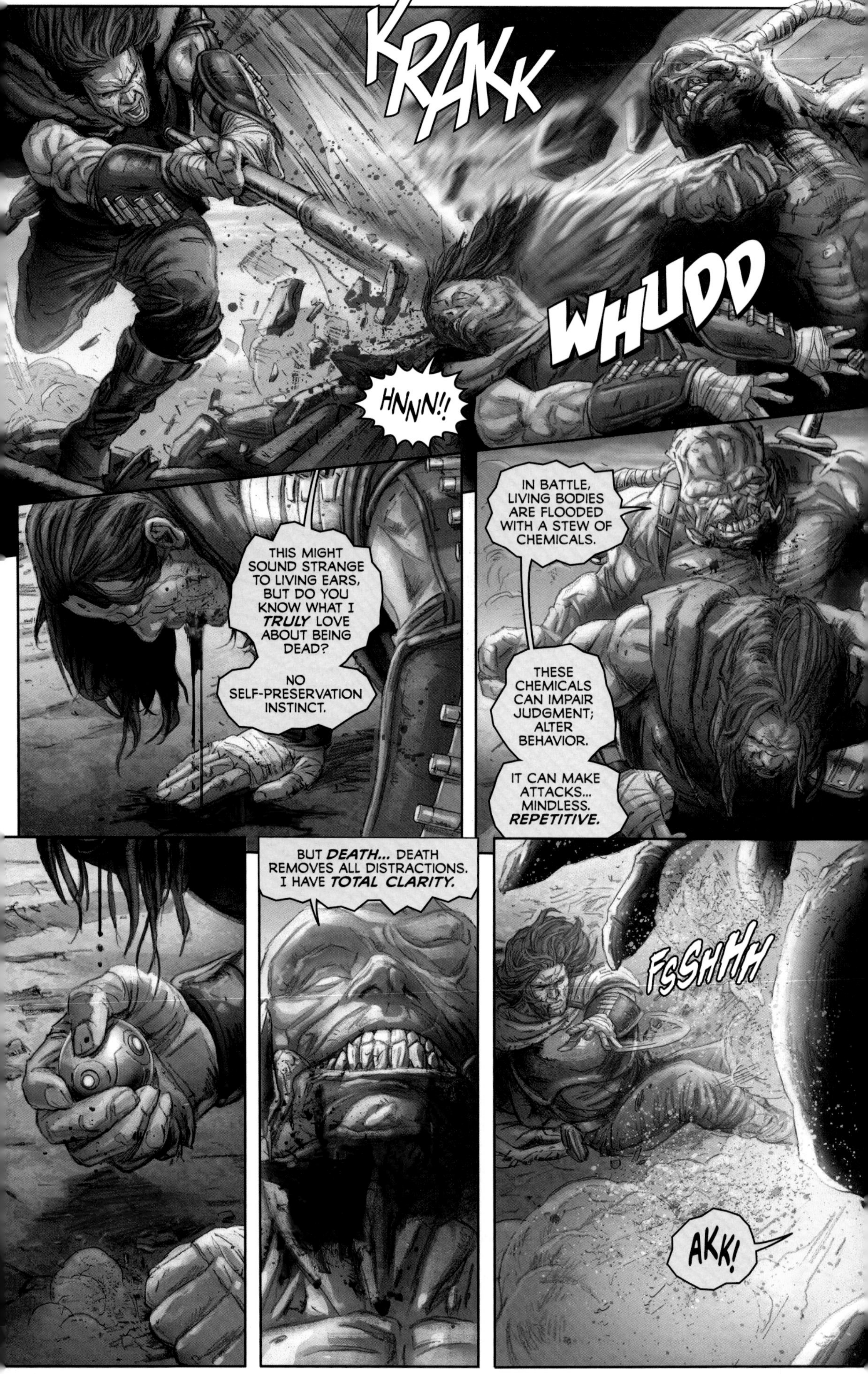

KRAKK
WHUDD
HNNN!!
THIS MIGHT SOUND STRANGE TO LIVING EARS, BUT DO YOU KNOW WHAT I *TRULY* LOVE ABOUT BEING DEAD?
NO SELF-PRESERVATION INSTINCT.
IN BATTLE, LIVING BODIES ARE FLOODED WITH A STEW OF CHEMICALS.
THESE CHEMICALS CAN IMPAIR JUDGMENT; ALTER BEHAVIOR.
IT CAN MAKE ATTACKS... MINDLESS. ***REPETITIVE.***
BUT ***DEATH...*** DEATH REMOVES ALL DISTRACTIONS. I HAVE ***TOTAL CLARITY.***
FSSHHH
AKK!

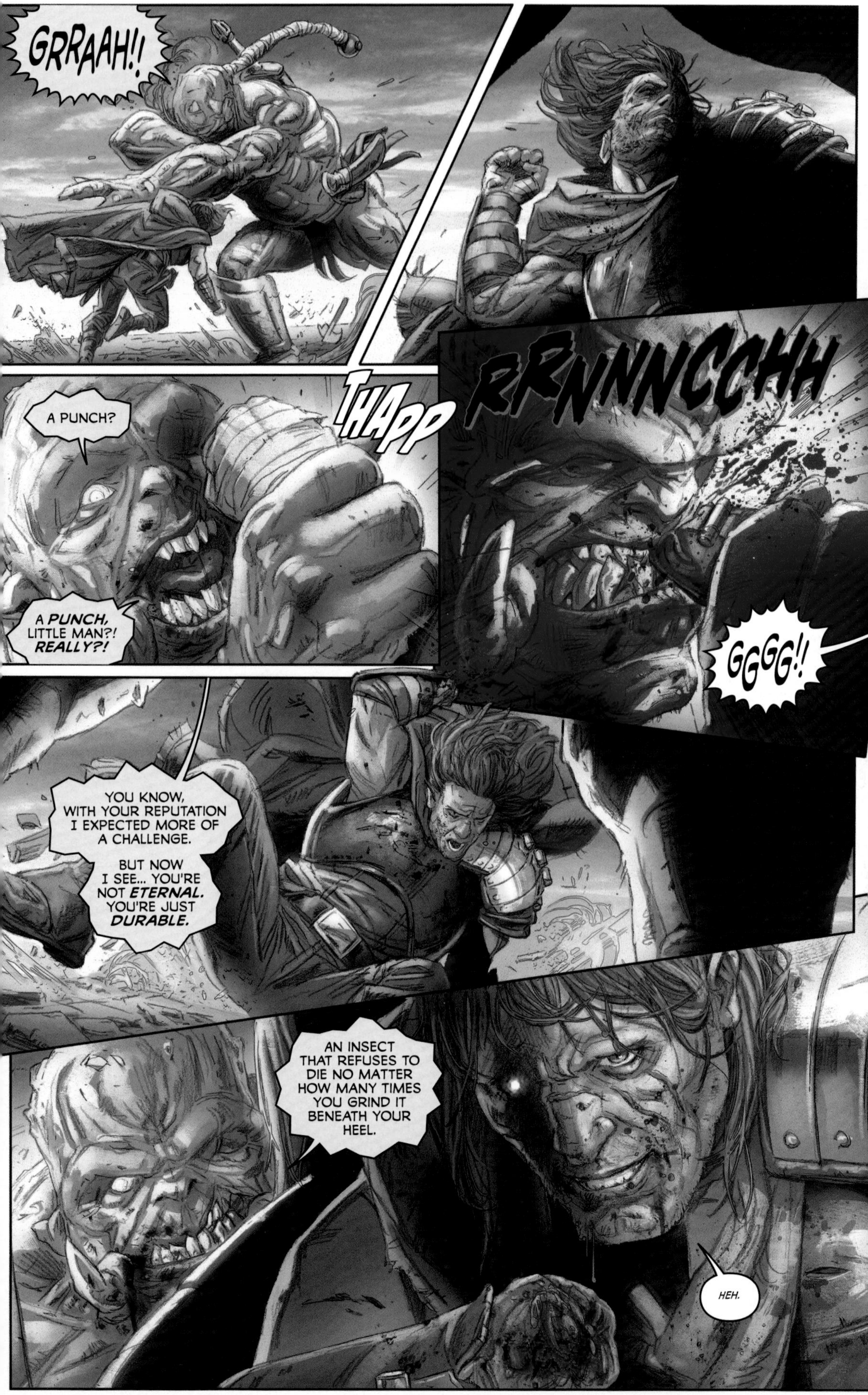
GRRAAH!!
A PUNCH?
A PUNCH, LITTLE MAN?! REALLY?!
THAPP
RRNNNCCHH
GGGG!!
YOU KNOW, WITH YOUR REPUTATION I EXPECTED MORE OF A CHALLENGE.
BUT NOW I SEE... YOU'RE NOT ETERNAL. YOU'RE JUST DURABLE.
AN INSECT THAT REFUSES TO DIE NO MATTER HOW MANY TIMES YOU GRIND IT BENEATH YOUR HEEL.
HEH.

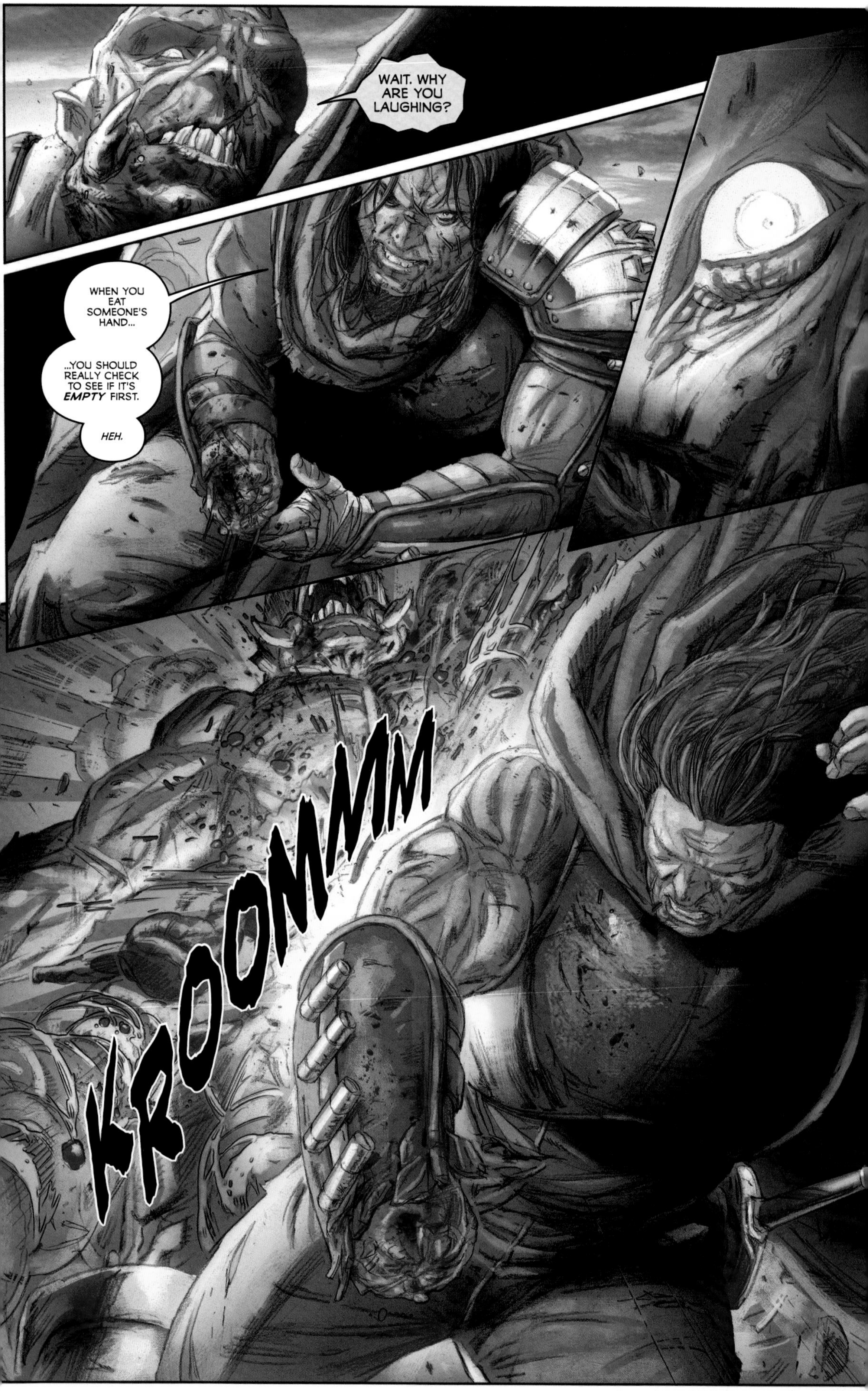

WAIT. WHY ARE YOU LAUGHING?
WHEN YOU EAT SOMEONE'S HAND...
...YOU SHOULD REALLY CHECK TO SEE IF IT'S *EMPTY* FIRST.
HEH.
KROOOMMM

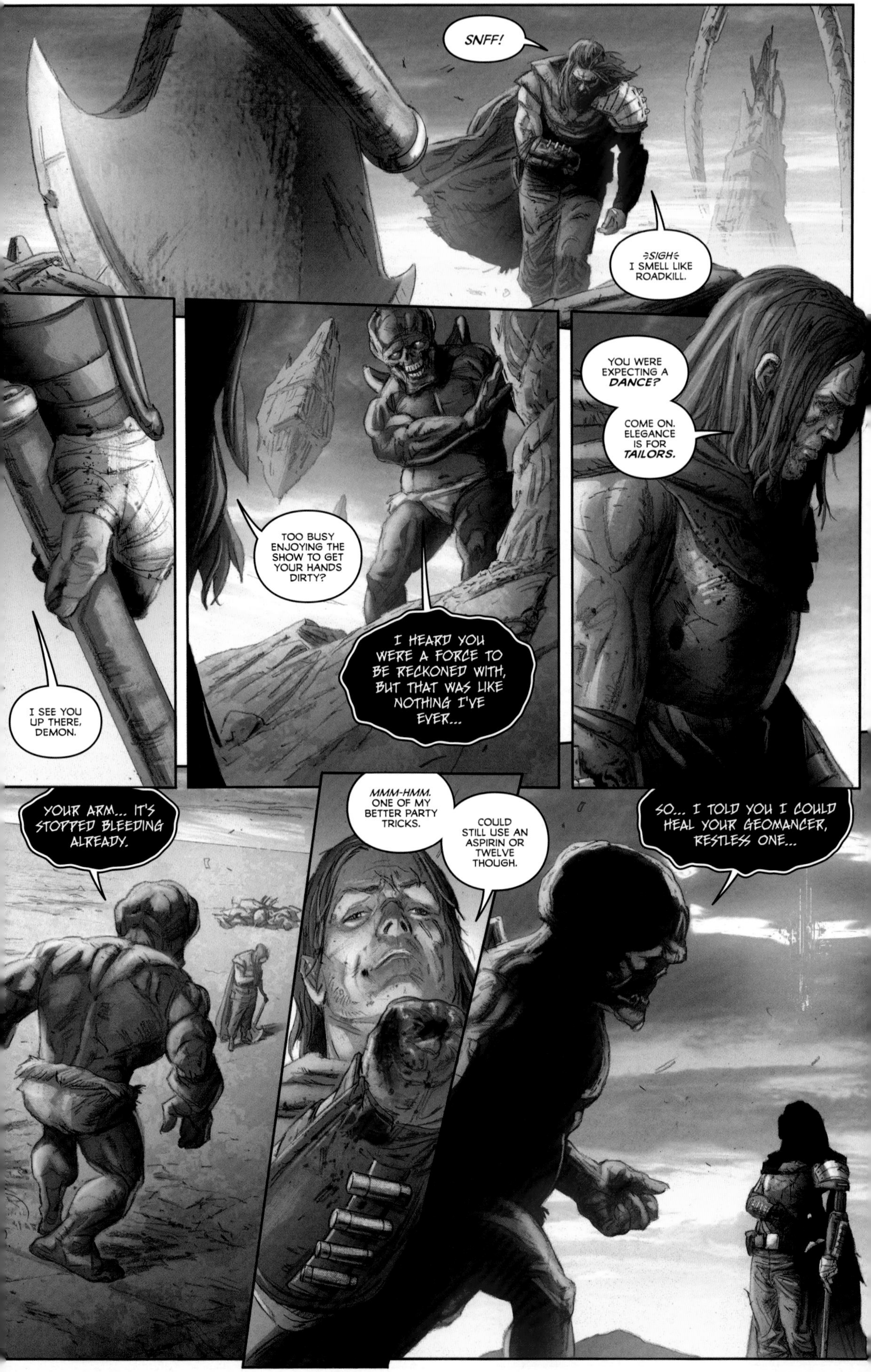
SNFF!
SIGH
I SMELL LIKE ROADKILL.
I SEE YOU UP THERE, DEMON.
TOO BUSY ENJOYING THE SHOW TO GET YOUR HANDS DIRTY?
I HEARD YOU WERE A FORCE TO BE RECKONED WITH, BUT THAT WAS LIKE NOTHING I'VE EVER...
YOU WERE EXPECTING A DANCE?
COME ON. ELEGANCE IS FOR TAILORS.
YOUR ARM... IT'S STOPPED BLEEDING ALREADY.
MMM-HMM. ONE OF MY BETTER PARTY TRICKS.
COULD STILL USE AN ASPIRIN OR TWELVE THOUGH.
SO... I TOLD YOU I COULD HEAL YOUR GEOMANCER, RESTLESS ONE...

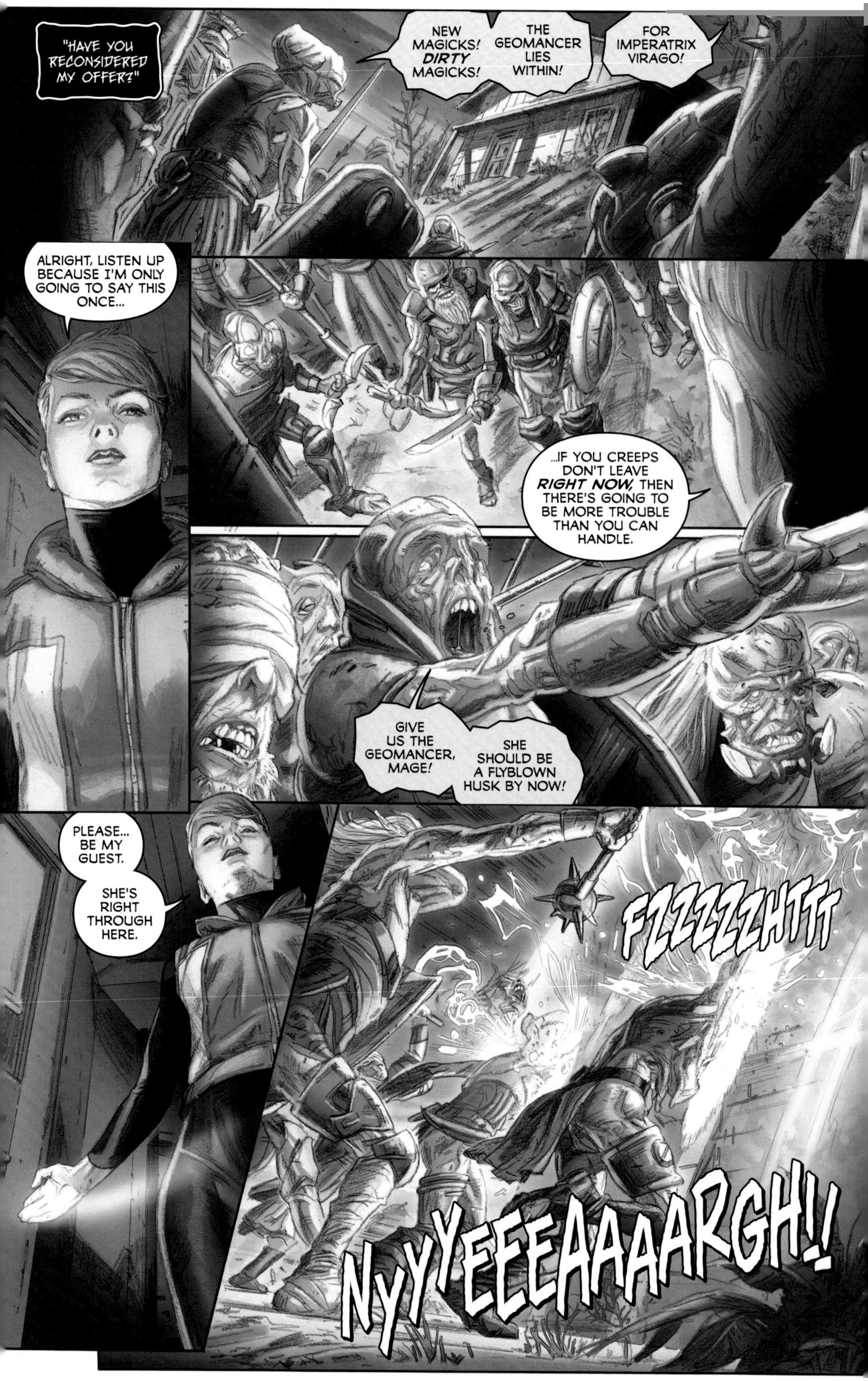
"HAVE YOU RECONSIDERED MY OFFER?"
NEW MAGICKS! DIRTY MAGICKS!
THE GEOMANCER LIES WITHIN!
FOR IMPERATRIX VIRAGO!
ALRIGHT, LISTEN UP BECAUSE I'M ONLY GOING TO SAY THIS ONCE...
...IF YOU CREEPS DON'T LEAVE RIGHT NOW, THEN THERE'S GOING TO BE MORE TROUBLE THAN YOU CAN HANDLE.
GIVE US THE GEOMANCER, MAGE!
SHE SHOULD BE A FLYBLOWN HUSK BY NOW!
PLEASE... BE MY GUEST.
SHE'S RIGHT THROUGH HERE.
FZZZZZHTTT
NyYYEEEAAAARGH!!

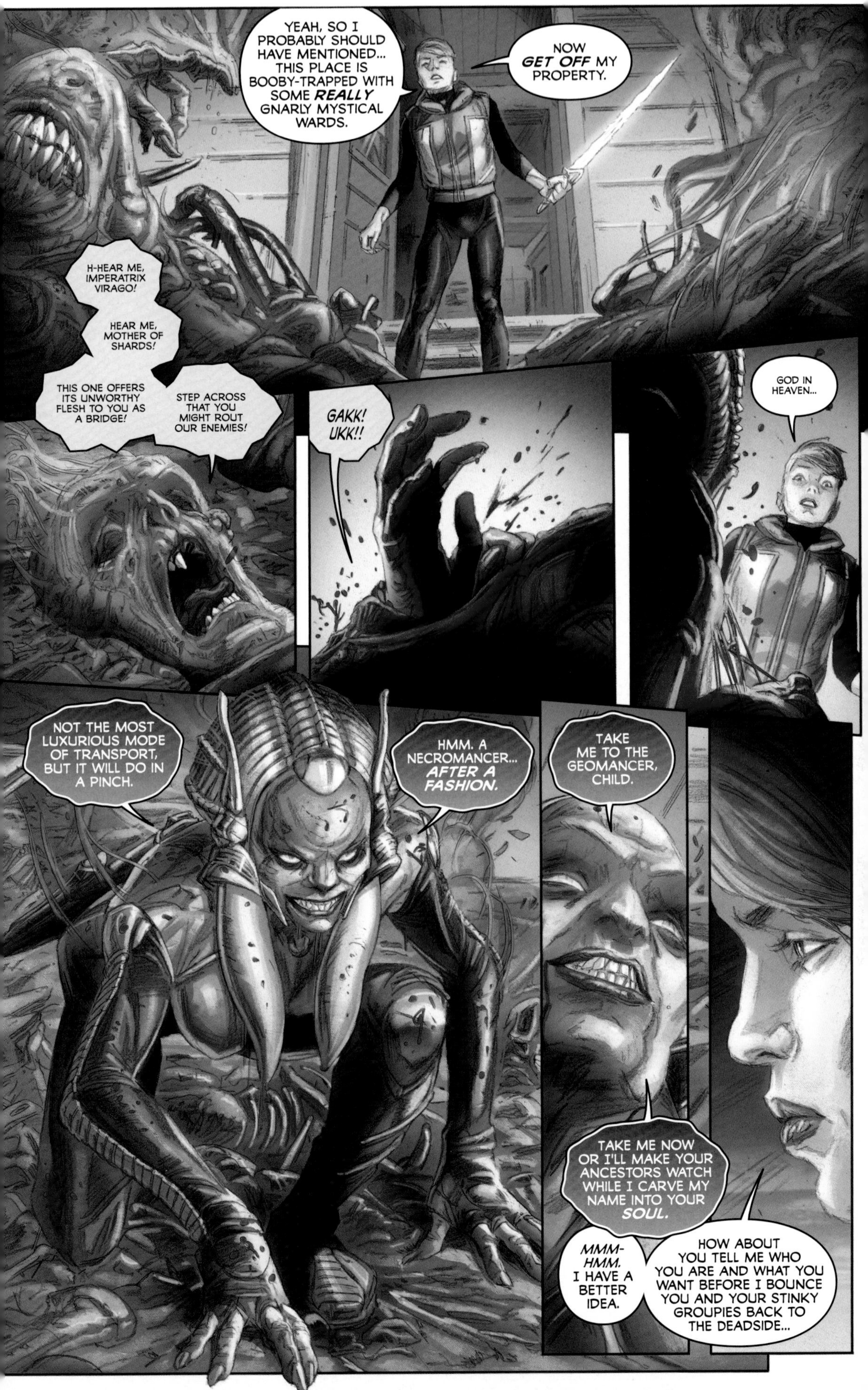
YEAH, SO I PROBABLY SHOULD HAVE MENTIONED... THIS PLACE IS BOOBY-TRAPPED WITH SOME *REALLY* GNARLY MYSTICAL WARDS.
NOW *GET OFF* MY PROPERTY.
H-HEAR ME, IMPERATRIX VIRAGO!
HEAR ME, MOTHER OF SHARDS!
THIS ONE OFFERS ITS UNWORTHY FLESH TO YOU AS A BRIDGE!
STEP ACROSS THAT YOU MIGHT ROUT OUR ENEMIES!
GAKK! UKK!!
GOD IN HEAVEN...
NOT THE MOST LUXURIOUS MODE OF TRANSPORT, BUT IT WILL DO IN A PINCH.
HMM. A NECROMANCER... *AFTER A FASHION.*
TAKE ME TO THE GEOMANCER, CHILD.
TAKE ME NOW OR I'LL MAKE YOUR ANCESTORS WATCH WHILE I CARVE MY NAME INTO YOUR *SOUL.*
MMM-HMM. I HAVE A BETTER IDEA.
HOW ABOUT YOU TELL ME WHO YOU ARE AND WHAT YOU WANT BEFORE I BOUNCE YOU AND YOUR STINKY GROUPIES BACK TO THE DEADSIDE...

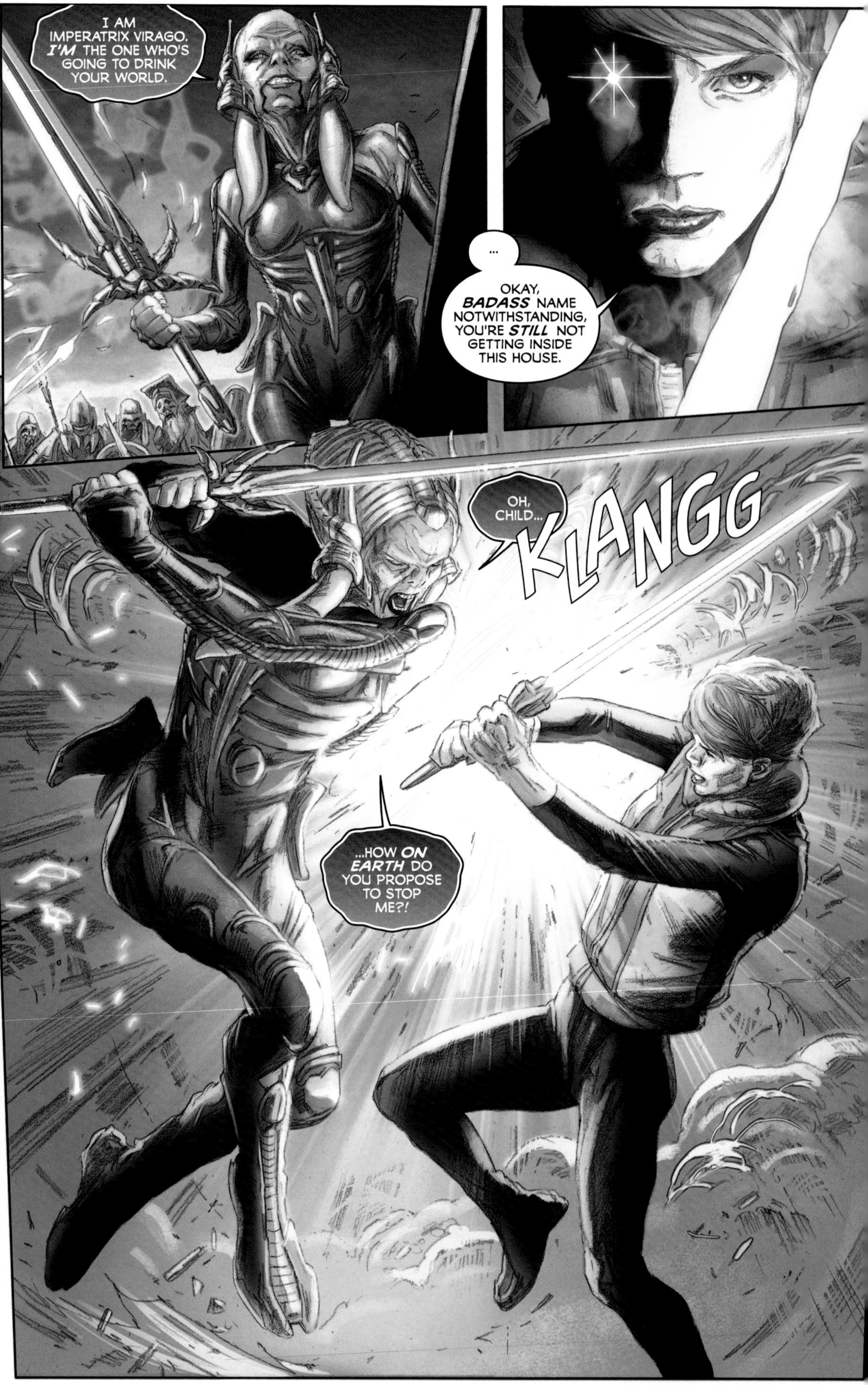
I AM IMPERATRIX VIRAGO. I'M THE ONE WHO'S GOING TO DRINK YOUR WORLD.
...
OKAY, BADASS NAME NOTWITHSTANDING, YOU'RE STILL NOT GETTING INSIDE THIS HOUSE.
OH, CHILD...
KLANGG
...HOW ON EARTH DO YOU PROPOSE TO STOP ME?!

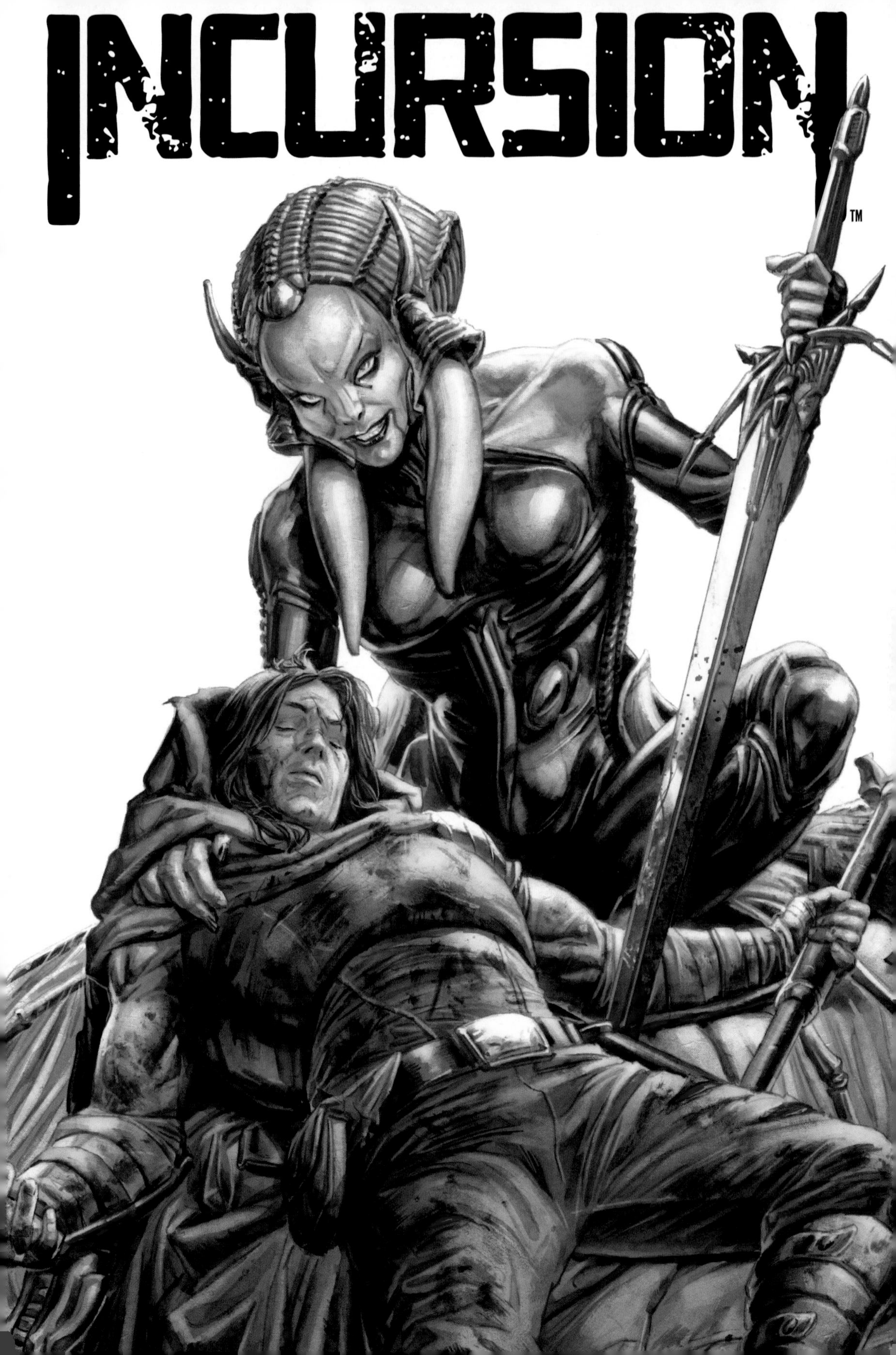
INCURSION™

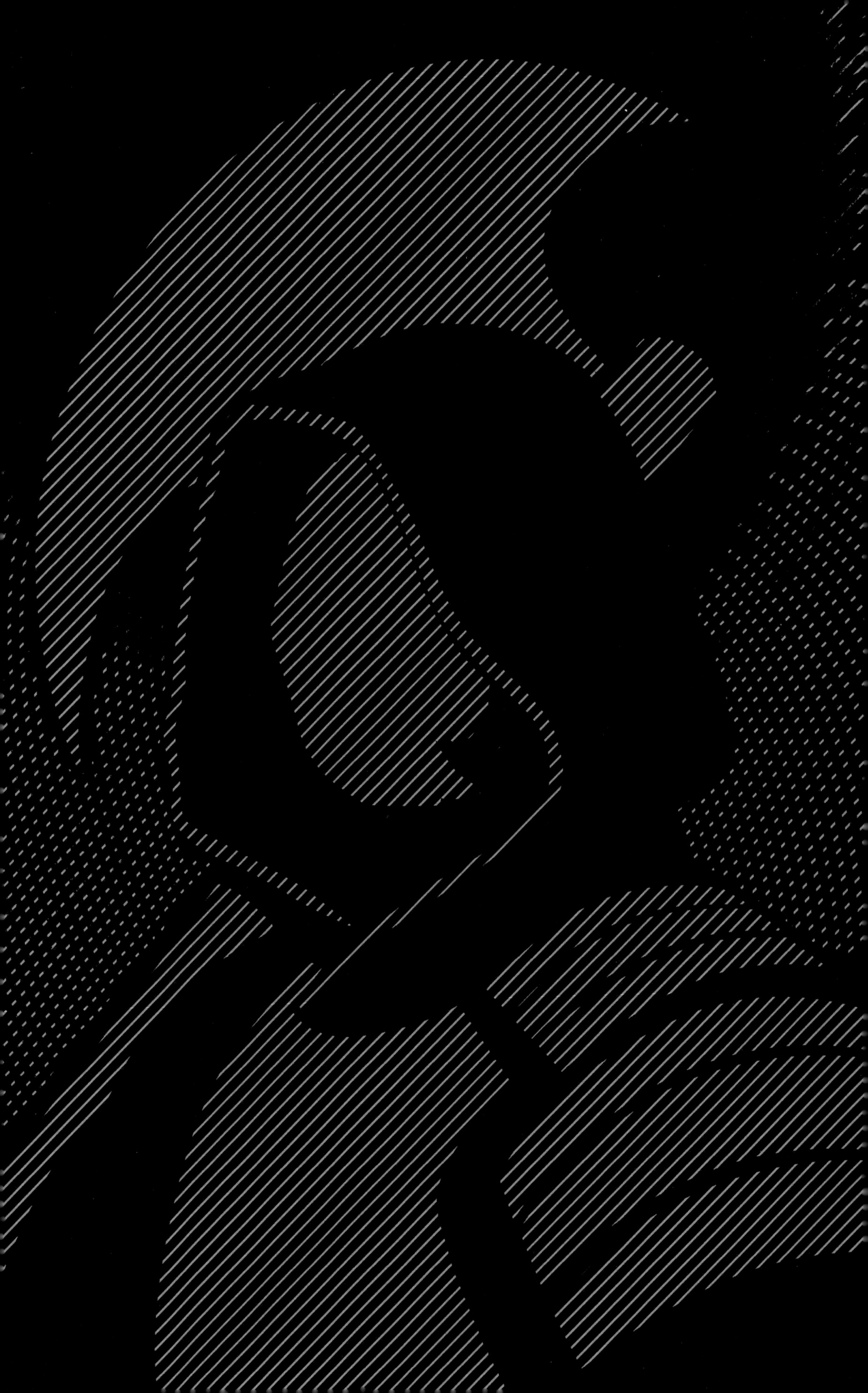

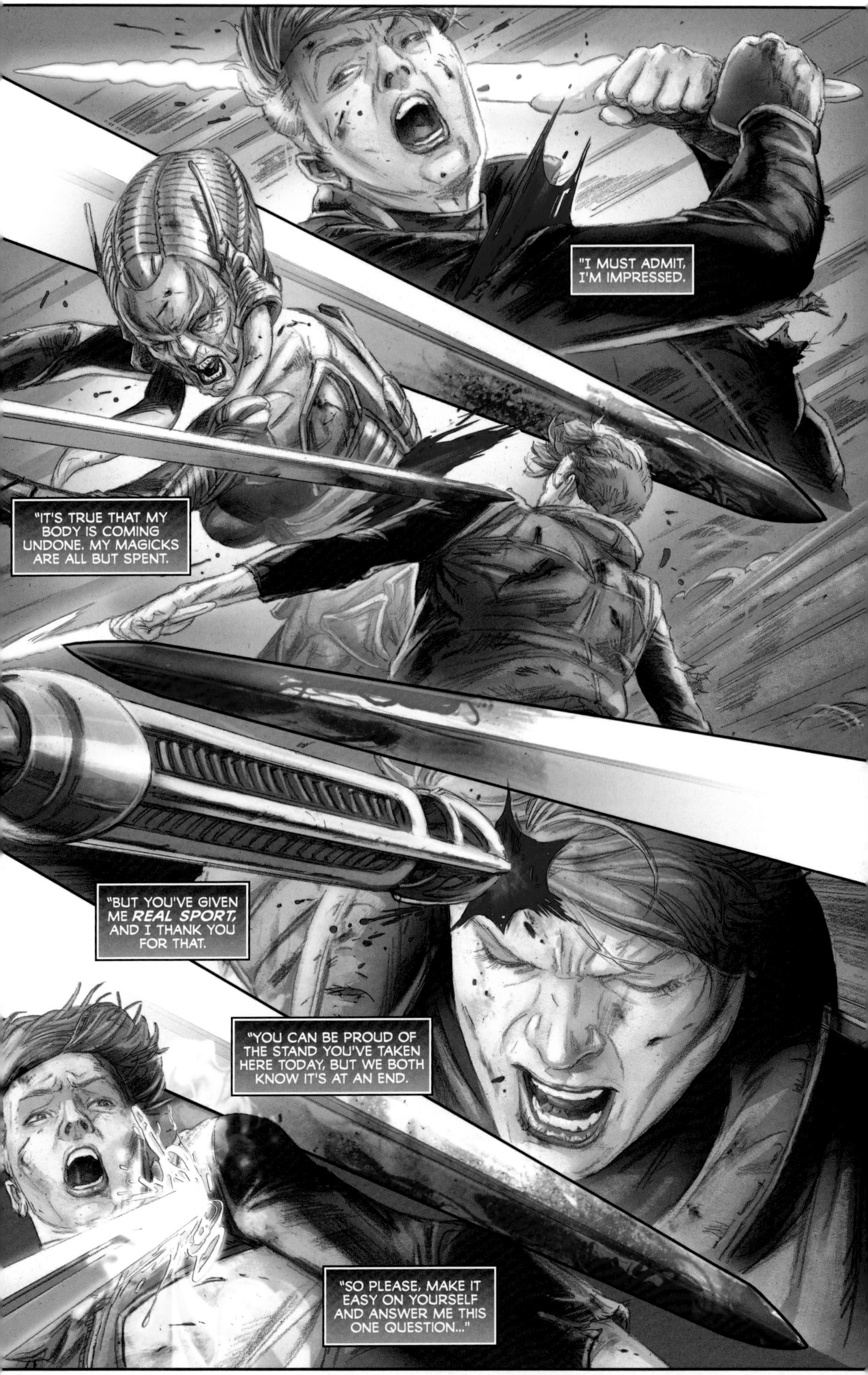
"I MUST ADMIT, I'M IMPRESSED.
"IT'S TRUE THAT MY BODY IS COMING UNDONE. MY MAGICKS ARE ALL BUT SPENT.
"BUT YOU'VE GIVEN ME *REAL SPORT,* AND I THANK YOU FOR THAT.
"YOU CAN BE PROUD OF THE STAND YOU'VE TAKEN HERE TODAY, BUT WE BOTH KNOW IT'S AT AN END.
"SO PLEASE, MAKE IT EASY ON YOURSELF AND ANSWER ME THIS ONE QUESTION..."

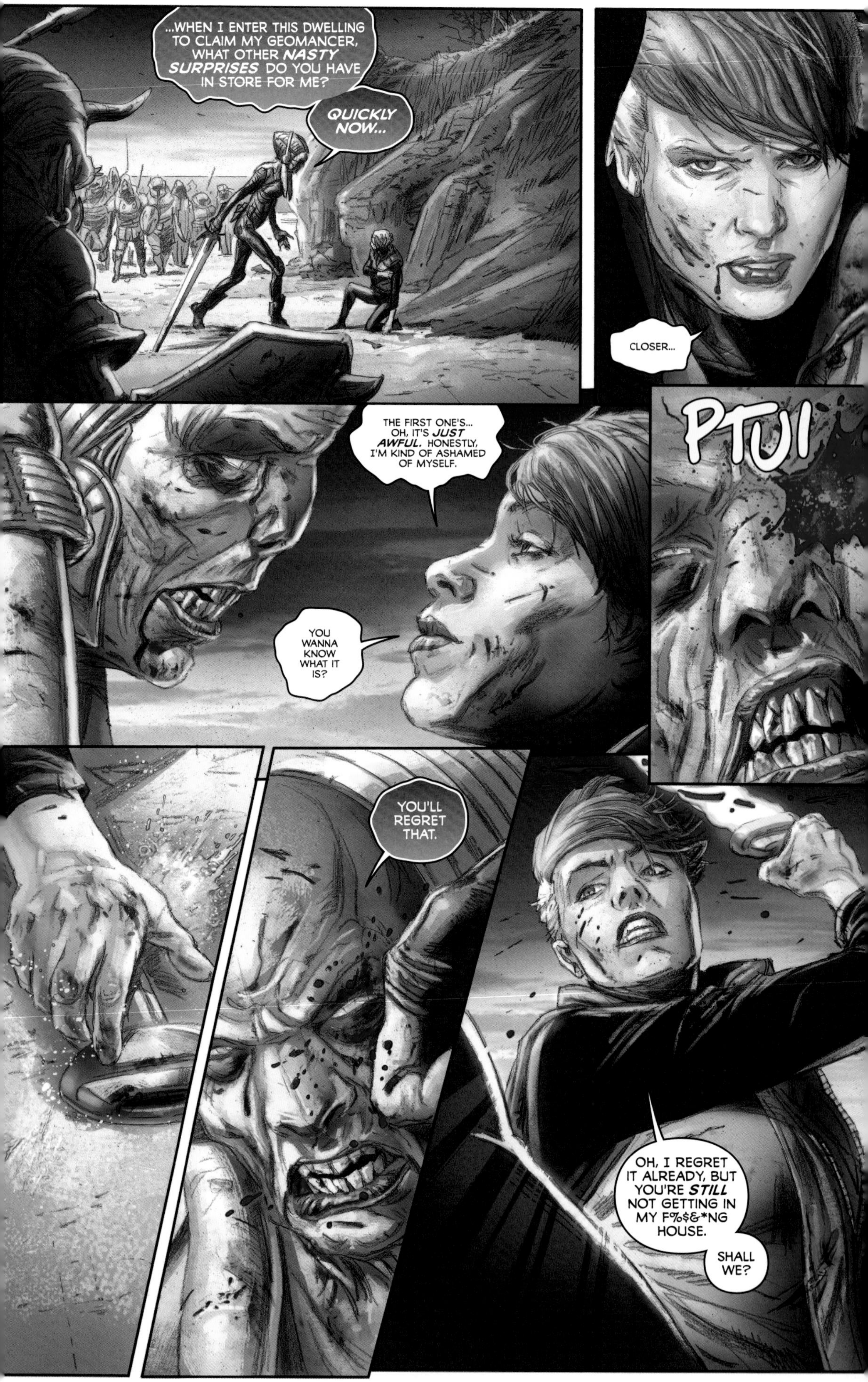
...WHEN I ENTER THIS DWELLING TO CLAIM MY GEOMANCER, WHAT OTHER NASTY SURPRISES DO YOU HAVE IN STORE FOR ME?
QUICKLY NOW...
CLOSER...
THE FIRST ONE'S... OH, IT'S JUST AWFUL. HONESTLY, I'M KIND OF ASHAMED OF MYSELF.
YOU WANNA KNOW WHAT IT IS?
PTUI
YOU'LL REGRET THAT.
OH, I REGRET IT ALREADY, BUT YOU'RE STILL NOT GETTING IN MY F%$&*NG HOUSE.
SHALL WE?

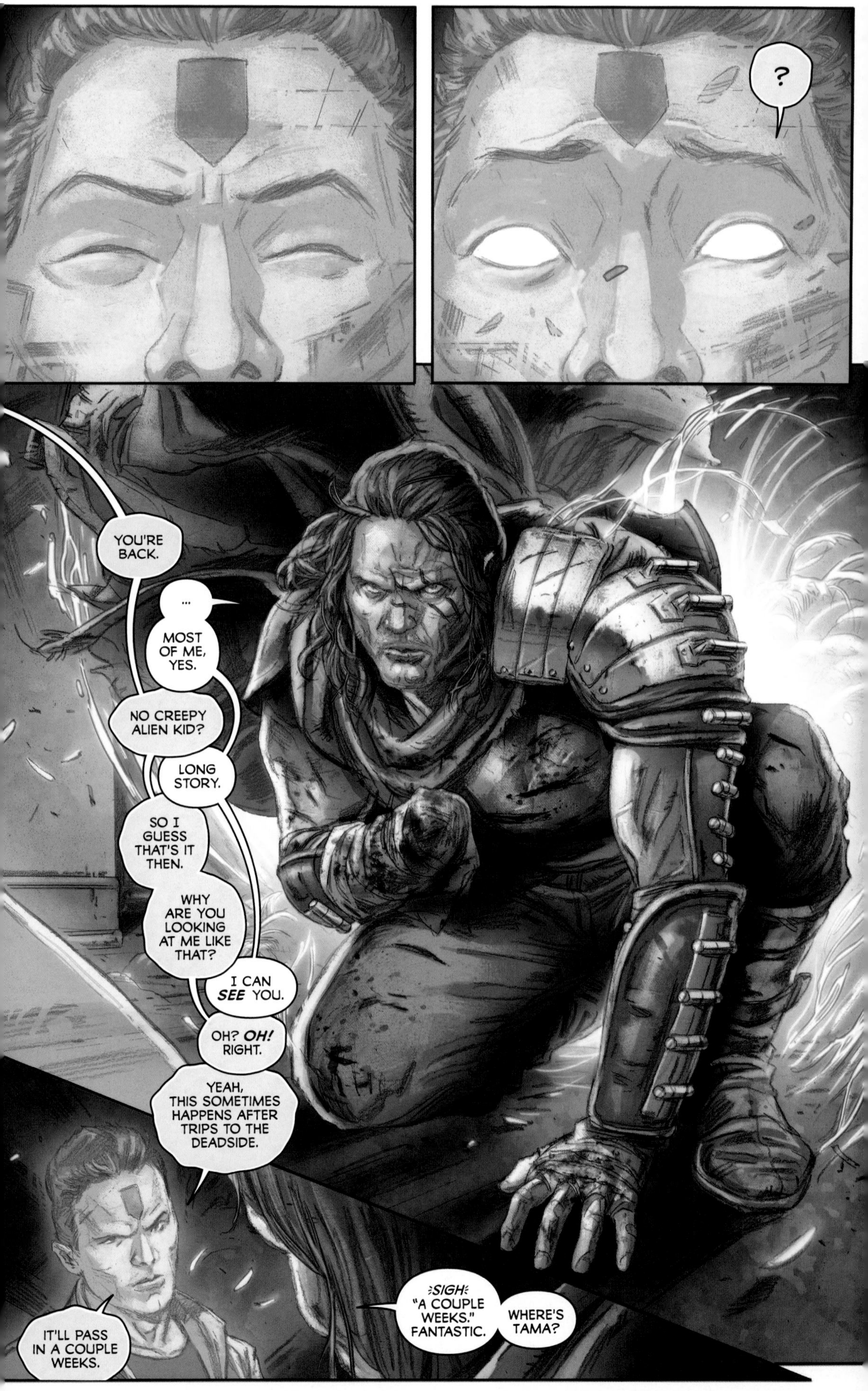
?
YOU'RE BACK.
...
MOST OF ME, YES.
NO CREEPY ALIEN KID?
LONG STORY.
SO I GUESS THAT'S IT THEN.
WHY ARE YOU LOOKING AT ME LIKE THAT?
I CAN SEE YOU.
OH? OH! RIGHT.
YEAH, THIS SOMETIMES HAPPENS AFTER TRIPS TO THE DEADSIDE.
IT'LL PASS IN A COUPLE WEEKS.
SIGH "A COUPLE WEEKS." FANTASTIC.
WHERE'S TAMA?

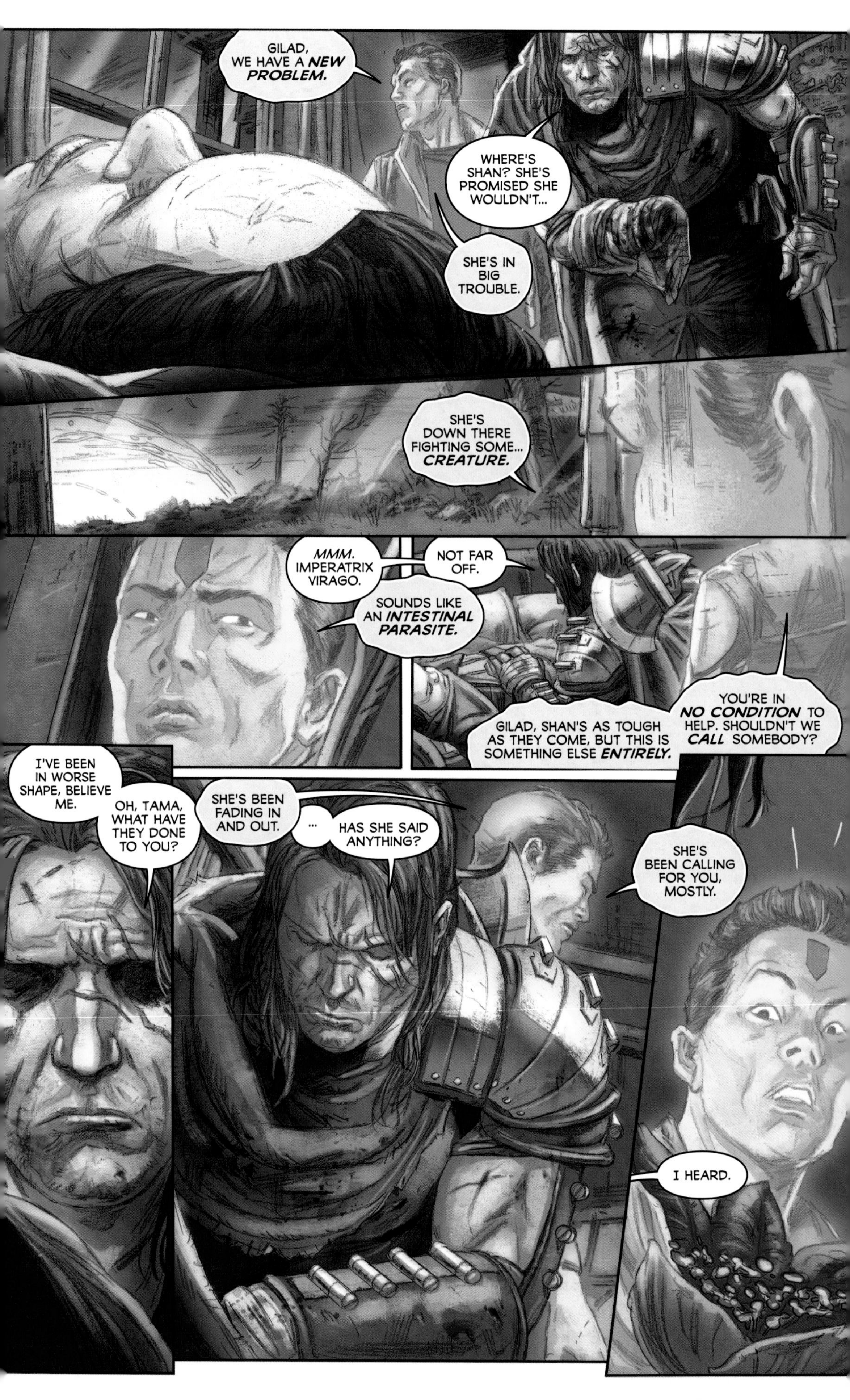
GILAD, WE HAVE A ***NEW PROBLEM.***
WHERE'S SHAN? SHE'S PROMISED SHE WOULDN'T...
SHE'S IN BIG TROUBLE.
SHE'S DOWN THERE FIGHTING SOME... ***CREATURE.***
MMM. IMPERATRIX VIRAGO.
NOT FAR OFF.
SOUNDS LIKE AN ***INTESTINAL PARASITE.***
GILAD, SHAN'S AS TOUGH AS THEY COME, BUT THIS IS SOMETHING ELSE ***ENTIRELY.***
YOU'RE IN ***NO CONDITION*** TO HELP. SHOULDN'T WE ***CALL*** SOMEBODY?
I'VE BEEN IN WORSE SHAPE, BELIEVE ME.
OH, TAMA, WHAT HAVE THEY DONE TO YOU?
SHE'S BEEN FADING IN AND OUT.
...
HAS SHE SAID ANYTHING?
SHE'S BEEN CALLING FOR YOU, MOSTLY.
I HEARD.

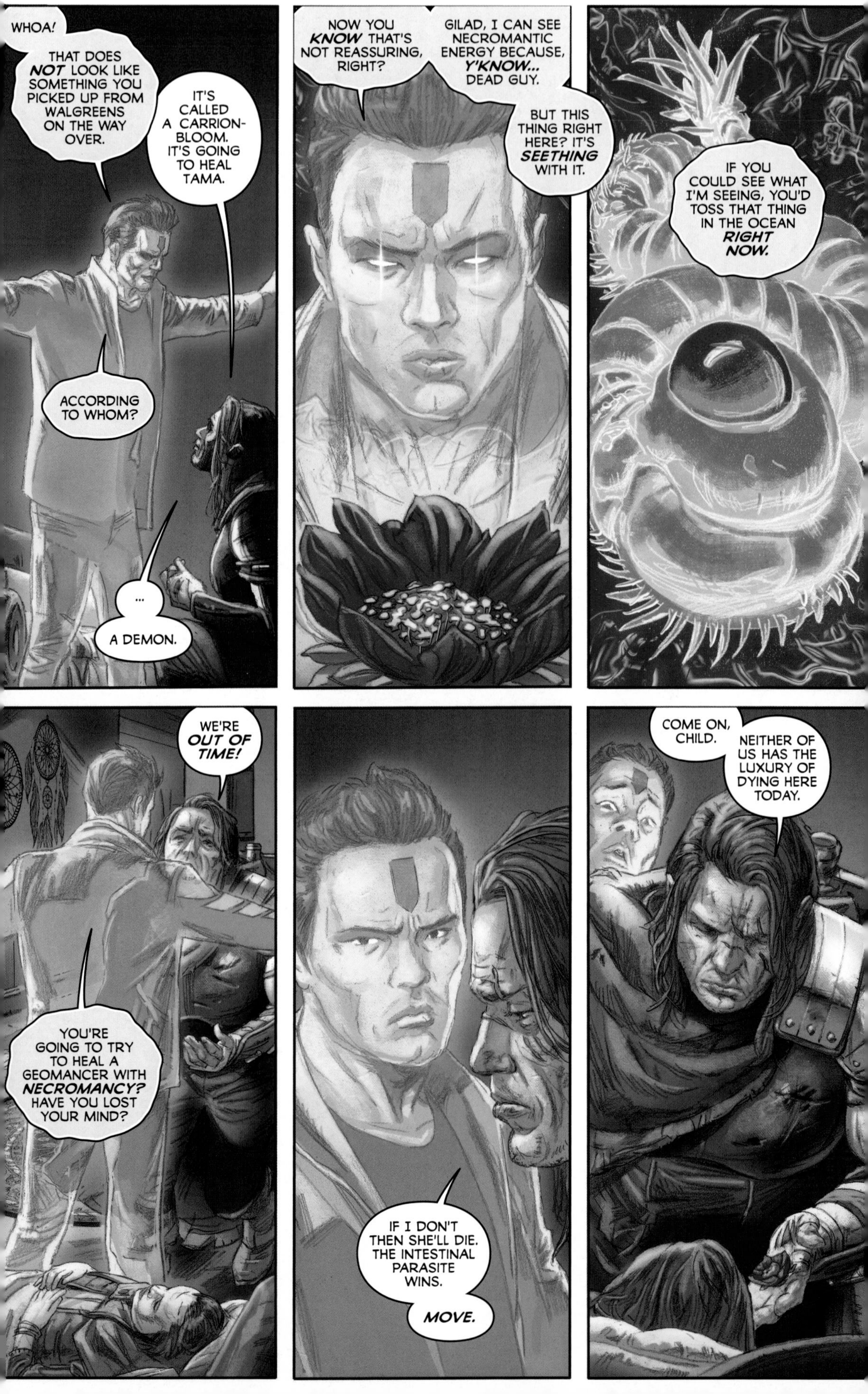
WHOA!
THAT DOES *NOT* LOOK LIKE SOMETHING YOU PICKED UP FROM WALGREENS ON THE WAY OVER.
IT'S CALLED A CARRION-BLOOM. IT'S GOING TO HEAL TAMA.
ACCORDING TO WHOM?
...
A DEMON.
NOW YOU *KNOW* THAT'S NOT REASSURING, RIGHT?
GILAD, I CAN SEE NECROMANTIC ENERGY BECAUSE, *Y'KNOW...* DEAD GUY.
BUT THIS THING RIGHT HERE? IT'S *SEETHING* WITH IT.
IF YOU COULD SEE WHAT I'M SEEING, YOU'D TOSS THAT THING IN THE OCEAN *RIGHT NOW.*
WE'RE *OUT OF TIME!*
YOU'RE GOING TO TRY TO HEAL A GEOMANCER WITH *NECROMANCY?* HAVE YOU LOST YOUR MIND?
IF I DON'T THEN SHE'LL DIE. THE INTESTINAL PARASITE WINS.
MOVE.
COME ON, CHILD.
NEITHER OF US HAS THE LUXURY OF DYING HERE TODAY.

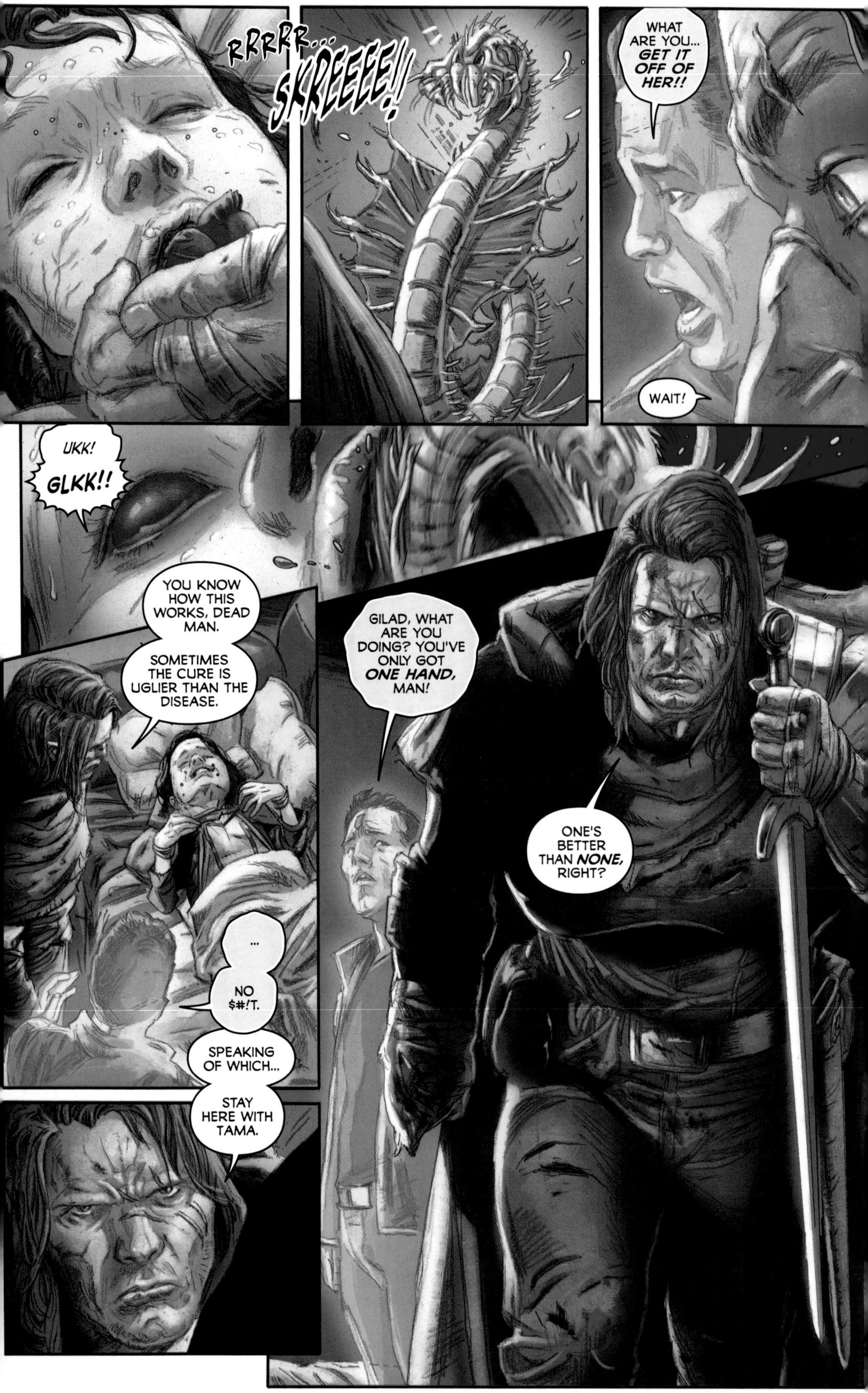
RRRRR...
SKREEEE!!
WHAT ARE YOU... GET IT OFF OF HER!!
WAIT!
UKK!
GLKK!!
YOU KNOW HOW THIS WORKS, DEAD MAN.
SOMETIMES THE CURE IS UGLIER THAN THE DISEASE.
...
NO $#!T.
SPEAKING OF WHICH...
STAY HERE WITH TAMA.
GILAD, WHAT ARE YOU DOING? YOU'VE ONLY GOT ONE HAND, MAN!
ONE'S BETTER THAN NONE, RIGHT?

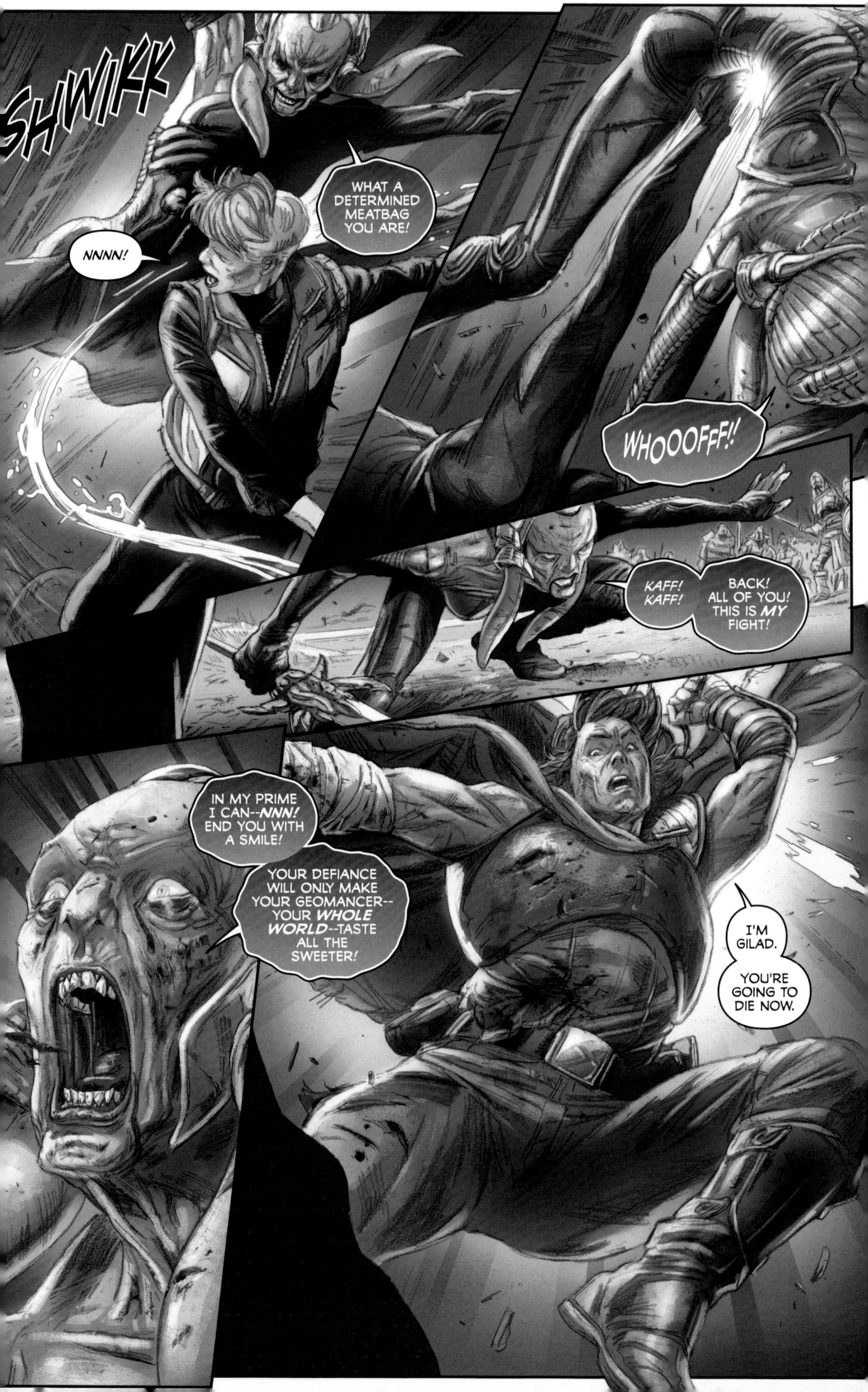
SHWIKK
WHAT A DETERMINED MEATBAG YOU ARE!
NNNN!
WHOOOFFF!!
KAFF! KAFF!
BACK! ALL OF YOU! THIS IS MY FIGHT!
IN MY PRIME I CAN--NNN! END YOU WITH A SMILE!
YOUR DEFIANCE WILL ONLY MAKE YOUR GEOMANCER--YOUR WHOLE WORLD--TASTE ALL THE SWEETER!
I'M GILAD.
YOU'RE GOING TO DIE NOW.

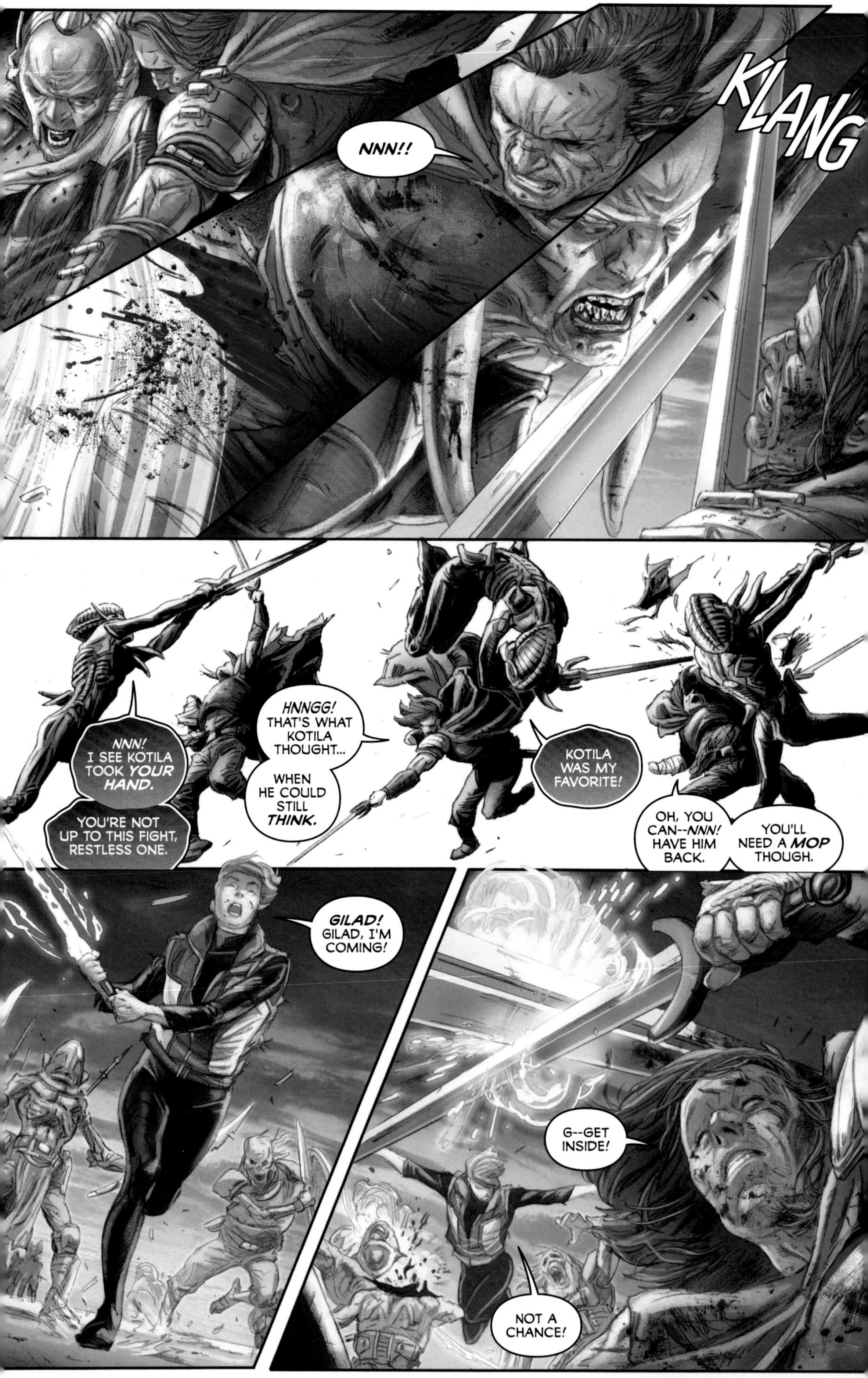
NNN!!
KLANG
NNN! I SEE KOTILA TOOK YOUR HAND.
YOU'RE NOT UP TO THIS FIGHT, RESTLESS ONE.
HNNGG! THAT'S WHAT KOTILA THOUGHT...
WHEN HE COULD STILL THINK.
KOTILA WAS MY FAVORITE!
OH, YOU CAN--NNN! HAVE HIM BACK.
YOU'LL NEED A MOP THOUGH.
GILAD! GILAD, I'M COMING!
G--GET INSIDE!
NOT A CHANCE!

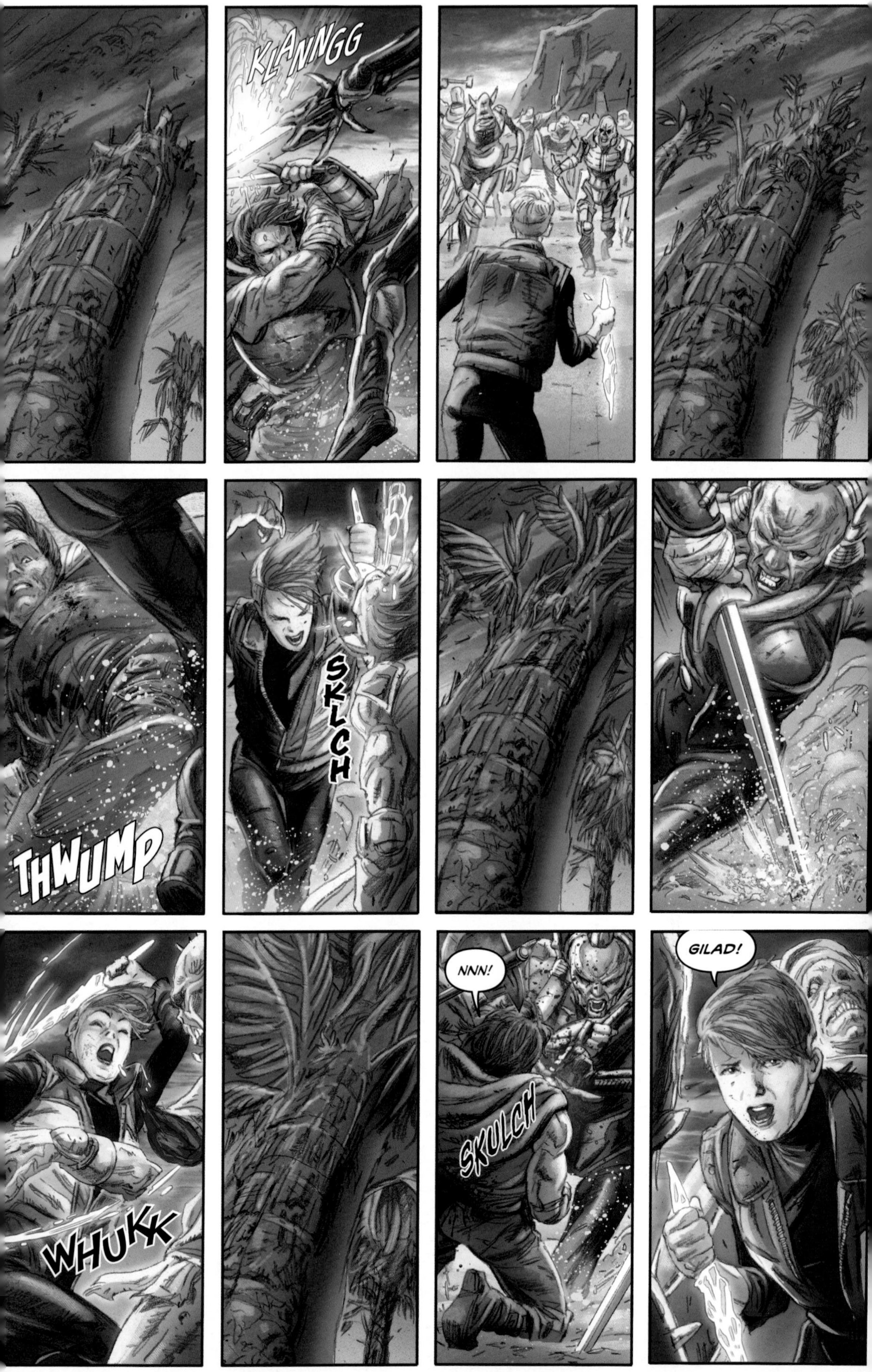
KLANNGG
THWUMP
SKLCH
WHUKK
NNN!
SKULCH
GILAD!

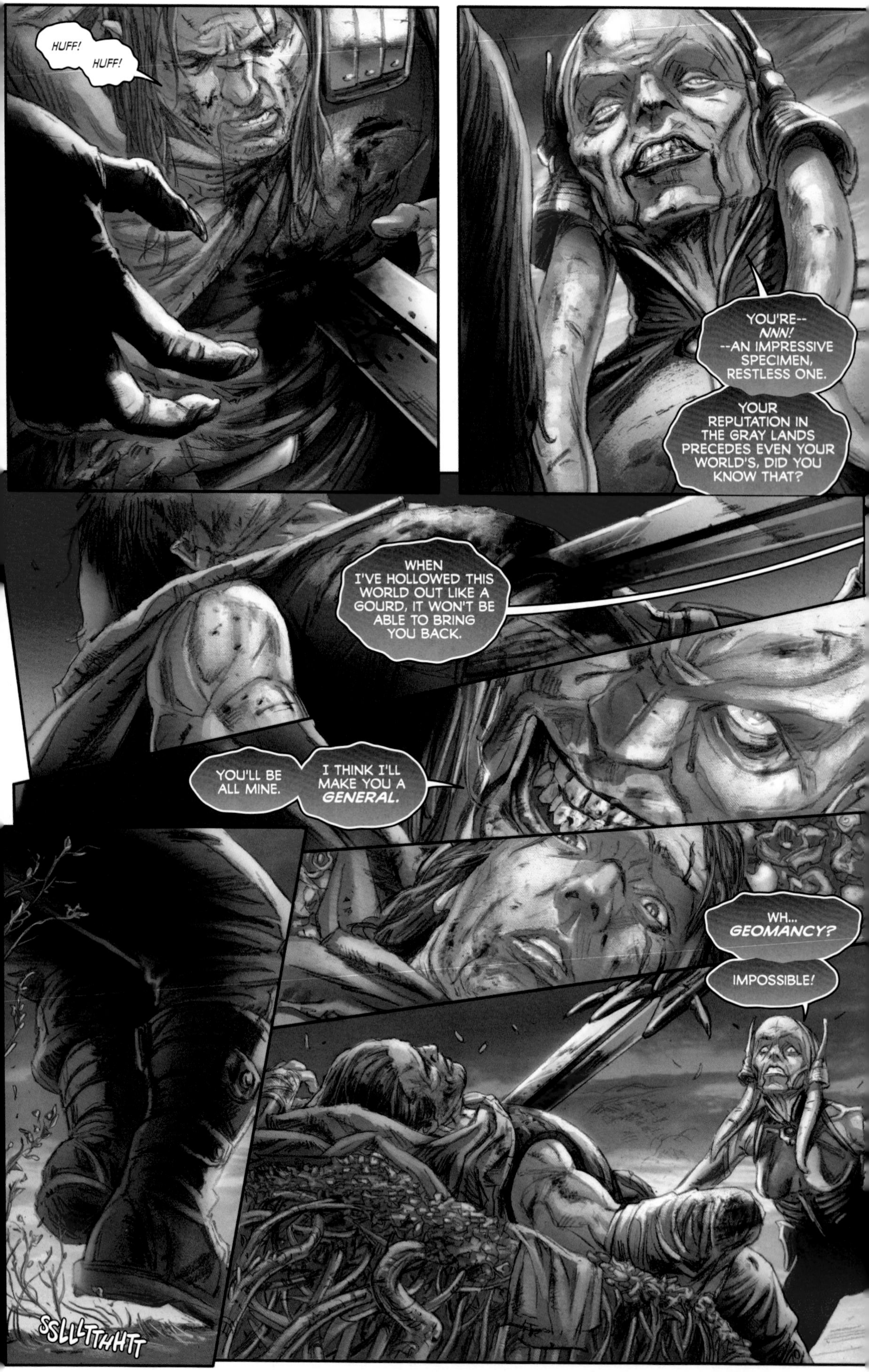
HUFF! HUFF!
YOU'RE-- NNN! --AN IMPRESSIVE SPECIMEN, RESTLESS ONE.
YOUR REPUTATION IN THE GRAY LANDS PRECEDES EVEN YOUR WORLD'S, DID YOU KNOW THAT?
WHEN I'VE HOLLOWED THIS WORLD OUT LIKE A GOURD, IT WON'T BE ABLE TO BRING YOU BACK.
I THINK I'LL MAKE YOU A GENERAL.
YOU'LL BE ALL MINE.
WH... GEOMANCY?
IMPOSSIBLE!
SSLLLTTHHTT

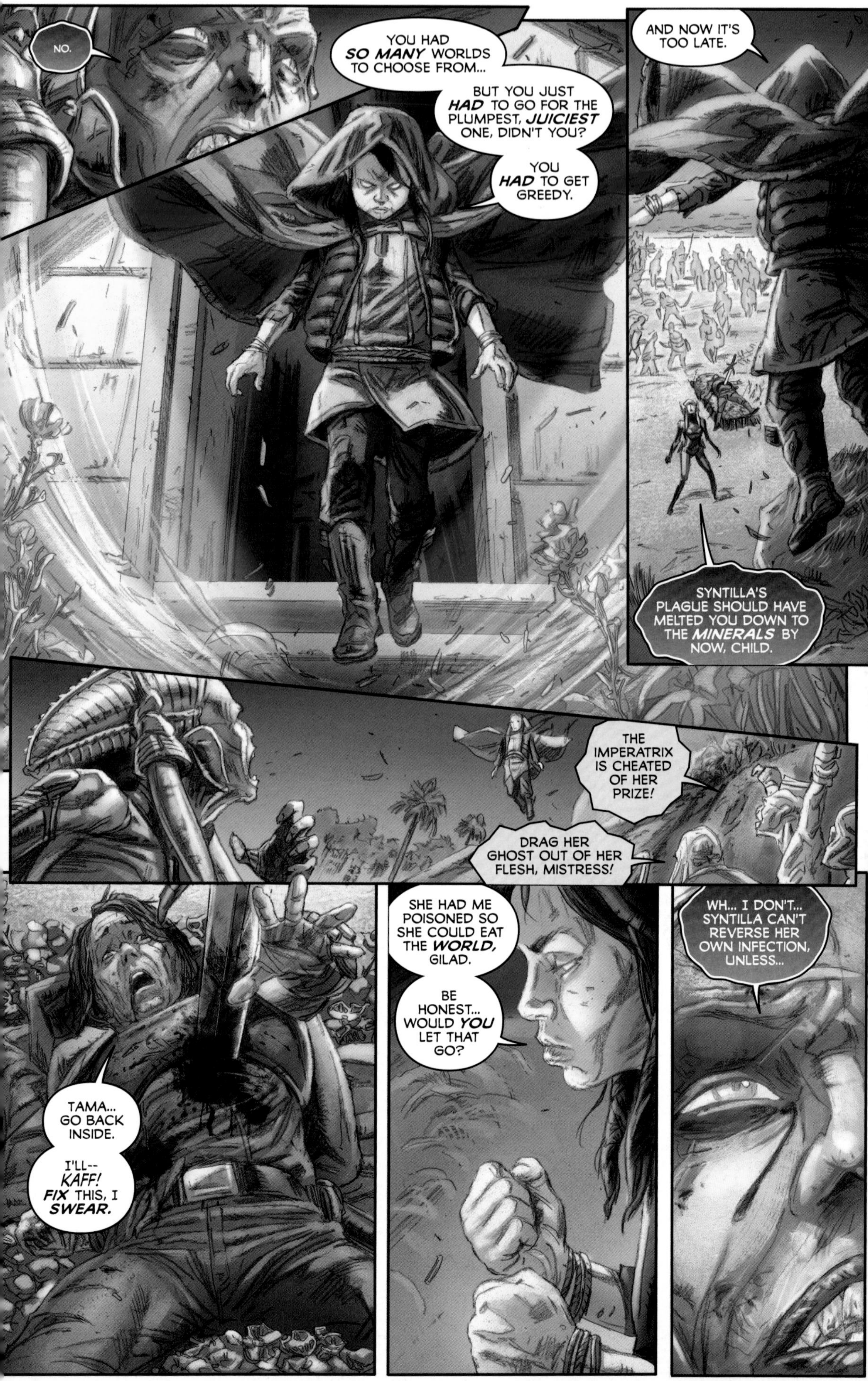
NO.
YOU HAD SO MANY WORLDS TO CHOOSE FROM...
BUT YOU JUST HAD TO GO FOR THE PLUMPEST, JUICIEST ONE, DIDN'T YOU?
YOU HAD TO GET GREEDY.
AND NOW IT'S TOO LATE.
SYNTILLA'S PLAGUE SHOULD HAVE MELTED YOU DOWN TO THE MINERALS BY NOW, CHILD.
THE IMPERATRIX IS CHEATED OF HER PRIZE!
DRAG HER GHOST OUT OF HER FLESH, MISTRESS!
TAMA... GO BACK INSIDE.
I'LL-- KAFF! FIX THIS, I SWEAR.
SHE HAD ME POISONED SO SHE COULD EAT THE WORLD, GILAD.
BE HONEST... WOULD YOU LET THAT GO?
WH... I DON'T... SYNTILLA CAN'T REVERSE HER OWN INFECTION, UNLESS...

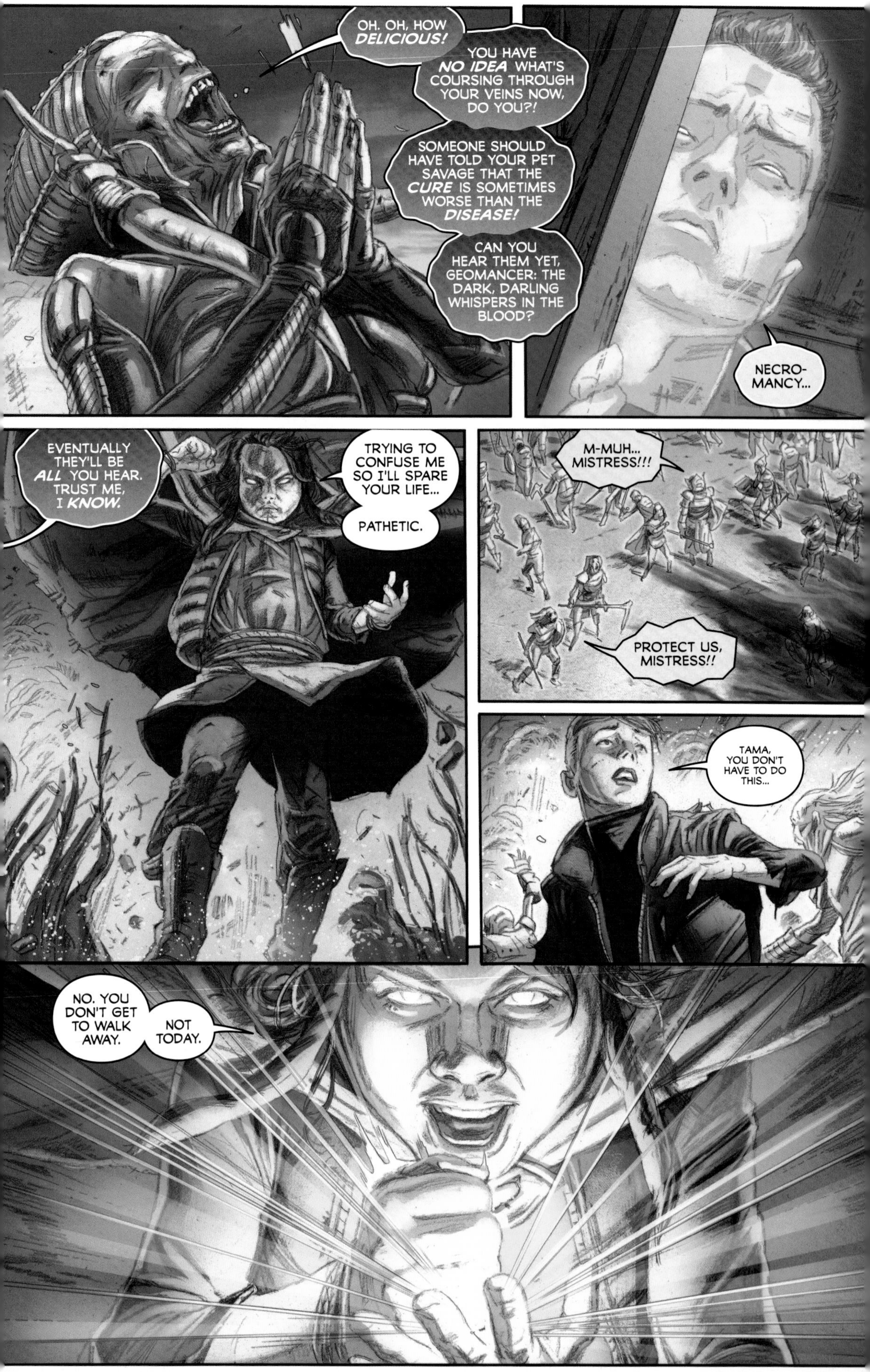
OH. OH, HOW DELICIOUS!
YOU HAVE NO IDEA WHAT'S COURSING THROUGH YOUR VEINS NOW, DO YOU?!
SOMEONE SHOULD HAVE TOLD YOUR PET SAVAGE THAT THE CURE IS SOMETIMES WORSE THAN THE DISEASE!
CAN YOU HEAR THEM YET, GEOMANCER: THE DARK, DARLING WHISPERS IN THE BLOOD?
NECRO-MANCY...
EVENTUALLY THEY'LL BE ALL YOU HEAR. TRUST ME, I KNOW.
TRYING TO CONFUSE ME SO I'LL SPARE YOUR LIFE...
PATHETIC.
M-MUH... MISTRESS!!!
PROTECT US, MISTRESS!!
TAMA, YOU DON'T HAVE TO DO THIS...
NO. YOU DON'T GET TO WALK AWAY.
NOT TODAY.

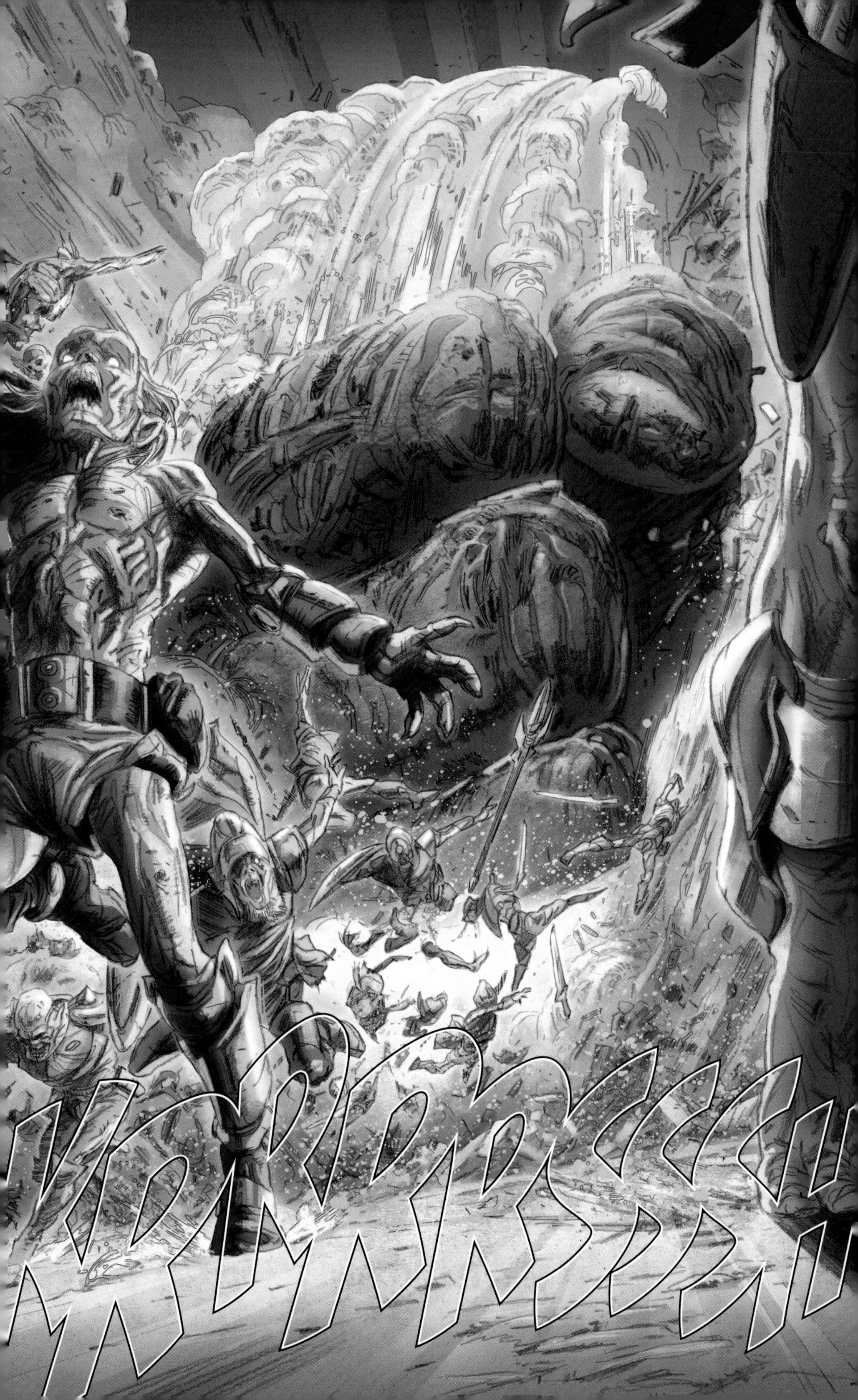

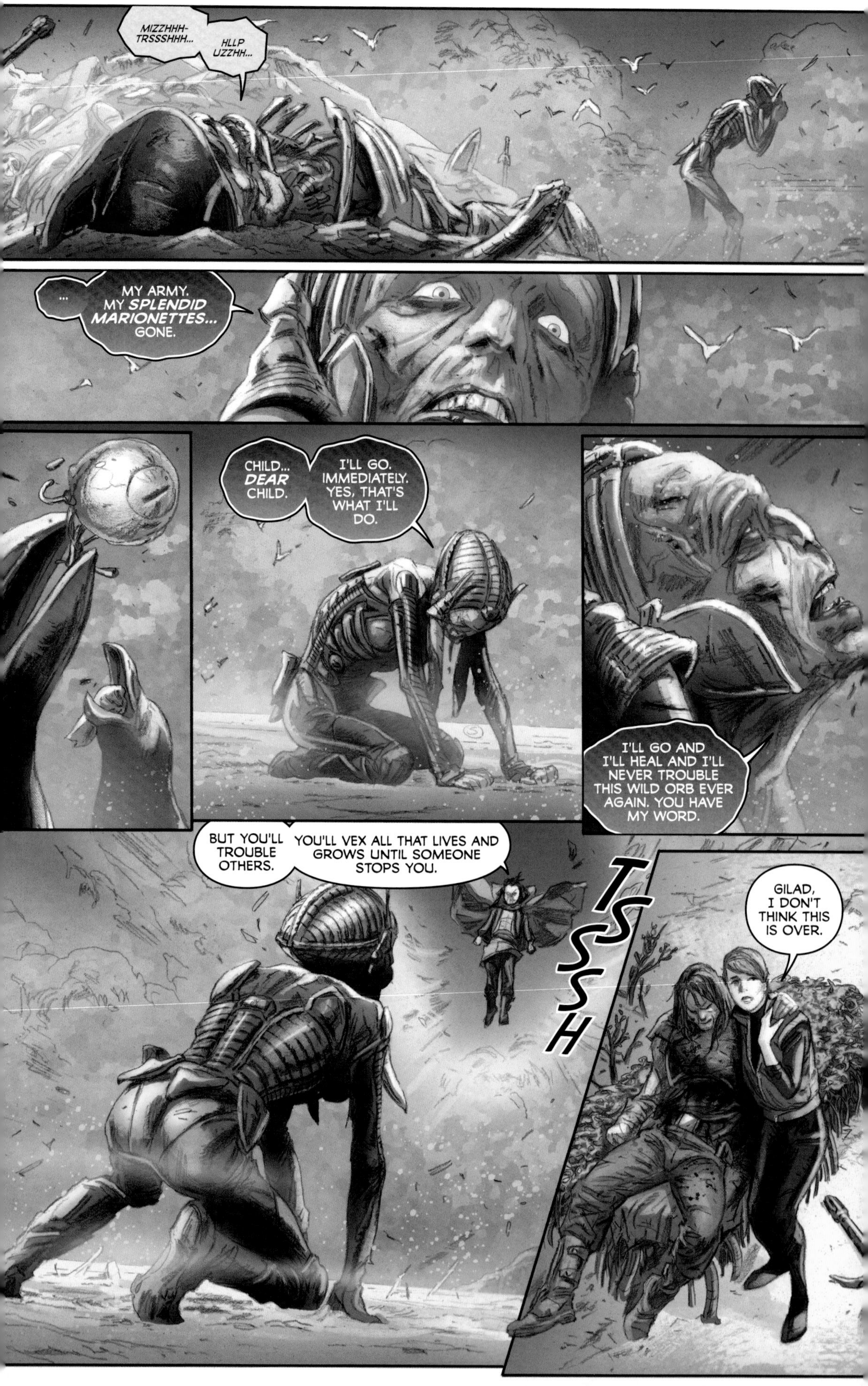
MIZZHHH-TRSSSHHH...
HLLP UZZHH...
... MY ARMY. MY *SPLENDID MARIONETTES...* GONE.
CHILD... *DEAR* CHILD.
I'LL GO. IMMEDIATELY. YES, THAT'S WHAT I'LL DO.
I'LL GO AND I'LL HEAL AND I'LL NEVER TROUBLE THIS WILD ORB EVER AGAIN. YOU HAVE MY WORD.
BUT YOU'LL TROUBLE OTHERS.
YOU'LL VEX ALL THAT LIVES AND GROWS UNTIL SOMEONE STOPS YOU.
TSSSH
GILAD, I DON'T THINK THIS IS OVER.

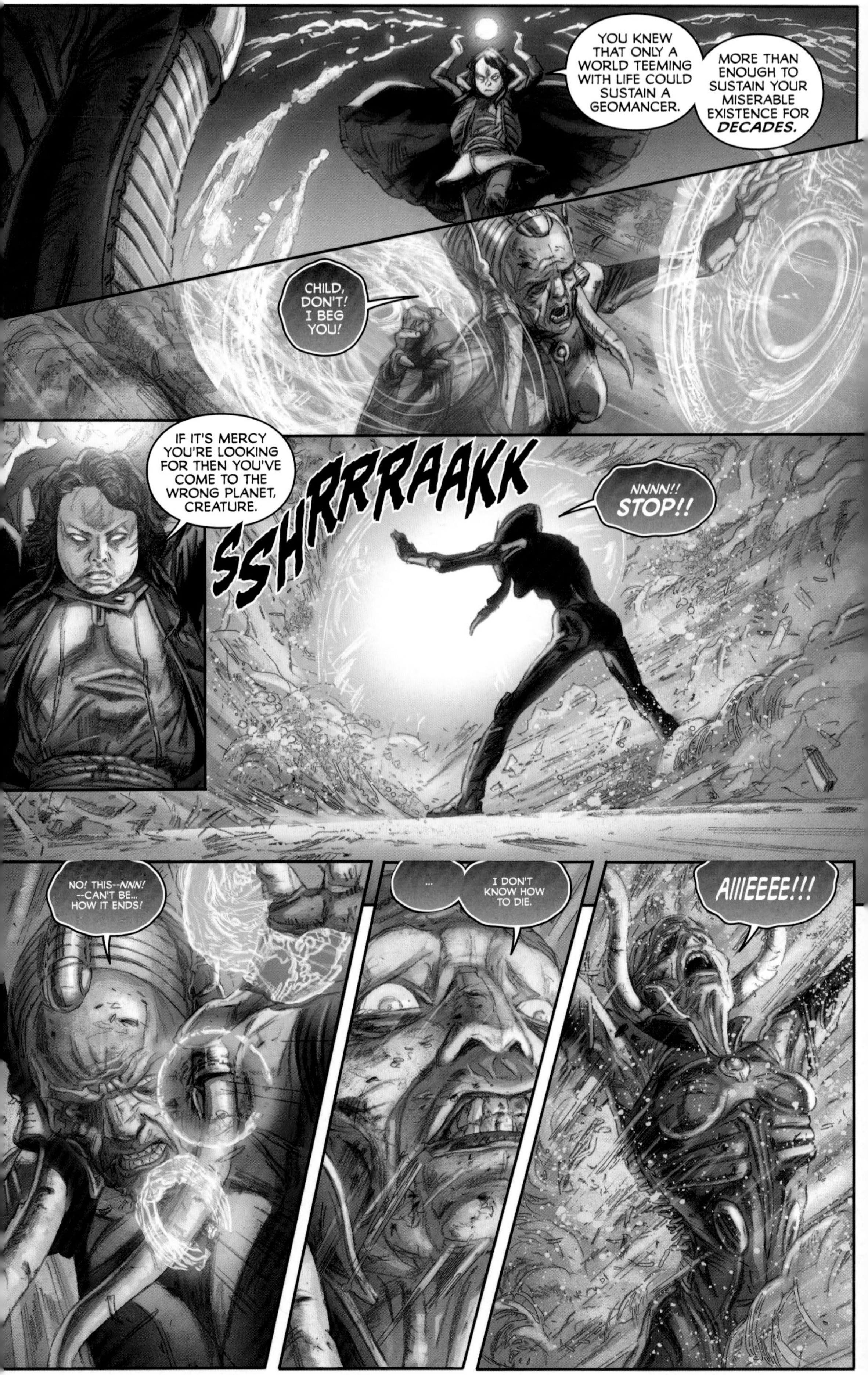
YOU KNEW THAT ONLY A WORLD TEEMING WITH LIFE COULD SUSTAIN A GEOMANCER.
MORE THAN ENOUGH TO SUSTAIN YOUR MISERABLE EXISTENCE FOR DECADES.
CHILD, DON'T! I BEG YOU!
IF IT'S MERCY YOU'RE LOOKING FOR THEN YOU'VE COME TO THE WRONG PLANET, CREATURE.
SSHRRRAAKK
NNNN!! STOP!!
NO! THIS--NNN! --CAN'T BE... HOW IT ENDS!
...
I DON'T KNOW HOW TO DIE.
AIIIEEEE!!!

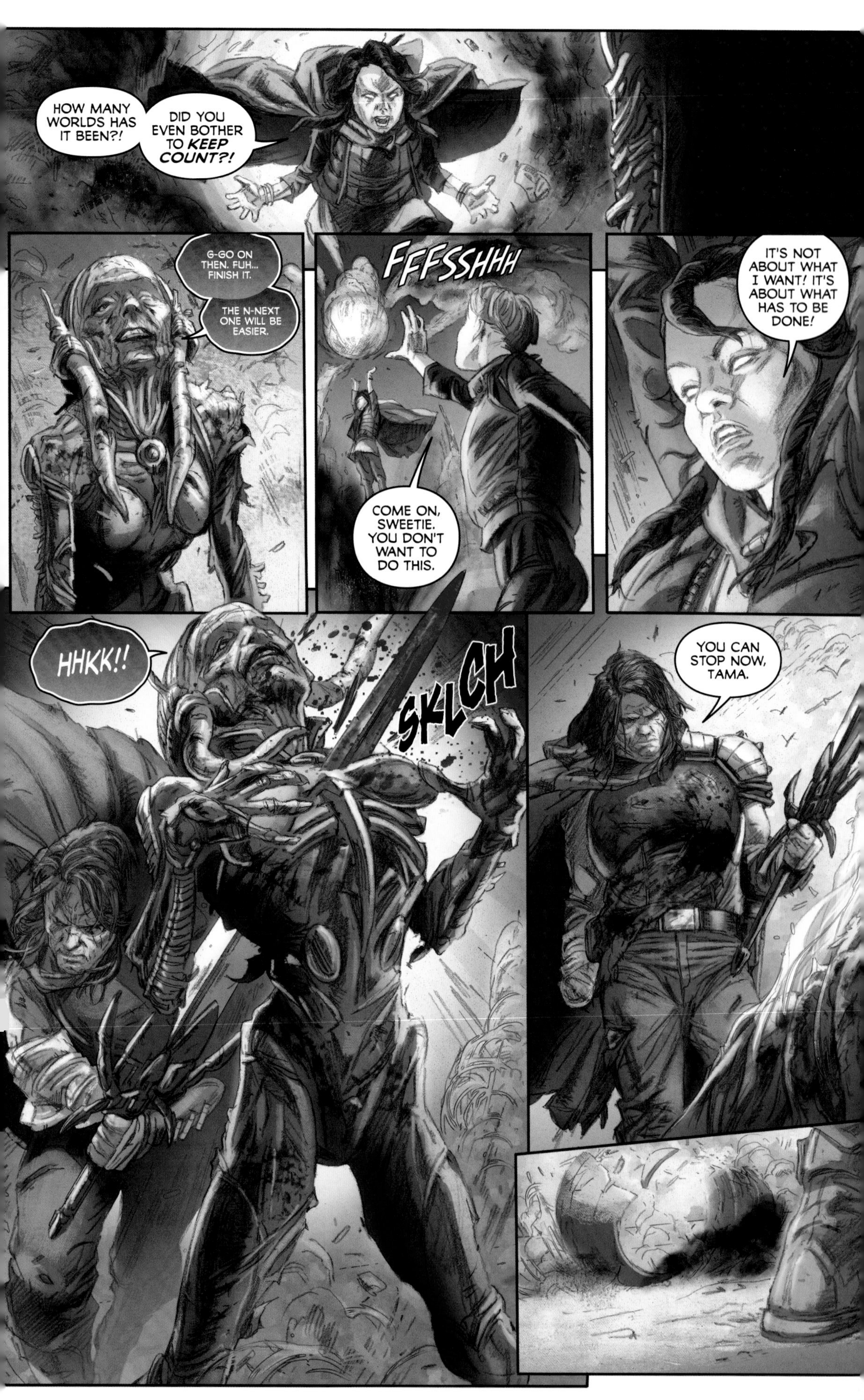
HOW MANY WORLDS HAS IT BEEN?!
DID YOU EVEN BOTHER TO KEEP COUNT?!
G-GO ON THEN. FUH... FINISH IT.
THE N-NEXT ONE WILL BE EASIER.
FFFSSHHH
COME ON, SWEETIE. YOU DON'T WANT TO DO THIS.
IT'S NOT ABOUT WHAT I WANT! IT'S ABOUT WHAT HAS TO BE DONE!
HHKK!!
SKLCH
YOU CAN STOP NOW, TAMA.

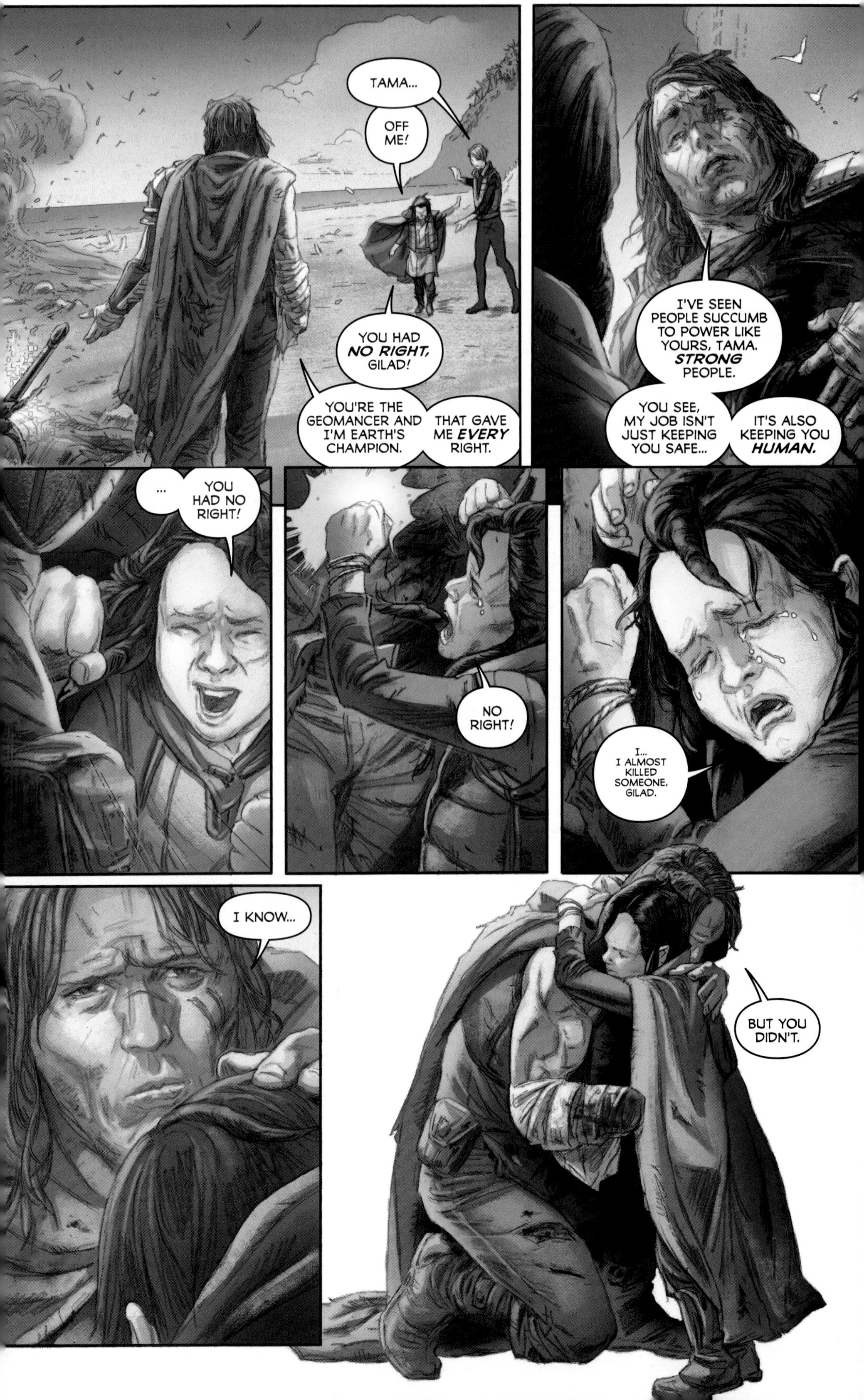
TAMA...
OFF ME!
YOU HAD NO RIGHT, GILAD!
YOU'RE THE GEOMANCER AND I'M EARTH'S CHAMPION.
THAT GAVE ME EVERY RIGHT.
I'VE SEEN PEOPLE SUCCUMB TO POWER LIKE YOURS, TAMA. STRONG PEOPLE.
YOU SEE, MY JOB ISN'T JUST KEEPING YOU SAFE...
IT'S ALSO KEEPING YOU HUMAN.
...
YOU HAD NO RIGHT!
NO RIGHT!
I... I ALMOST KILLED SOMEONE, GILAD.
I KNOW...
BUT YOU DIDN'T.

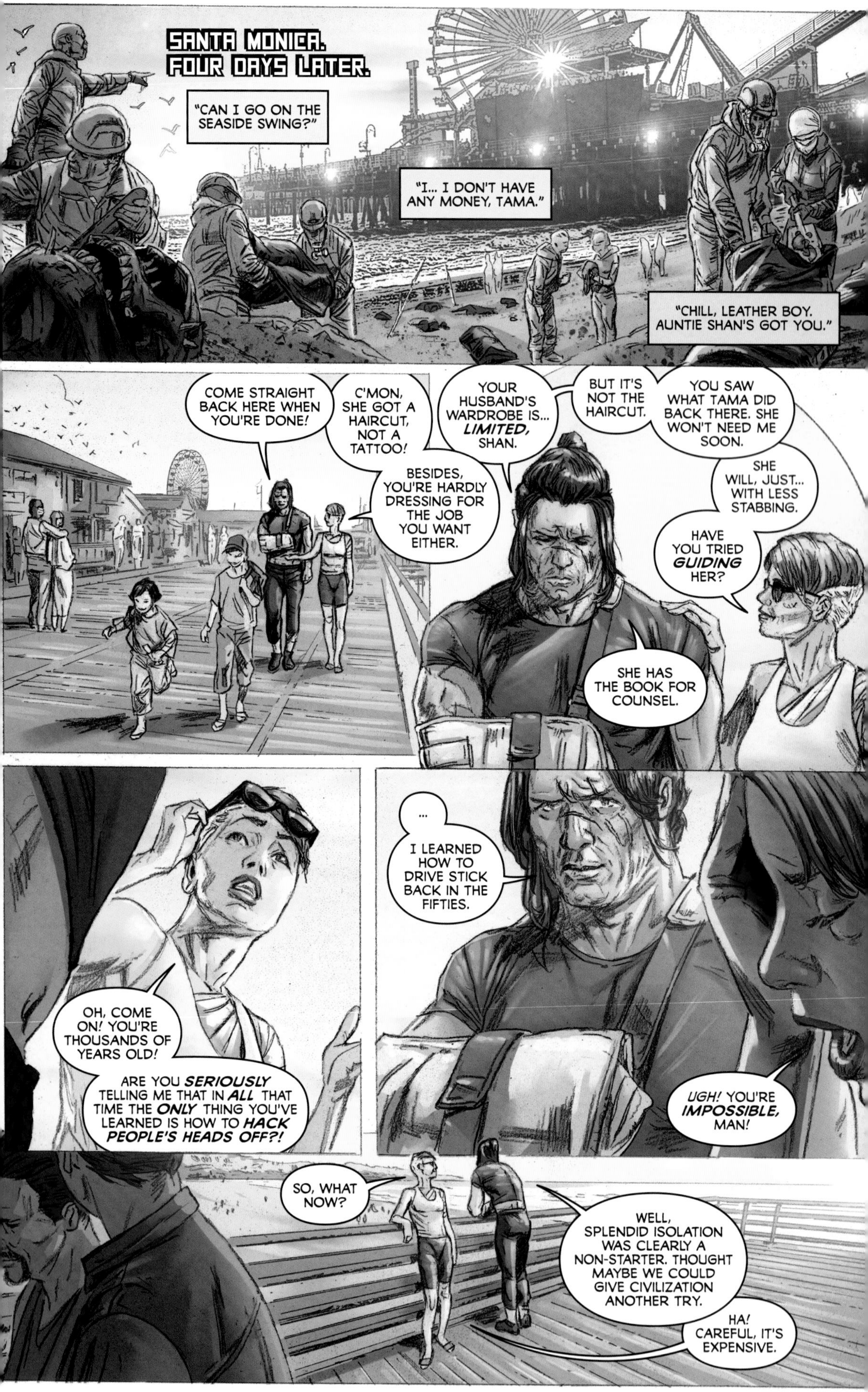
SANTA MONICA. FOUR DAYS LATER.
"CAN I GO ON THE SEASIDE SWING?"
"I... I DON'T HAVE ANY MONEY, TAMA."
"CHILL, LEATHER BOY. AUNTIE SHAN'S GOT YOU."
COME STRAIGHT BACK HERE WHEN YOU'RE DONE!
C'MON, SHE GOT A HAIRCUT, NOT A TATTOO!
BESIDES, YOU'RE HARDLY DRESSING FOR THE JOB YOU WANT EITHER.
YOUR HUSBAND'S WARDROBE IS... LIMITED, SHAN.
BUT IT'S NOT THE HAIRCUT.
YOU SAW WHAT TAMA DID BACK THERE. SHE WON'T NEED ME SOON.
SHE WILL, JUST... WITH LESS STABBING.
HAVE YOU TRIED GUIDING HER?
SHE HAS THE BOOK FOR COUNSEL.
OH, COME ON! YOU'RE THOUSANDS OF YEARS OLD!
ARE YOU SERIOUSLY TELLING ME THAT IN ALL THAT TIME THE ONLY THING YOU'VE LEARNED IS HOW TO HACK PEOPLE'S HEADS OFF?!
...
I LEARNED HOW TO DRIVE STICK BACK IN THE FIFTIES.
UGH! YOU'RE IMPOSSIBLE, MAN!
SO, WHAT NOW?
WELL, SPLENDID ISOLATION WAS CLEARLY A NON-STARTER. THOUGHT MAYBE WE COULD GIVE CIVILIZATION ANOTHER TRY.
HA! CAREFUL, IT'S EXPENSIVE.

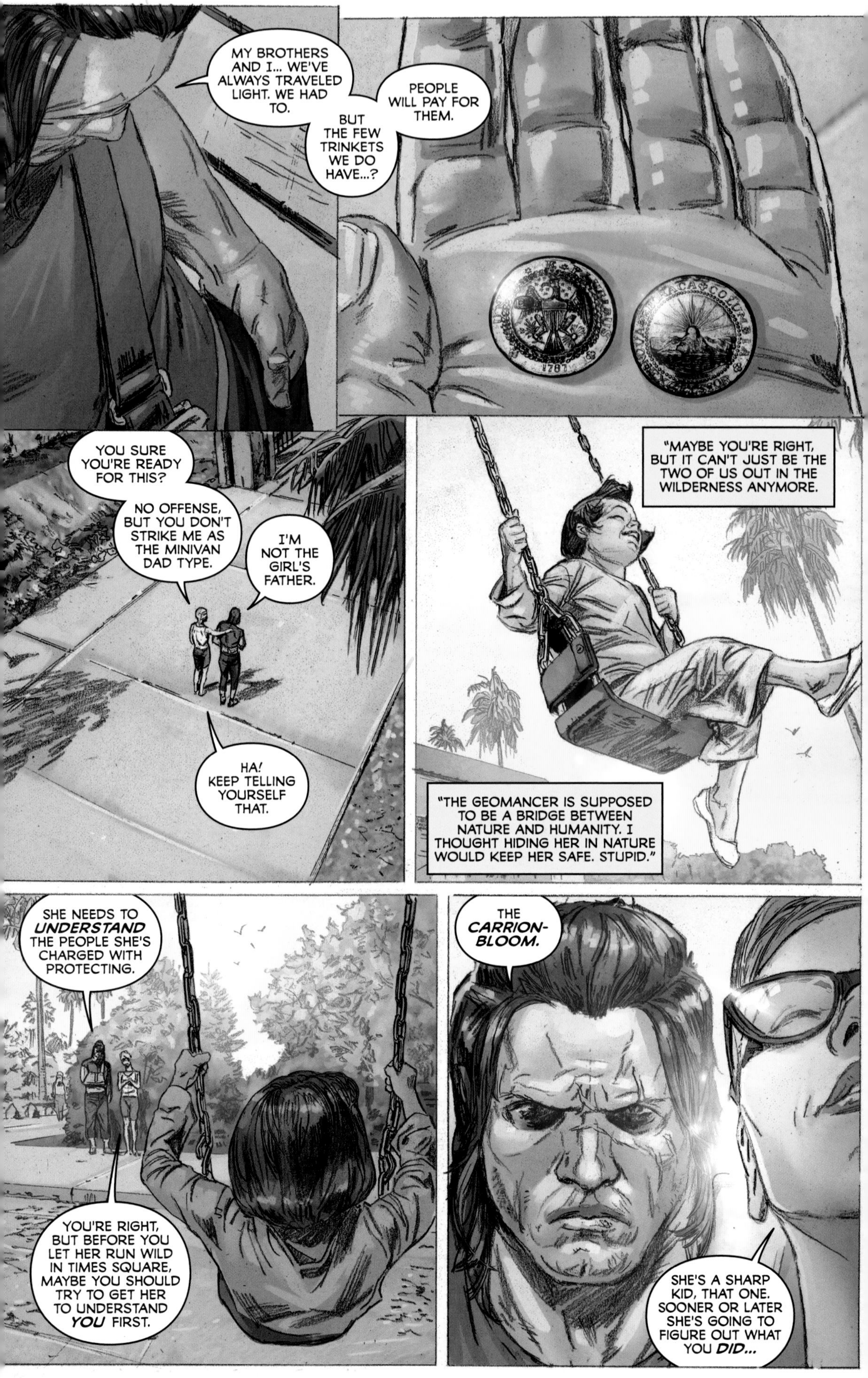
MY BROTHERS AND I... WE'VE ALWAYS TRAVELED LIGHT. WE HAD TO.
BUT THE FEW TRINKETS WE DO HAVE...?
PEOPLE WILL PAY FOR THEM.
1787
YOU SURE YOU'RE READY FOR THIS?
NO OFFENSE, BUT YOU DON'T STRIKE ME AS THE MINIVAN DAD TYPE.
I'M NOT THE GIRL'S FATHER.
HA! KEEP TELLING YOURSELF THAT.
"MAYBE YOU'RE RIGHT, BUT IT CAN'T JUST BE THE TWO OF US OUT IN THE WILDERNESS ANYMORE.
"THE GEOMANCER IS SUPPOSED TO BE A BRIDGE BETWEEN NATURE AND HUMANITY. I THOUGHT HIDING HER IN NATURE WOULD KEEP HER SAFE. STUPID."
SHE NEEDS TO ***UNDERSTAND*** THE PEOPLE SHE'S CHARGED WITH PROTECTING.
YOU'RE RIGHT, BUT BEFORE YOU LET HER RUN WILD IN TIMES SQUARE, MAYBE YOU SHOULD TRY TO GET HER TO UNDERSTAND ***YOU*** FIRST.
THE ***CARRION-BLOOM.***
SHE'S A SHARP KID, THAT ONE. SOONER OR LATER SHE'S GOING TO FIGURE OUT WHAT YOU ***DID...***

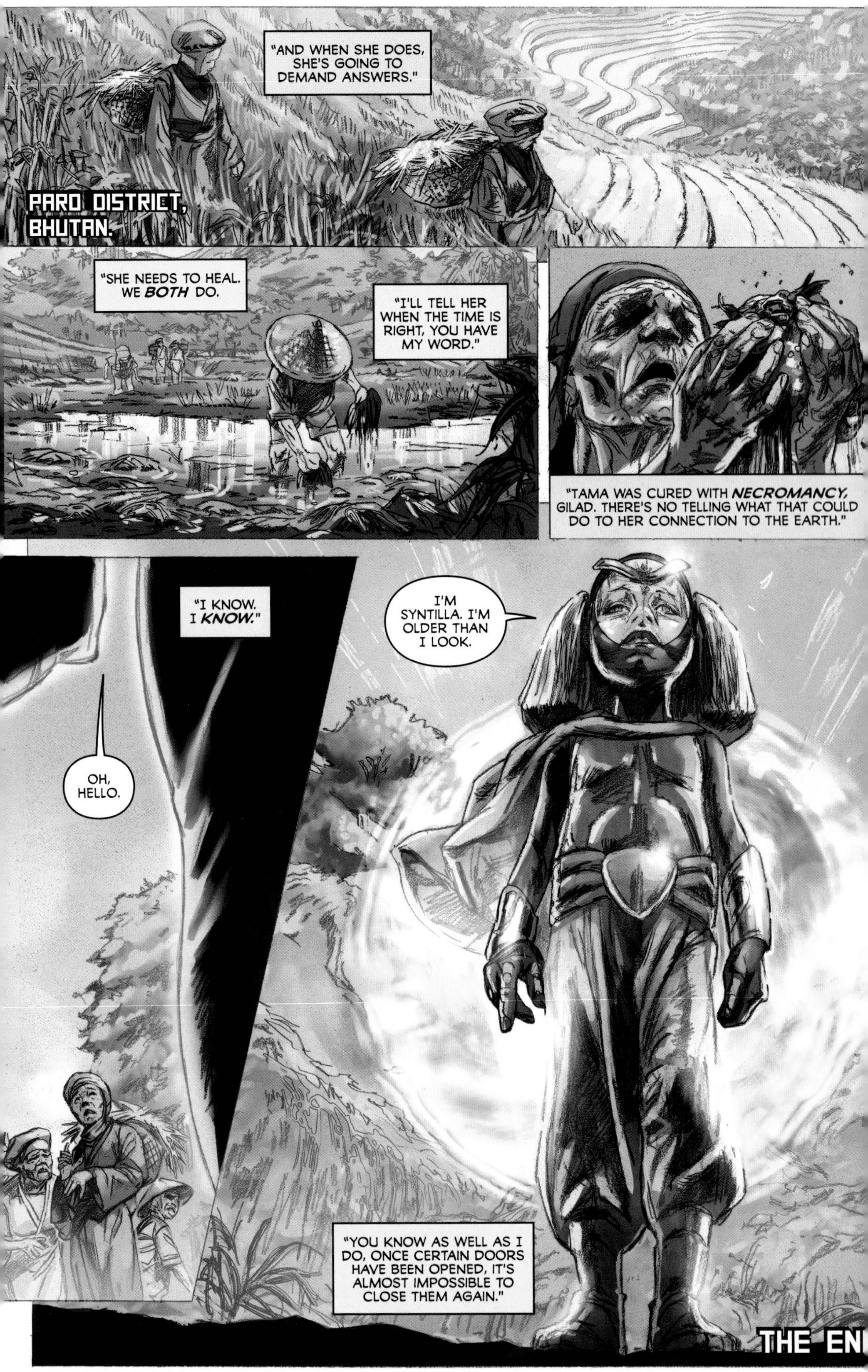
"AND WHEN SHE DOES, SHE'S GOING TO DEMAND ANSWERS."
PARO DISTRICT, BHUTAN.
"SHE NEEDS TO HEAL. WE BOTH DO.
"I'LL TELL HER WHEN THE TIME IS RIGHT, YOU HAVE MY WORD."
"TAMA WAS CURED WITH NECROMANCY, GILAD. THERE'S NO TELLING WHAT THAT COULD DO TO HER CONNECTION TO THE EARTH."
"I KNOW. I KNOW."
OH, HELLO.
I'M SYNTILLA. I'M OLDER THAN I LOOK.
"YOU KNOW AS WELL AS I DO, ONCE CERTAIN DOORS HAVE BEEN OPENED, IT'S ALMOST IMPOSSIBLE TO CLOSE THEM AGAIN."
THE EN

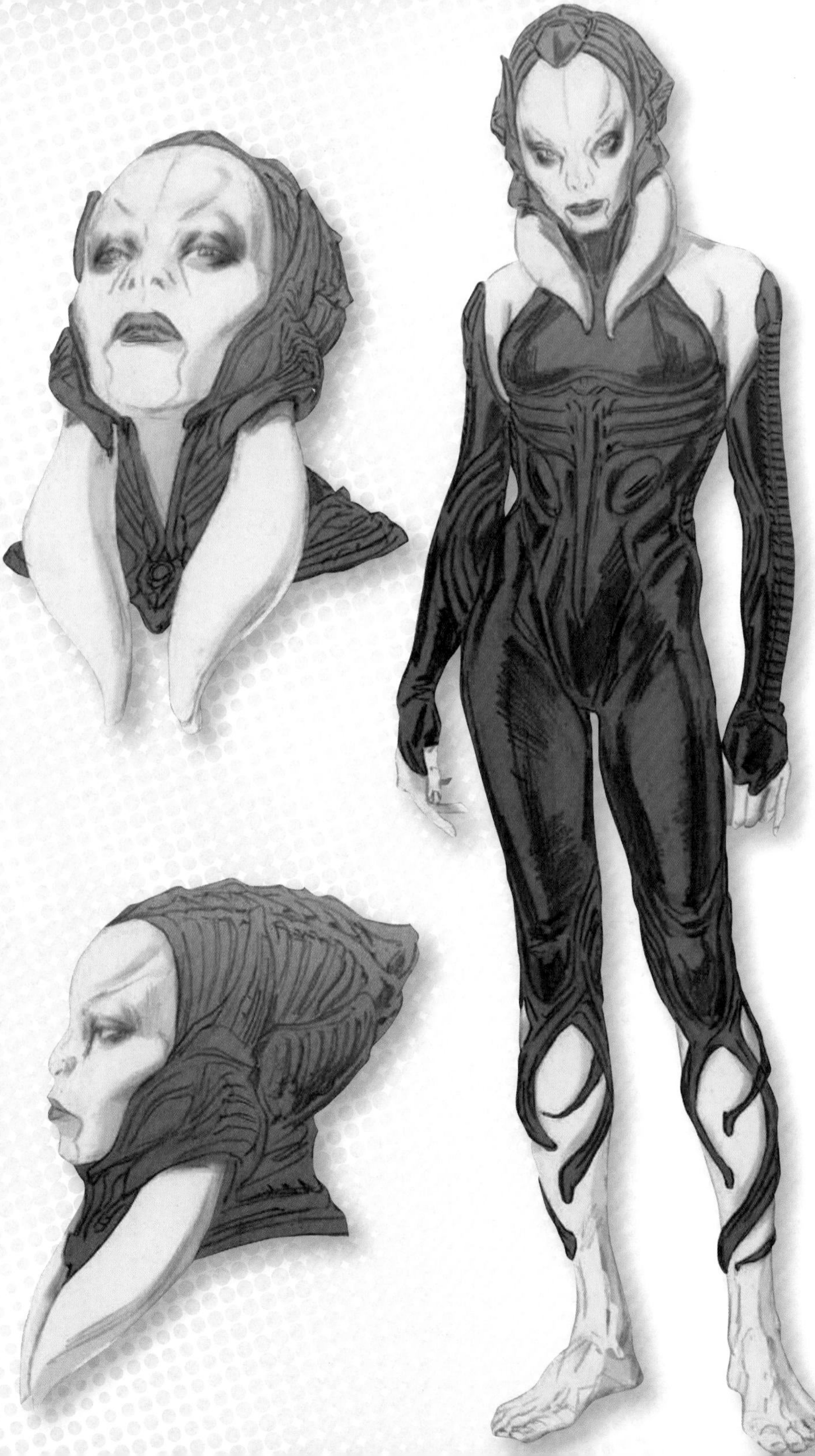

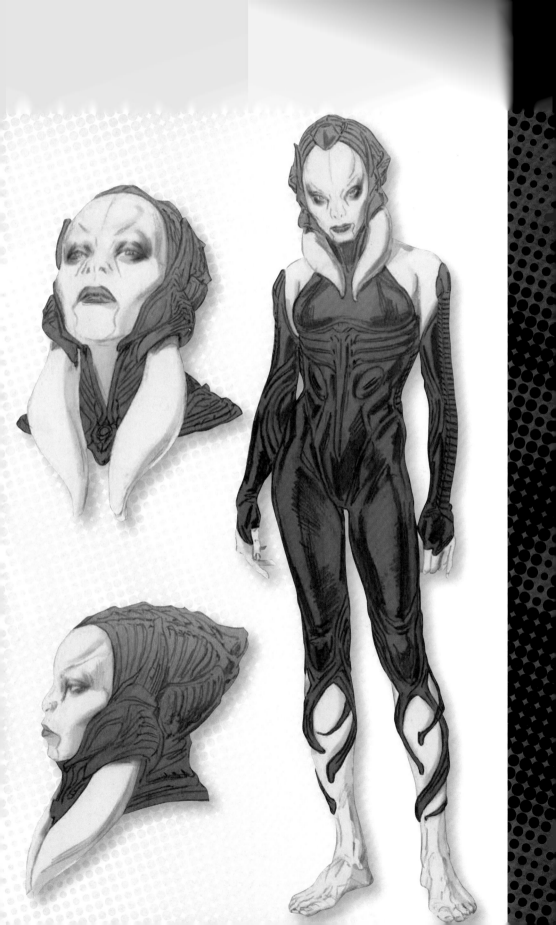

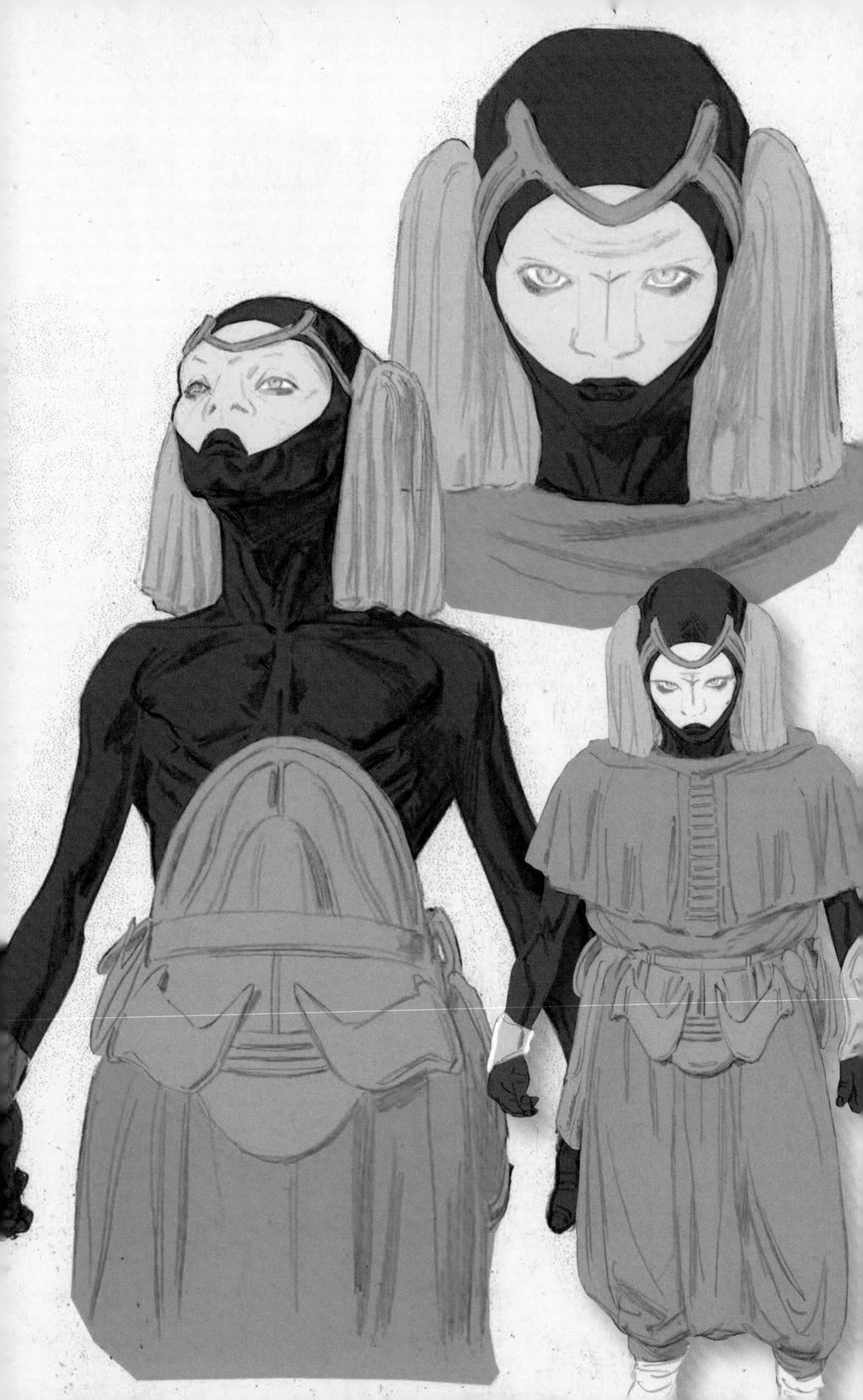

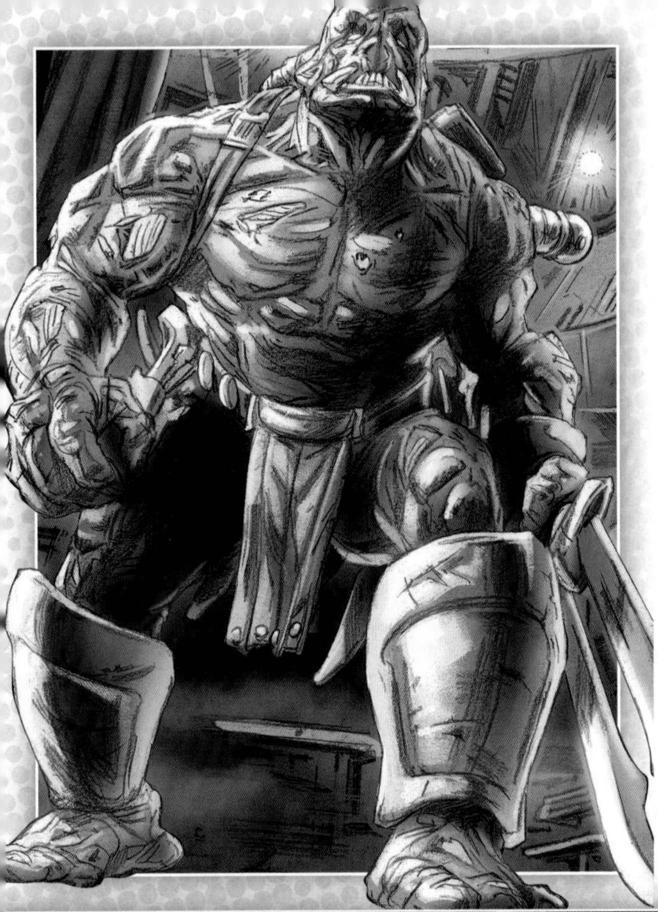

A hulking colossus – a slab of muscle and knives – KOTILA has huge mandibles and razor-sharp teeth. Scar over one eye. Dead tissue exposing (ample) musculature beneath the skin.

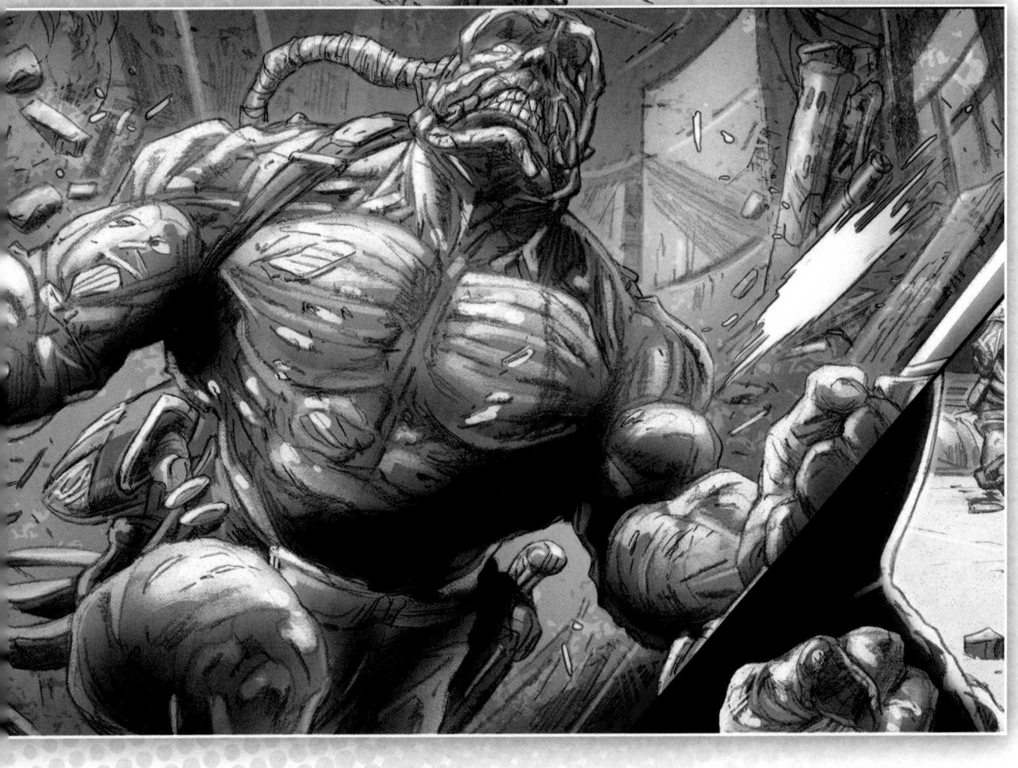

DEFLATION MIGRATION:
Zoom in to the upper atmosphere. Jellyfish-like alien PLANTS float in the sky; like giant helium balloons, trailing pale tendrils. Many are deflating, sinking, dying...

SHE'S OLDER THAN SHE LOOKS:
Wide. Little SYNTILLA (an alien child, same race as IMPERATRIX VIRAGO) approaches, her back to us in close foreground, panel left. Out across the balcony, Virago turns to us. The dead scientist lies at her feet, beheaded.

BUNKER HILL:
Low angle now, looking up past Gilad as he trudges up out of the trees into a clearing. He's heading towards a DERELICT G.A.T.E. site set into the mountainside. Most of the facility is tunneled back into the rock-face; all we see is the front end. A squat, ugly concrete bunker, dappled with moss and weeds.

HUG OF WAR:
Tama bows her head, upset. Gilad puts a reassuring hand on her shoulder. She needs a hug; but Gilad is a warrior, not a hugger.

RIPPLE EFFECT:
Small. Profile shot. Tight on SYNTILLA's hand as she gently presses her forefinger against the thick door of the bunker. A liquid ripple immediately begins to radiate outward from the tip of her finger.

IN VEIN:
Where SYNTILLA is stroking TAMA, black veins begin to appear; an infection beginning to spread throughout her body.

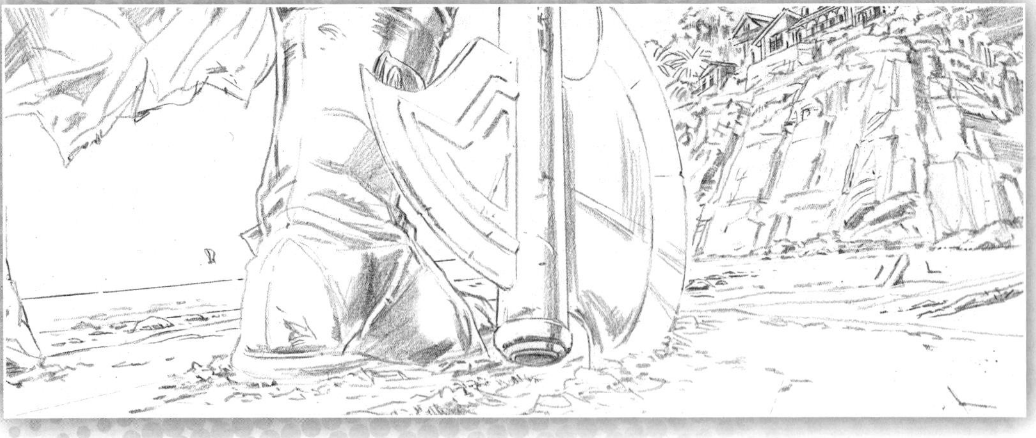

CALIFORNIA GRIEVIN':
Zoom into the beach under a stormy, blackened sky. Heavy human footsteps in the sand accompanied by a single straight line – GILAD's footprints accompanied by a straight groove scored by his axe. On the horizon high above the beach is the property of the DOCTORS MIRAGE.

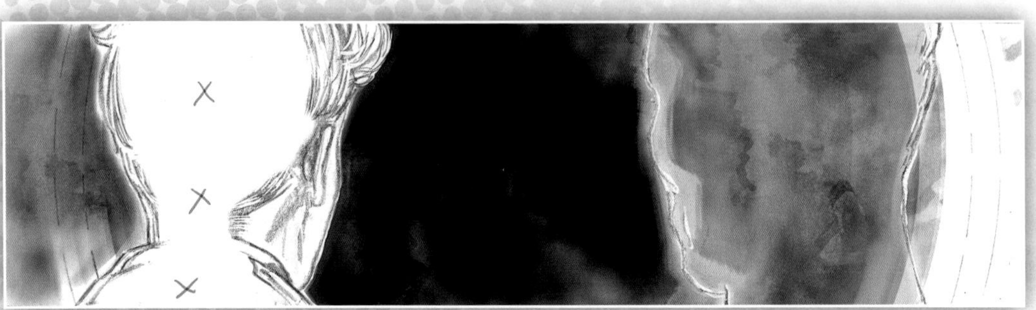

PORTAL PERIL:
Wide. SHAN and HWEN standing side by side with their backs to us, from the shoulders up. They are both staring at the swirling Deadside portal in front of them, which is also the focal point of the panel. Deadside portals are black, so HWEN and SHAN can't see that they've – whoops! – effectively teleported GILAD into mid-air.

AXE ON, AXE OFF:
Big. AMY swinging the axe handle over her head with GILAD still attached, using his own momentum to smash him into the hard Deadside rock, gouging out a small crater on impact. A shower of slate and clinker flies everywhere. A squat, ugly concrete bunker, dappled with moss and weeds.

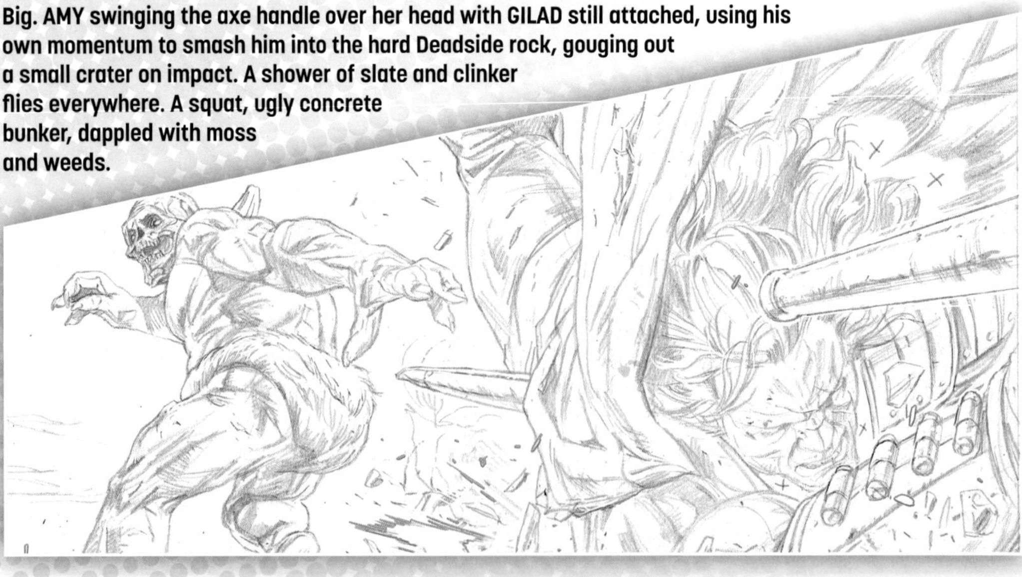

COME PLAGUE WITH US:
Big. SYNTILLA giggling as she touches the ground on a distant world, infecting it with the same plague that's consuming TAMA. The black veins snake toward us from her fingertips, blighting everything in their path.

ETERNAL WARPATH:
Wide. GILAD fighting his way through the Eternal Warfields of the Deadside – a hellscape of never-ending war, i.e. GILAD's element. He has hacked his way through the panel with abandon. Many corpses in GILAD's wake.

GEL CELL:
Big. GILAD is now in the DREAMING SPIRE – Syntilla's sleep chamber. Children's toys and dollhouses from a variety of alien worlds are strewn all over the floor, including a caged alien bird. We should have the profound sense that Syntilla is a caged creature forcibly infantilized, like the tragic, doomed Christiane in George Franju's 'Les Yeux Sans Visage' ('Eyes Without A Face'). At the center of the scene is a suspended animation chamber, at once ornate and menacing – a giant larval cocoon crossed with a Fabergé egg.

ANATOMY OF A SCENE
WITH ASSISTANT EDITOR **DREW BAUMGARTNER**

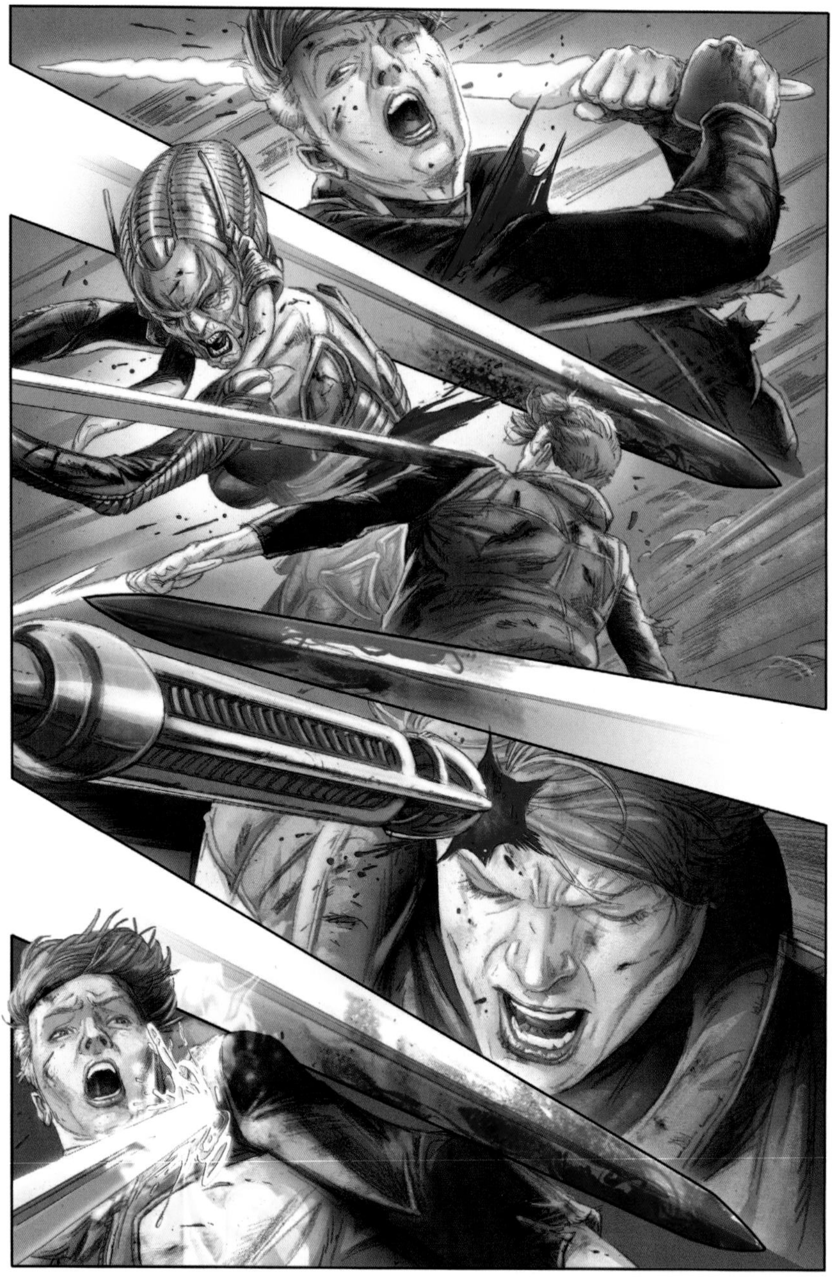

What an opening page! Alex Paknadel's script called for this page to be divided up by Doctor Mirage and Virago's clashing weapons, but Doug Braithwaite made the smart decision to make it all Virago's sword. It's a small change, but it immediately helps set the tone for this battle, clearly casting Virago as the aggressor. My favorite detail, though, is the way colorist Diego Rodriguez blends Virago's blade into the white gutter of the margins. It's a great design element, but it also emphasize's Virago's otherworldliness -- Doctor Mirage isn't being wounded by just any sword, but one that exists outside of time and space. It all helps build Virago up as this unstoppable force that Doctor Mirage won't be able to hold back for much longer.

ARTWORK BY **DOUG BRAITHWAITE** WITH **DIEGO RODRIGUEZ** Originally presented in *INCURSION #4 PRE-ORDER EDITION*.

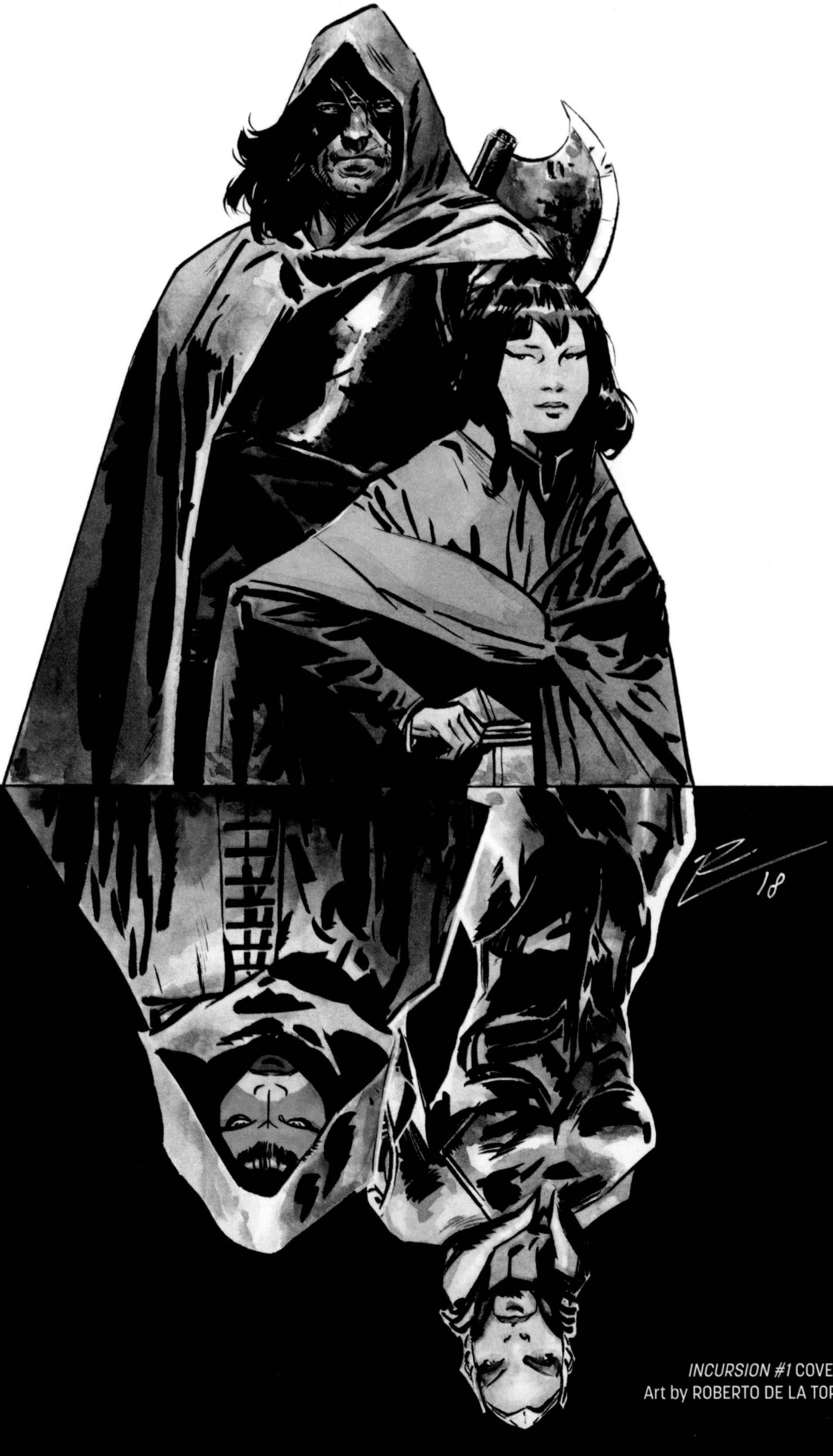

INCURSION #1 COVER B
Art by ROBERTO DE LA TORRE

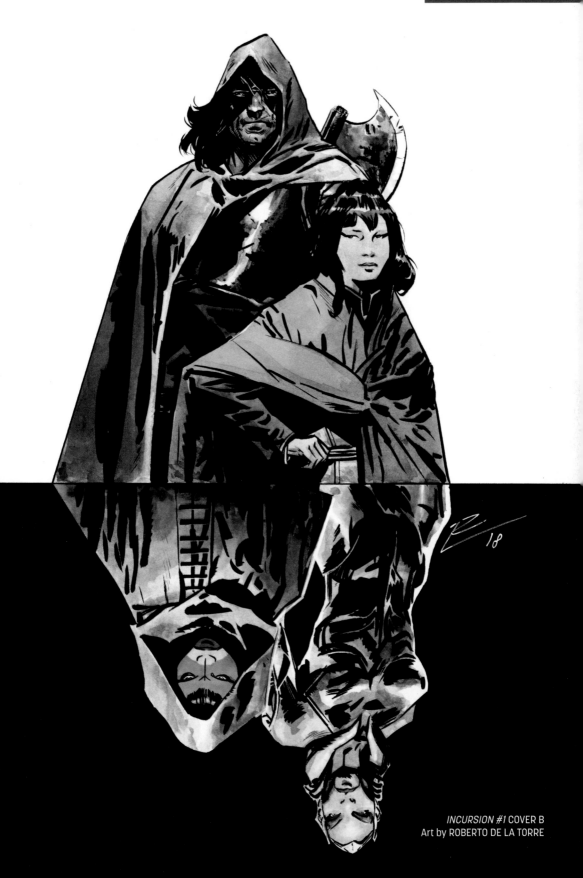

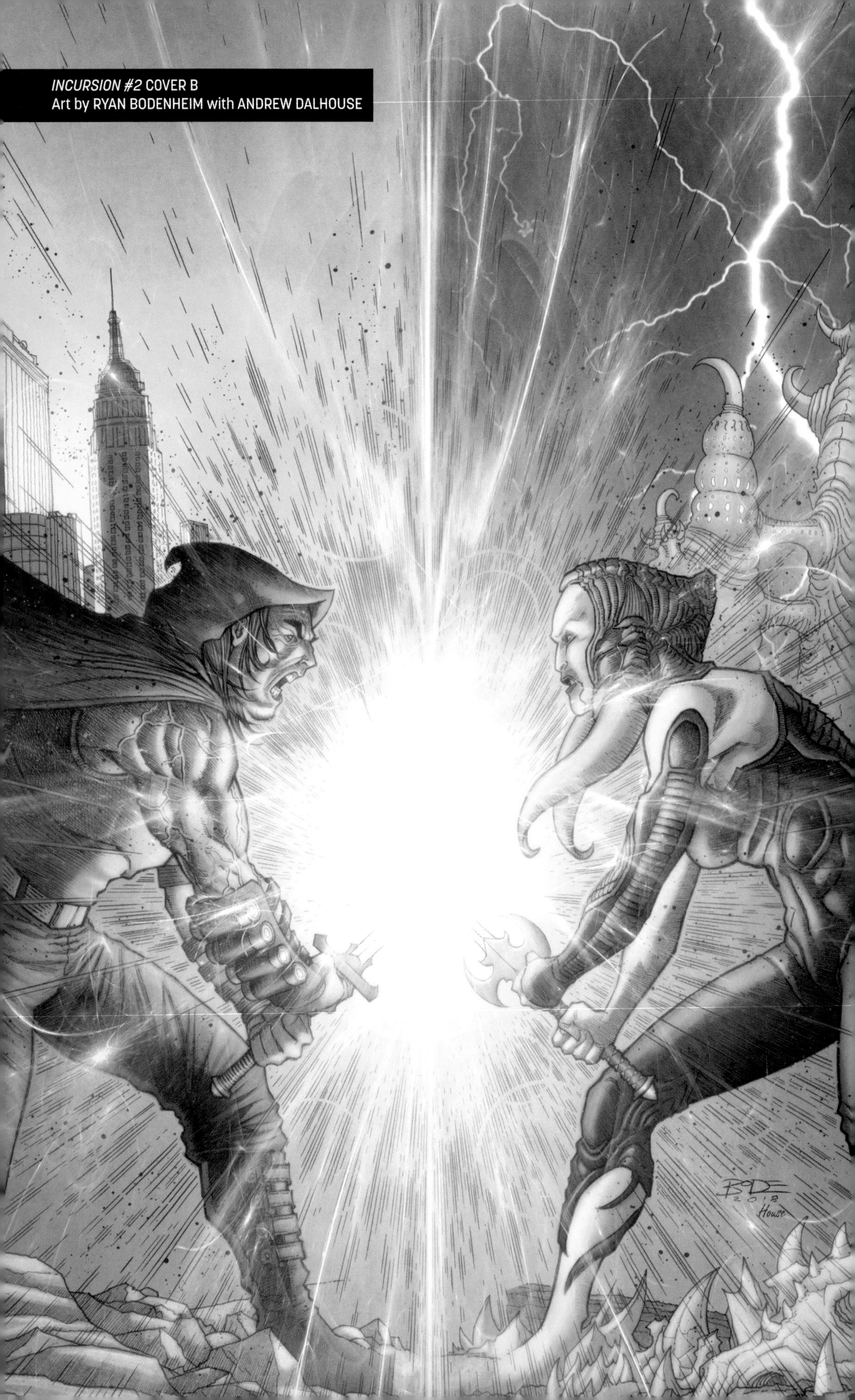
BODE
2018
House

INCURSION #2 COVER B
Art by RYAN BODENHEIM with ANDREW DALHOUSE

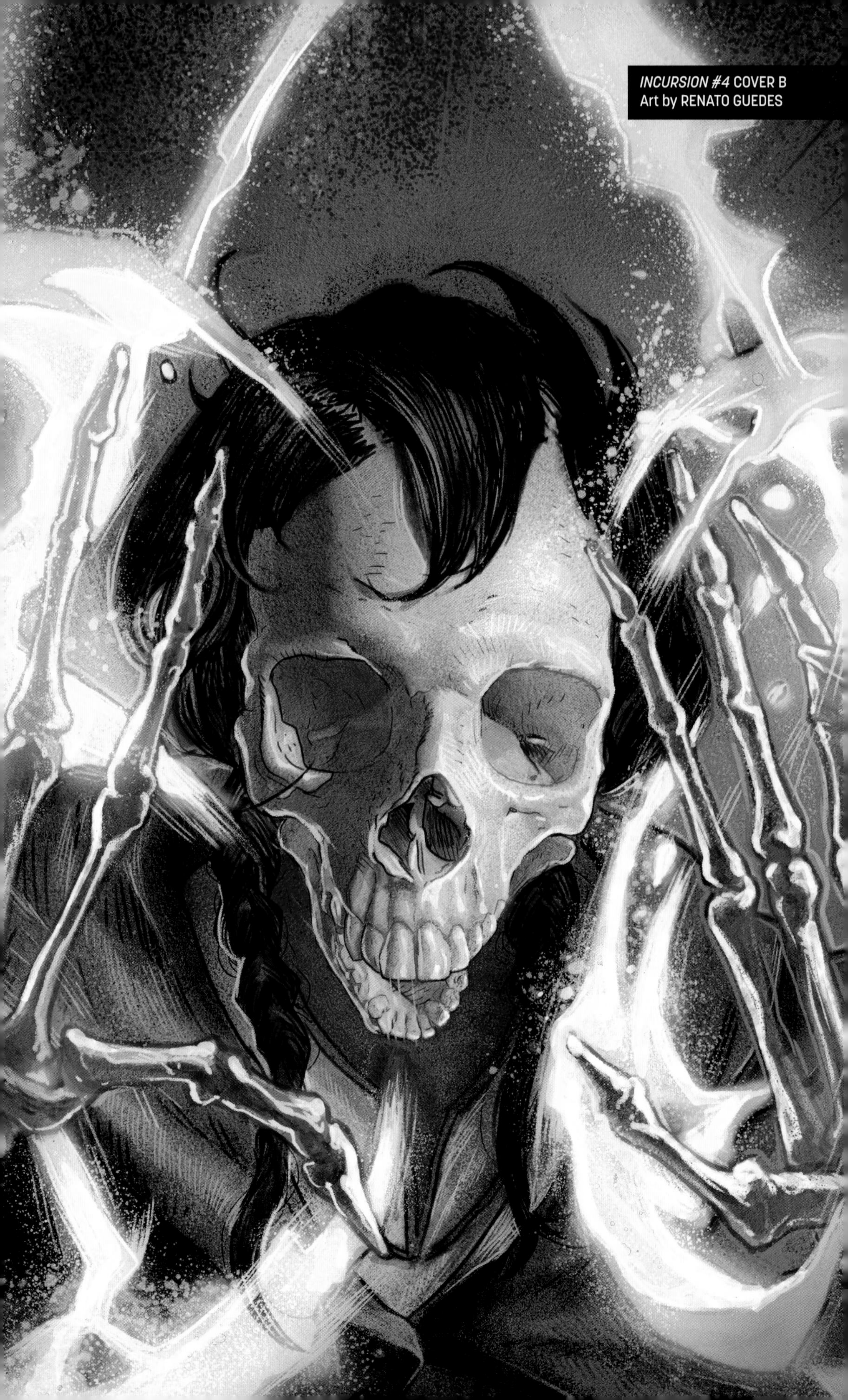

INCURSION #4 COVER B
Art by RENATO GUEDES

iNCURSION #1 PRE-ORDER EDITION COVER
Art by TONCI ZONJIC

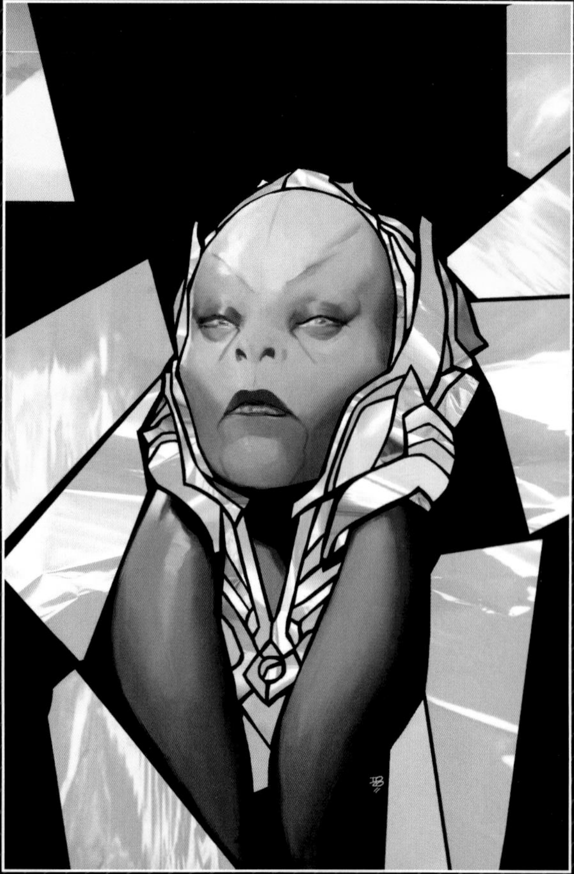

iNCURSION #2 PRE-ORDER EDITION COVER
Art by TONCI ZONJIC

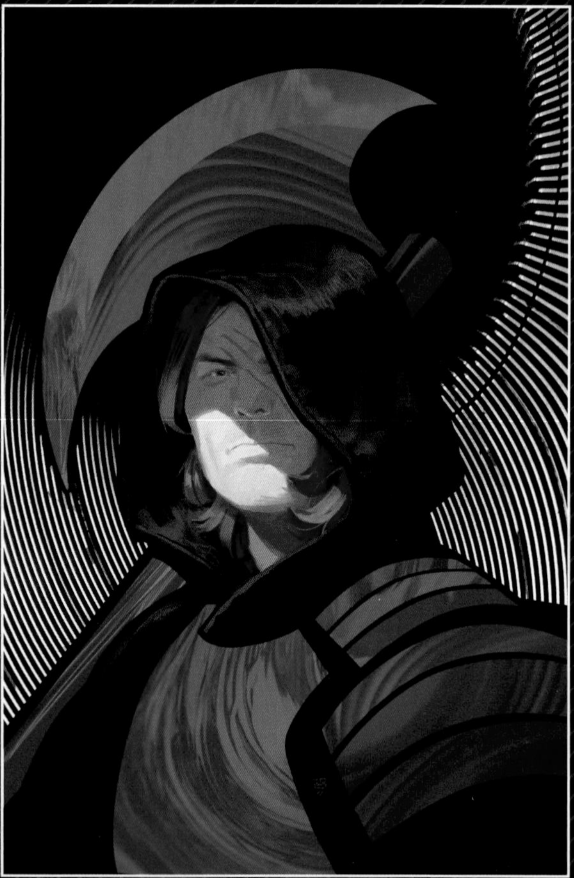

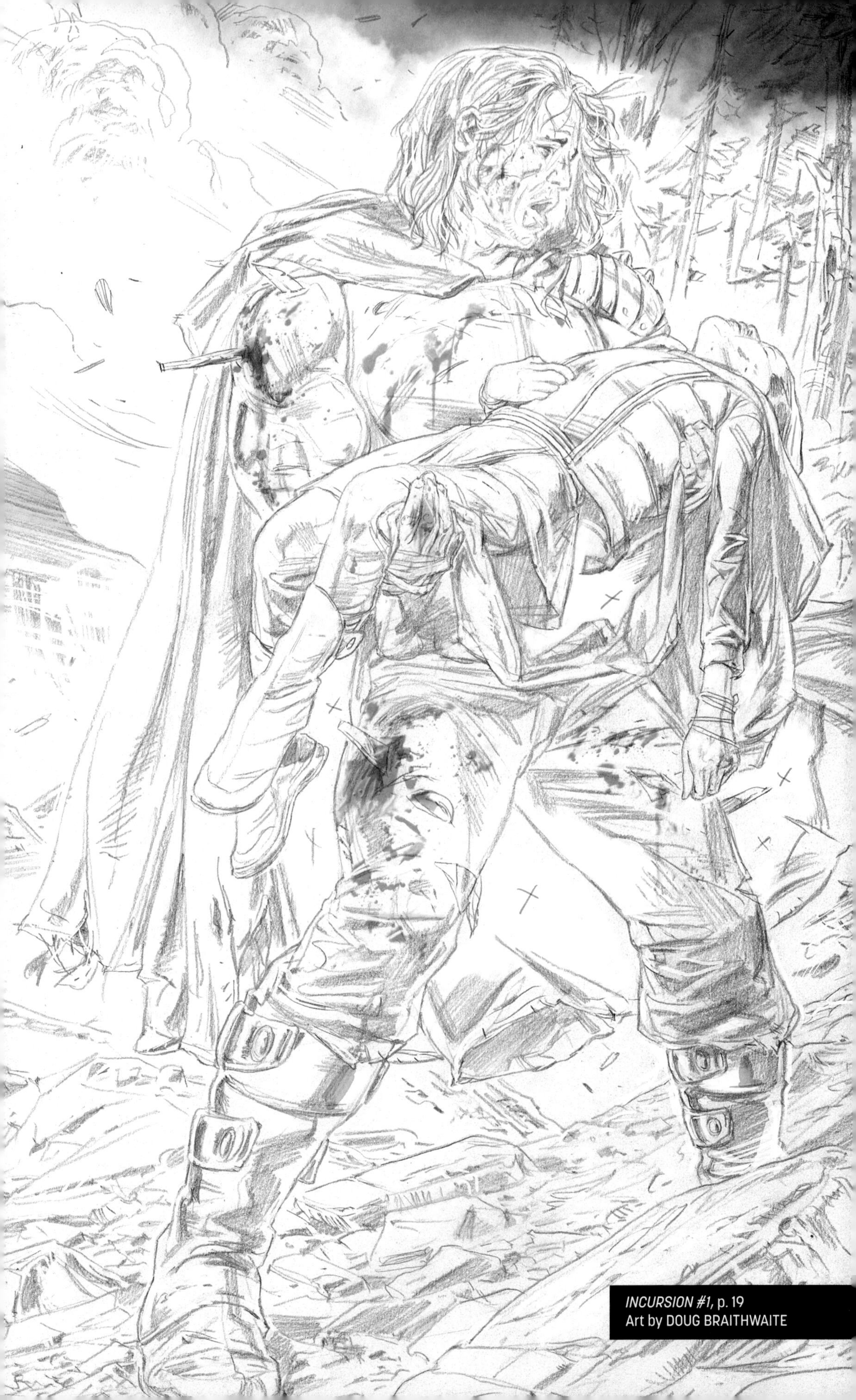

INCURSION #1, p. 19
Art by DOUG BRAITHWAITE

INCURSION #2 / Pg 14-15 (FULL BLEED)

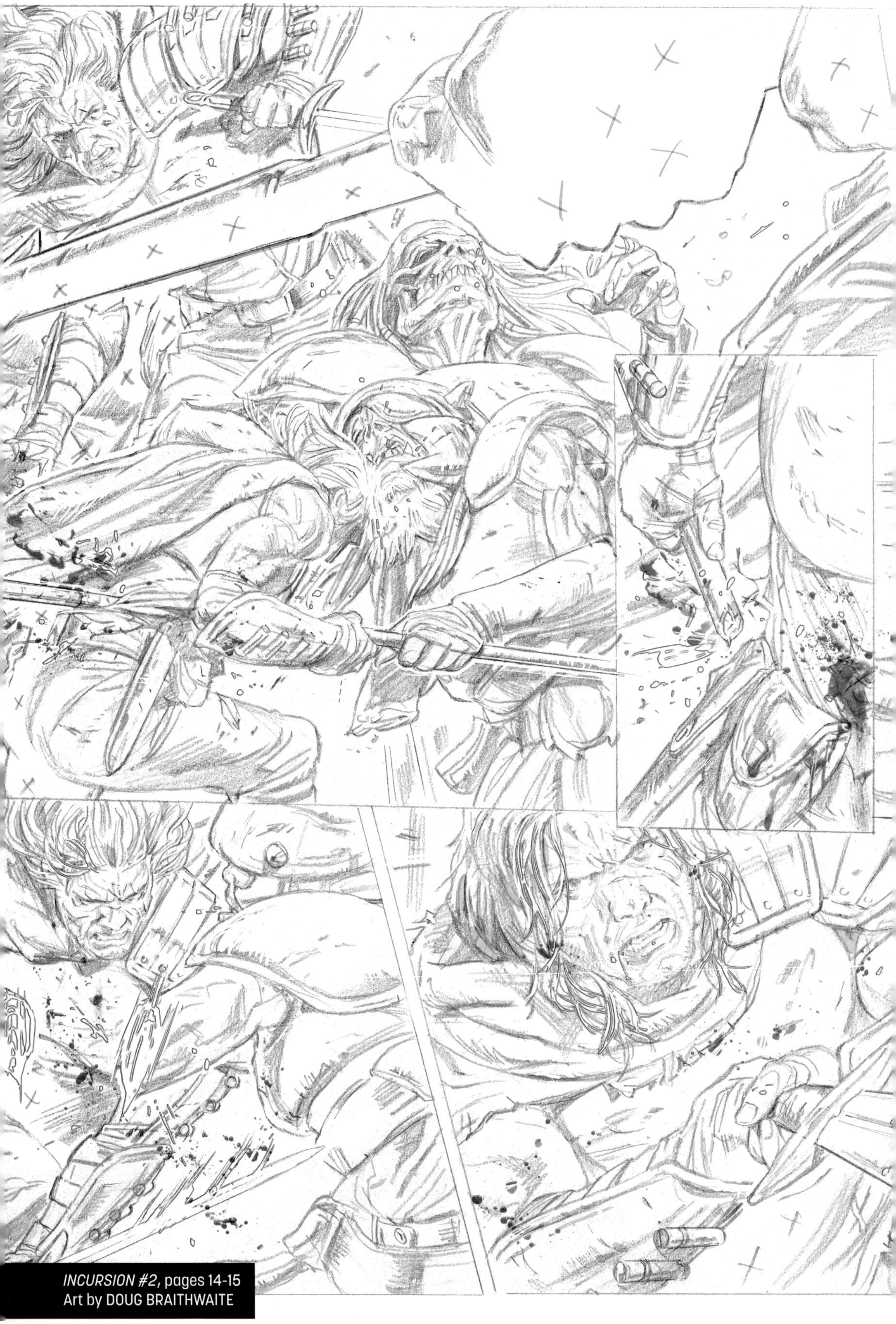

INCURSION #2, pages 14-15
Art by DOUG BRAITHWAITE

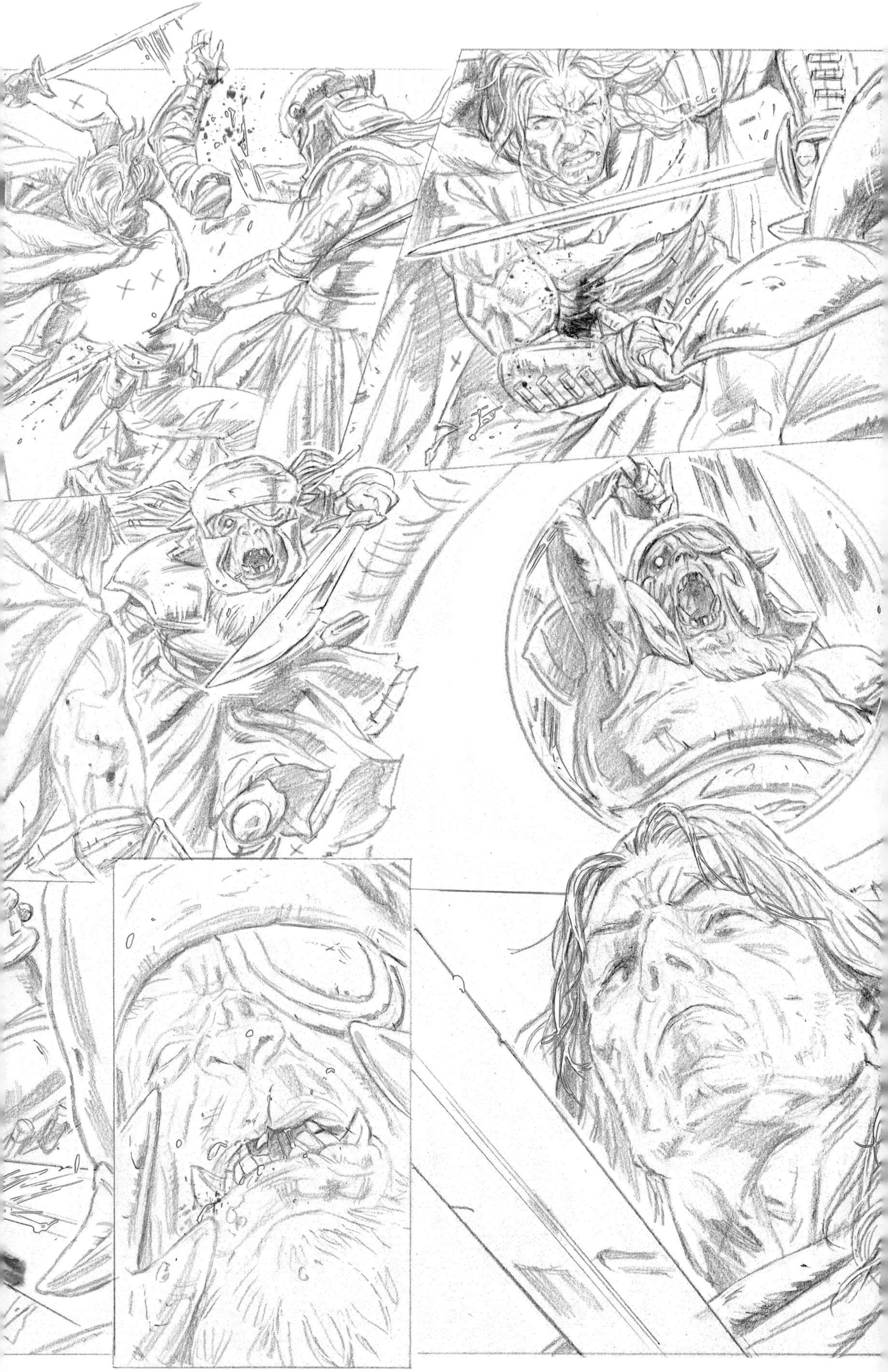

INCURSION #4, p. 11, 12, and (facing) 13
Art by DOUG BRAITHWAITE

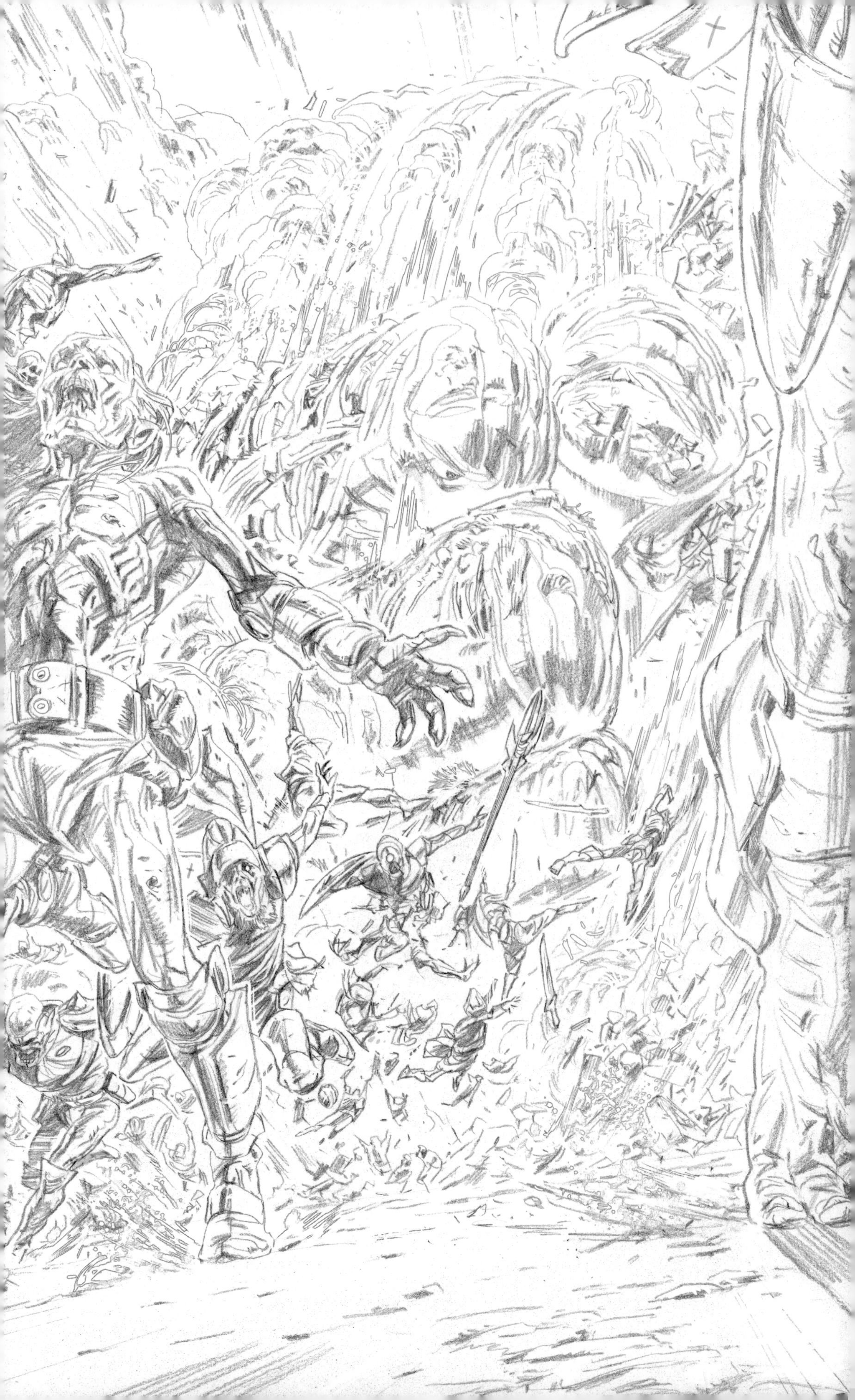

EXPLORE THE VALIANT

ACTION & ADVENTURE

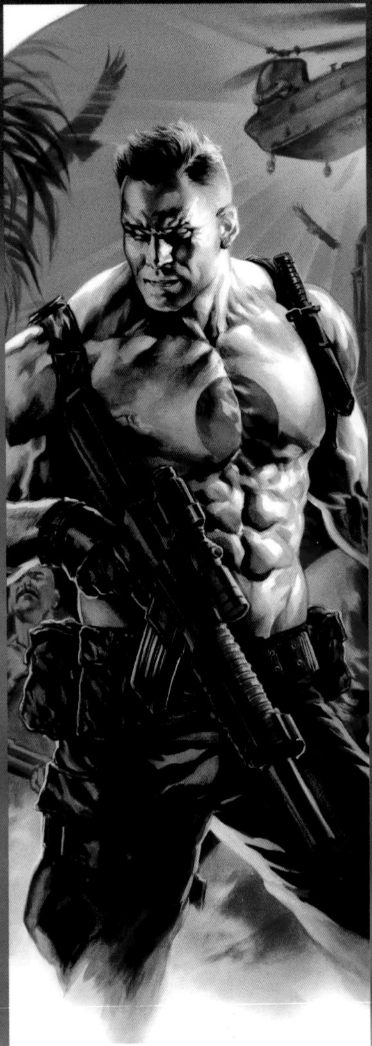

BLOODSHOT SALVATION VOL. 1: THE BOOK OF REVENGE
ISBN: 978-1-68215-255-3
NINJA-K VOL. 1: THE NINJA FILES
ISBN: 978-1-68215-259-1
SAVAGE
ISBN: 978-1-68215-189-1
WRATH OF THE ETERNAL WARRIOR VOL. 1: RISEN
ISBN: 978-1-68215-123-5
X-O MANOWAR (2017) VOL. 1: SOLDIER
ISBN: 978-1-68215-205-8

BLOCKBUSTER ADVENTURE

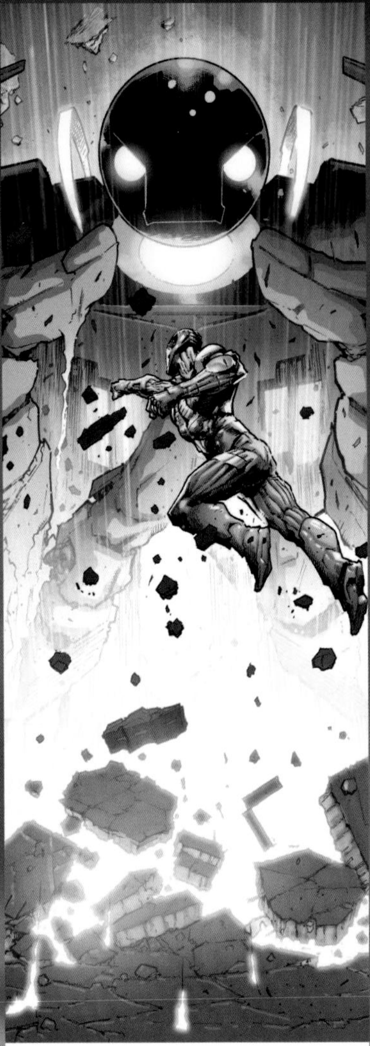

4001 A.D.
ISBN: 978-1-68215-143-3
ARMOR HUNTERS
ISBN: 978-1-939346-45-2
BOOK OF DEATH
ISBN: 978-1-939346-97-1
HARBINGER WARS
ISBN: 978-1-939346-09-4
THE VALIANT
ISBN: 978-1-939346-60-5

COMEDY

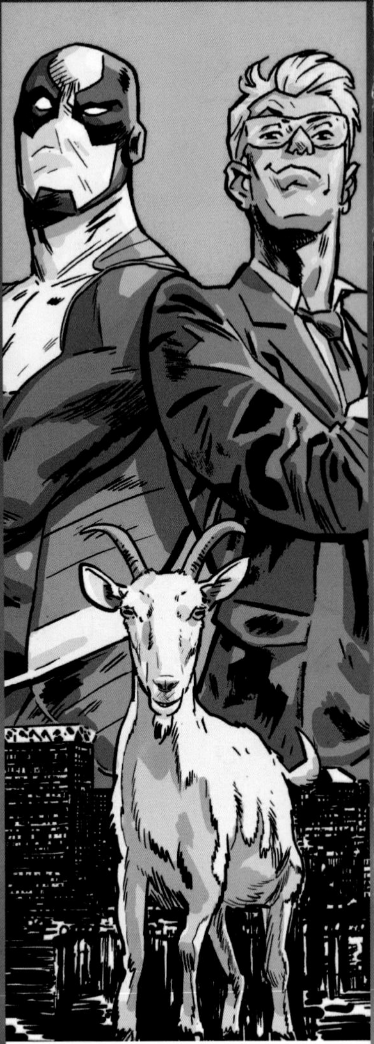

A&A: THE ADVENTURES OF ARCHER & ARMSTRONG VOL. 1: IN THE BAG
ISBN: 978-1-68215-149-5
THE DELINQUENTS
ISBN: 978-1-939346-51-3
QUANTUM AND WOODY! (2017) VOL. 1: KISS KISS, KLANG KLANG
ISBN: 978-1-68215-269-0

UNIVERSE FOR ONLY $9.99

HORROR & MYSTERY

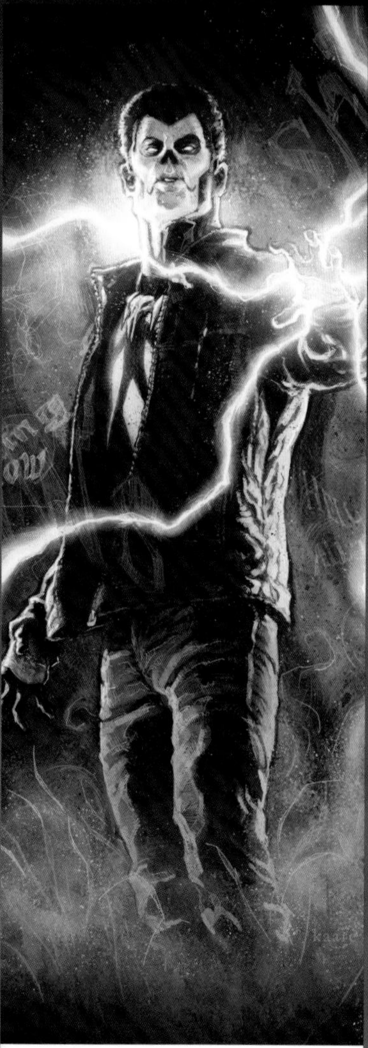

BRITANNIA
ISBN: 978-1-68215-185-3
THE DEATH-DEFYING DOCTOR MIRAGE
ISBN: 978-1-939346-49-0
RAPTURE
ISBN: 978-1-68215-225-6
SHADOWMAN (2018) VOL. 1: FEAR OF THE DARK
ISBN: 978-1-68215-239-3

SCIENCE FICTION & FANTASY

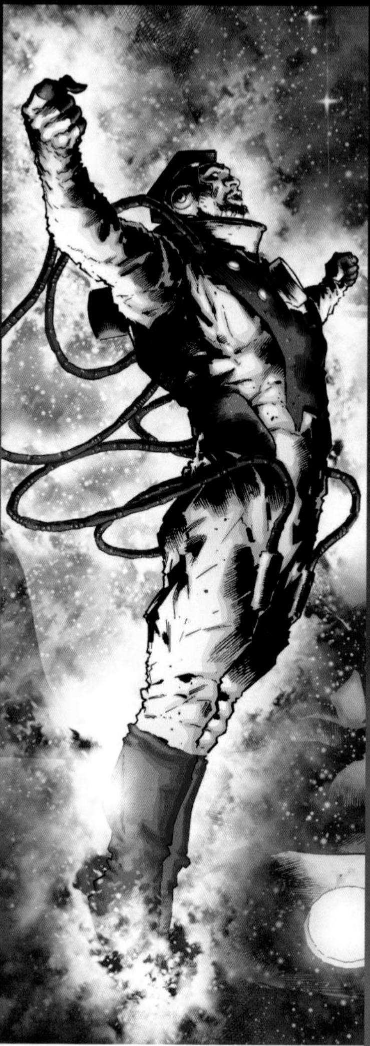

DIVINITY
ISBN: 978-1-939346-76-6
IMPERIUM VOL. 1: COLLECTING MONSTERS
ISBN: 978-1-939346-75-9
IVAR, TIMEWALKER VOL. 1: MAKING HISTORY
ISBN: 978-1-939346-63-6
RAI VOL. 1: WELCOME TO NEW JAPAN
ISBN: 978-1-939346-41-4
WAR MOTHER
ISBN: 978-1-68215-237-9

TEEN ADVENTURE

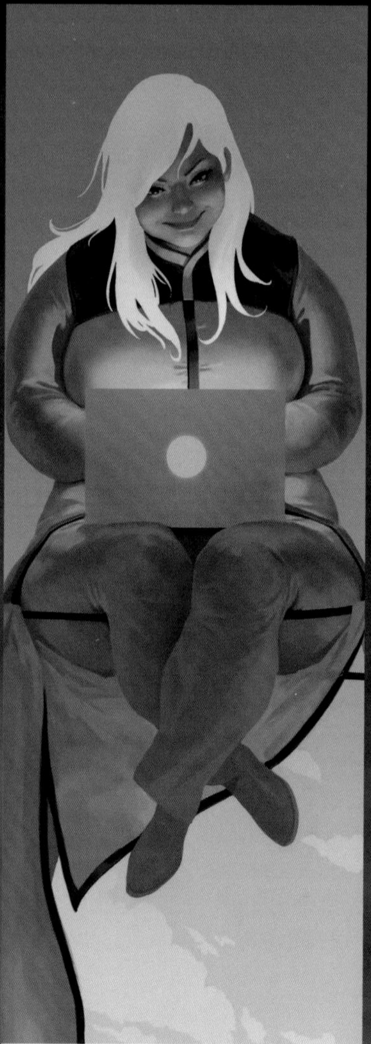

FAITH VOL. 1: HOLLYWOOD AND VINE
ISBN: 978-1-68215-121-1
GENERATION ZERO VOL. 1: WE ARE THE FUTURE
ISBN: 978-1-68215-175-4
HARBINGER RENEGADE VOL. 1: THE JUDGMENT OF SOLOMON
ISBN: 978-1-68215-169-3
LIVEWIRE VOL. 1: FUGITIVE
ISBN: 978-1-68215-301-7
SECRET WEAPONS
ISBN: 978-1-68215-229-4

Discover the entire Valiant Universe of titles at VALIANTENTERTAINMENT.COM/ALL-SERIES/

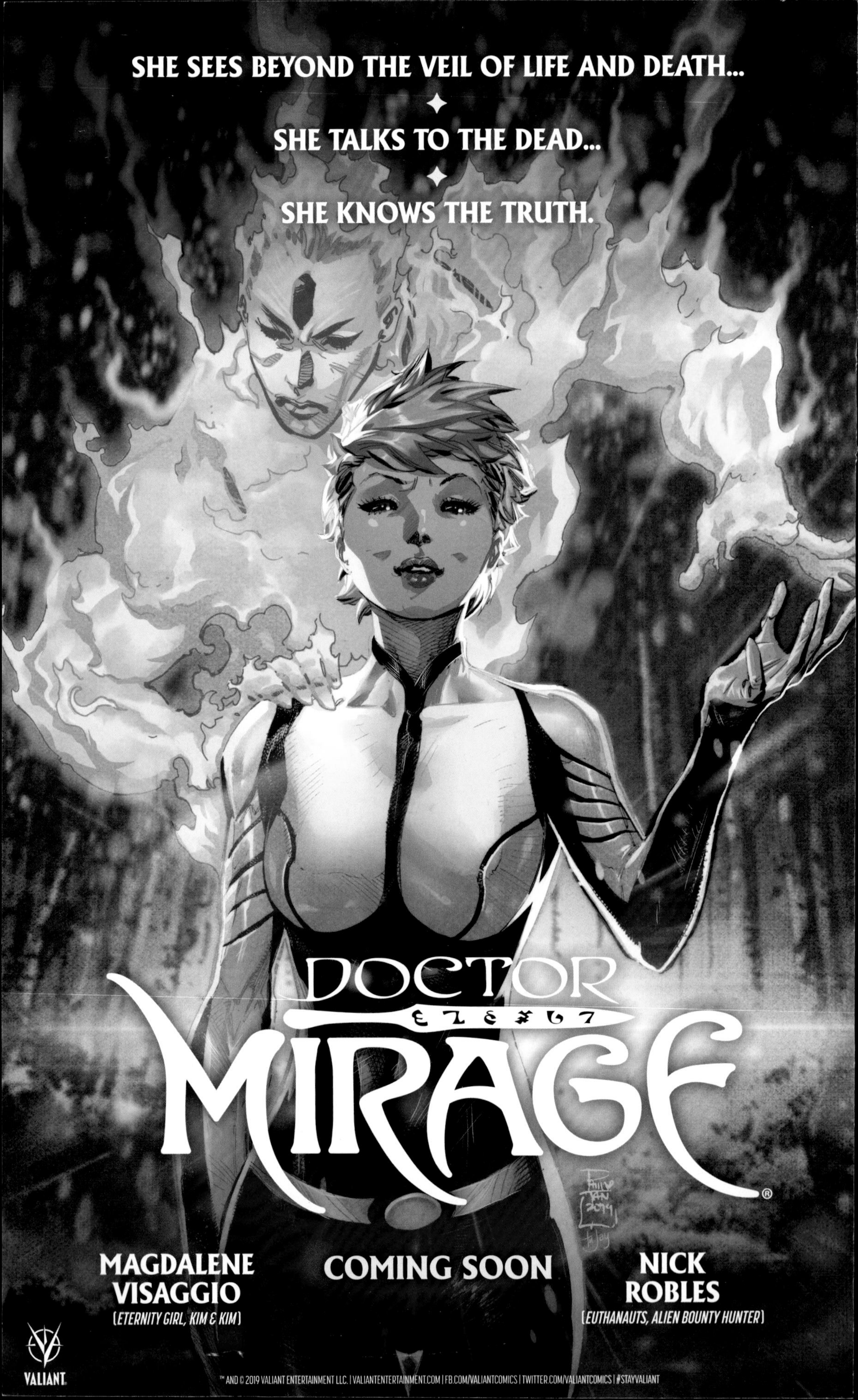
SHE SEES BEYOND THE VEIL OF LIFE AND DEATH...
SHE TALKS TO THE DEAD...
SHE KNOWS THE TRUTH.
DOCTOR MIRAGE®
MAGDALENE VISAGGIO
(ETERNITY GIRL, KIM & KIM)
COMING SOON
NICK ROBLES
(EUTHANAUTS, ALIEN BOUNTY HUNTER)
VALIANT
™ AND © 2019 VALIANT ENTERTAINMENT LLC. | VALIANTENTERTAINMENT.COM | FB.COM/VALIANTCOMICS | TWITTER.COM/VALIANTCOMICS | #STAYVALIANT